THE SELECTED POEMS OF BUDDHADEVA BOSE

Cover of the first issue of *Kavita*, 1935.

THE SELECTED POEMS OF BUDDHADEVA BOSE

Translated and Introduced by
Ketaki Kushari Dyson

OXFORD
UNIVERSITY PRESS

YMCA Library Building, Jai Singh Road, New Delhi 110001

Oxford University Press is a department of the University of Oxford. It furthers the University's objective of excellence in research, scholarship, and education by publishing worldwide in

Oxford   New York

Auckland   Cape Town   Dar es Salaam   Hong Kong   Karachi
Kuala Lumpur   Madrid   Melbourne   Mexico City   Nairobi
New Delhi   Shanghai   Taipei   Toronto

With offices in

Argentina   Austria   Brazil   Chile   Czech Republic   France   Greece
Guatemala   Hungary   Italy   Japan   Poland   Portugal   Singapore
South Korea   Switzerland   Thailand   Turkey   Ukraine   Vietnam

Oxford is a registered trade mark of Oxford University Press
in the UK and in certain other countries

Published in India
by Oxford University Press, New Delhi

© Oxford University Press 2003

The moral rights of the author have been asserted
Database right Oxford University Press (maker)

First published 2003
Oxford India Paperbacks 2009

All rights reserved. No part of this publication may be reproduced, stored in a retrieval system, or transmitted, in any form or by any means, without the prior permission in writing of Oxford University Press, or as expressly permitted by law, or under terms agreed with the appropriate reprographics rights organization. Enquiries concerning reproduction outside the scope of the above should be sent to the Rights Department, Oxford University Press, at the address above

You must not circulate this book in any other binding or cover and you must impose this same condition on any acquirer

ISBN-13: 978-0-19-806249-3
ISBN-10: 0-19-806249-4

Typeset in Lapidary 333 BT
by Eleven Arts, Keshav Puram, Delhi 110 035
Printed at Pauls Press, New Delhi 110 020
Published by Oxford University Press
YMCA Library Building, Jai Singh Road, New Delhi 110 001

To the future of poetry in the twenty-first century

Contents

Acknowledgements	xi
Introduction	xiii
Translator's Testament	lxv

THE POEMS

From *Bandir Bandana* (1930)	1
A Prisoner's Song of Praise	1
No Other Wishes	4
Love and Life (Nos 1 and 6)	4
From *Kankabati* (1937)	6
One Hand	6
This Is All	7
From *Natun Pata* (1940)	8
This Winter	8
There Isn't Time	9
Gods are Two (No. 1)	10
New Day	11
Still the Koel Calls (No. 2)	12
Rain and Storm	14
Sea-bathing (No. 1)	15
Peace by the Lake	16
Morning in Chilka	17
Everest	18

Sunrise on Tiger Hill	19
Moon	21
To My Poems (Nos 2 and 3)	22
New Leaves	25
If Rebirth Were Really True	26

From *Ek Paisay Ekti* (1942) — 28
- Thoughts on a Day of Bhadra — 28
- The Rains Come To Santiniketan — 28
- Farewell at Midday — 29

From *Baishe Srabon* (1942) — 30
- For Rabindranath — 30

From *Damayanti* (1943) — 31
- O Africa, Covered in Shadows — 31
- Padma — 32
- A Day of Asharh — 37
- Hilsa — 38

From *Rupantar* (1944) — 39
- Transformation — 39

From *Draupadir Sari* (1948) — 40
- Magic Desk — 40
- Afternoon — 40
- Sunday Afternoon — 41
- The Refugee — 42

From *Sheeter Prarthana: Basanter Uttar* (1955) — 50
- After Death: Before Birth — 50
- After Forty — 58
- Monsoon Day — 58
- 30 January 1948 — 61
- Calcutta — 62
- Prayer of A Winter Night — 66

From *Baromaser Chhora* (1956) — 71
    Mimi, On Your Birthday — 71

From *Je-Andhar Alor Adhik* (1958) — 72
    To Memory: 1 — 72
    To Memory: 2 — 72
    To the Sea: Spoken from a Ship — 73
    The Epiphany — 74
    The Surrender — 74
    To Arjun: from a Nameless Woman — 76
    To a Dog — 77
    Sonnet of 3 a.m.: 1 — 77
    Sonnet of 3 a.m.: 2 — 78
    The Desert Journey — 79
    Why? — 79
    'Two Birds' — 80
    In Reply to the Seasons — 80
    For My Forty-eighth Winter: 2 — 81
    Anuradha — 82
    The Moment of Liberation — 84

From *Morche-pora Pereker Gan* (1966) — 85
    The Weeping Beauty — 85
    Life on the Margin — 86
    Other Germs — 87
    Icarus — 89
    Only by Holding on to You — 90
    From Another Land — 92
    Other Debts — 92
    You, Strangers, Who Write Me Letters — 93
    Hölderlin — 94
    Song of a Man in Love — 95
    When the Burnt Day is Done — 96

The Music of Mortality	97
The Song of a Rusty Nail	99

From *Ekdin: Chirodin o Anyanyo Kavita* (April 1971) 103

Bloomington, Indiana	103
The Dead	104
Young Men and Young Women	106
Shopkeepers	108
Day of Rain	110
Night	111
Nostalgia	114
My Life	115
My Tower	117
The Constraint of Seasonality	118
The Expatriate	120
Ela-di	122
A Farewell at Howrah Station	124
One Day: For Ever	128

From *Swagatobiday o Anyanyo Kavita* (June 1971) 131

Fishing	131
He and Others	132
Lament	134
The Aged Poet	138
The Poet's Old Age	139
The Death of a Prostitute	140
A Juncture of Time	141
Welcome and Farewell	145
A Poem for Savitri	149

Notes to the Poems	155
Appendix	177
Bibliography	204

Acknowledgements

I would like to express my warmest thanks to Damayanti Basu Singh, the younger daughter of Buddhadeva Bose, for asking me to translate a selection of her father's poetry into English. By doing so, she opened for me the door to a delightful, absorbing, and challenging literary task: it has been both a pleasure and an honour to work on this project. Damayanti has also answered many queries in connection with this work and read through the first drafts of the introductory sections of this book, for which I am truly grateful. Very sincere thanks are also due to her elder sister, Meenakshi Datta, and their mother, Protiva Bose, the widow of the poet, for reminiscing to me about the poet one wonderful afternoon of rain and sun in July 1997.

Inevitably, the work generated queries of all kinds. In particular, I must thank Sibnarayan Ray, Samir Sengupta, and Sounak Chacraverti for answering a number of them. I also wish to thank Robert Rowles of Kidlington for helping me to sort out the answers to another set of questions in connection with the Appendix. Damayanti's husband Raminder Singh and my husband Robert Dyson have given their invaluable technical support to procedures involving computers and electronic transmissions.

In the past as well as in recent years various friends have given me books to read, which, though they had not been given to me with the explicit intention of aiding the present project, have nevertheless turned out to be useful in the same. Such are the gifts of serendipity, and I am grateful for them. In addition, I must thank Ashoke Sen and Sounak Chacraverti for giving me certain books which were directly relevant to this project.

A number of these translations (or their first versions) were first published in the special issue of the Calcutta magazine *Boidagdhya* (May 1999) commemorating Buddhadeva Bose. A couple were first published in the web magazine *Parabaas*. A few others have been published in the following British magazines: *Tears in the Fence, Fire,* and *Poetry Review.* One of the poems is due to appear in an article I have written for the *Encyclopedia of Literary Modernism,* edited by Paul Poplawski, Greenwood Press, Westport CT and

London, 2003. Some of the translations have been discussed in the poetry workshop I attend locally in the Oxford area; I am thankful for comments and suggestions which have come from my workshop colleagues from time to time.

In 1999–2000 the Association of Senior Members of St Hilda's College, Oxford, kindly gave me a small grant towards this project; this assistance is gratefully remembered. Finally, I wish to thank Oxford University Press India for their decision to publish this volume.

K. K. D.
Kidlington, Oxon.

Introduction

Buddhadeva Bose (1908–74) is a major Bengali writer of the twentieth century, someone whom intellectuals in both the Bengals are finally beginning to recognize as the most multitalented amongst those who, for the sake of convenience, are termed the 'post-Tagore' generation. 'Looking back,' says the distinguished writer and scholar Sibnarayan Ray, 'it now seems that amongst all these geniuses [i.e. of the post-Tagore generation] Buddhadeva Bose had the most multifaceted genius.'[1] 'I can say without any hesitation,' says the eminent Bangladeshi poet Shamsur Rahman, 'that after Rabindranath no other writer has appeared in Bengali literature who can match the multifaceted genius of Buddhadeva Bose.'[2] Like Rabindranath Tagore, Buddhadeva Bose was a versatile writer, comfortable in every genre. A brilliant poet, who also wrote novels, short stories, plays in both prose and verse, and non-fictional prose such as travelogues, memoirs, and literary essays, he was also an editor-publisher, a translator, a writer for children, and a consummate critic. Standard bibliographies list 153 titles published by him up to the time of his death, including three in English, amongst which are the much-admired *An Acre of Green Grass* (1948) and *Tagore: Portrait of a Poet* (1962). Four other titles were published immediately after his death. There is a huge amount of material in periodicals, not gathered in book-form.

At the beginning of the twentieth century the Bengali literary scene was naturally dominated by the towering figure of Rabindranath Tagore (1861–1941). When Bose was growing up, it was very difficult for aspiring writers to get away from Tagore's ubiquitous influence. Tagore had shaped the modern literary Bengali they had inherited and which they were willy-nilly bound to use: there was no getting away from that. They were creative spirits caught in the shadow of a genius who, by virtue of an interplay between his own gifts and the circumstances of the times he lived in, had stamped himself firmly on their backdrop. Like creative spirits everywhere, they chafed under such a powerful shadow and wished to put their own marks on that backcloth, to give writing, its content and style, a new direction in consonance with the shifting perspectives of their own times. Such were Tagore's powers of self-renewal during his long life that it was aptly said, even in his lifetime, that the first new voice in Bengali literature after Tagore was Tagore himself: the Tagore of the prose poems of *Lipika* (1922), of the novella *Shesher Kavita* (1929), and of the striking collections of poetry with a new turn published in the last decade of his life, say, from *Punashcha* (1932) onwards. Indeed, the language of contemporary Bengali poetry can be seen as derived in a line of direct descent from the poetry shaped in the thirties by a number of innovative poets, including the late Tagore and those who took his pioneering efforts further.

The twenties saw a younger generation of writers getting distinctly restless, fretting at always being in the rain-shadow area of the mountain called Tagore, and keen to express the anxieties, uncertainties, and convictions of their times. The fiery, rebellious Nazrul Islam (1899–1976), poet, singer, songwriter-composer, was a popular new voice during this period, though he did not develop into a full-blown 'modernist' and stands somewhat apart from the main line of development. Often erroneously regarded as an archetypal Bangladeshi poet, Nazrul, born in the district of Burdwan in western Bengal, was a product of the old undivided Bengal and of a period when the notion of a Bangladeshi identity had not emerged. Nazrul's output was particularly prolific in songs: the corpus of songs which he has left is considered to be even larger than Tagore's substantial song-oeuvre. His creative life was cut tragically short by an illness that robbed him of his cognitive faculties; he fell silent well before the partition of Bengal. He was physically there, continued to live in the Indian side of Bengal, but was not able to create any longer. Then in his last few years he was claimed by liberated Bangladesh as its 'national poet' and taken across the border, and it was in Bangladesh that he died. I find this concept of a 'national poet' fraught with dangers. Poets need to be seen as belonging to all the world, and their work as the heritage of all humanity. Nazrul was undeniably the first major Bengali Muslim poet of the twentieth century, yet it is doubtful if, as a secular person, he would have cared very much himself about a religious identity-tag.

Genuinely modernist efforts in Bengali writing began to consolidate themselves through literary magazines of the twenties such as *Kallol* (Roaring Waves, founded in Calcutta in 1923), *Kali-Kalam* (Pen and Ink, founded in Calcutta in 1926), and *Pragati* (Progress, founded in Dhaka in 1927). Buddhadeva Bose, in 1927 just a student, was one of the two editors of the last-named magazine, of which he had already launched a hand-written version in 1925. The co-editor was Ajit Datta, friend, fellow student, and fellow poet. Published for a little over two years, the printed *Pragati* made a remarkable contribution to the emerging modernist movement. It was a platform where Bose, barely nineteen and already vilified by puritans as an obscene writer because of one of his short stories published in *Kallol,* tried, as a representative of the youngest generation of writers, to arrive at some kind of negotiation with Tagore: 'a negotiation—that is to say, an arrangement, or it might be called, from our point of view, an act of getting ready, so that we did not remain for ever trapped in his vast net, so that he could become bearable and usable for us.'[3] A degree of rebellion against Tagore was a major ingredient of the twenties turmoil. Tagore's greatness and relevance were never challenged, but certain features of his world-view were. As Sibnarayan Ray puts it:

Against his intuitive apprehension of cosmic and personal harmony the accent now was increasingly on the inevitability, even the desirability, of conflict and disorder; to his joy of existence were opposed passionate feelings of frustration, anguish and anger; his aesthetic gracefulness was challenged by underlining the social reality of violence, exploitation and squalor; and the mystic-religious dimension which related his love lyrics, especially of the middle period of his career, to the tradition of the Vaishnavas, Bauls and Sufis, was rejected in favour of a more overtly sex-oriented, secular and tormented eroticism.[4]

This is the core of the modernist project in Bengal. Not that Tagore also was not evolving continuously as an artist and a thinker, and indeed, as a doer as well, interacting with his changing environment, going through conflicts, and dealing with them to the best of his abilities. His pace of overall development scarcely ever slackened. He founded a university, stimulated rural regeneration, intervened in political debates, raised awareness of the dangers of 'nationalism' and 'non-cooperation', and so on. But his starting-point had been different, and that was bound to make a difference. When those born forty or fifty years after him came of age, they were negotiating with a slightly different Bengal, a slightly different India, a slightly different world. In his excellent Introduction to *I have seen Bengal's face,* Sibnarayan Ray gives us an overview of these threads of change, and it would be worthwhile to cast a glance at them. These include: the decline of imperial Britain's economic power as a consequence of the First World War; the beginning of a limited industrialization in India with the emergence of an urban proletariat; peasant unrest and the impact of Gandhi's mass-based political struggle; the growth of educated unemployment; the rise of tension between Hindus and Muslims in Bengal; the ideological impact of the Russian Revolution and the dream nurtured by it that the Indian social order could be quickly changed through the adoption of communism; and the impact of Freud's thinking on the intelligentsia of Bengal.[5] So here, clearly, was a world different from the nineteenth-century world that Tagore had himself inherited. It is therefore not surprising that, in so far as the business of writing was concerned, a new generation of writers would want to tackle things in their own way; meanwhile Tagore was still alive, very much there, an immensely prestigious name, and a very influential presence: not just a father-figure, but by virtue of his extra-literary activities a great deal more—a guru and a grandfather. From the literary point of view, it was essentially a generational game, made keener because Tagore was so long-lived. Interestingly, the mature Tagore did indeed become one of the principal pioneers of modernism in Indian visual art, but in literature, more pregnant with mundane 'meanings', the picture was more complicated. Novels like *Ghare-Baire* (1916) and *Char Adhyay* (1934) provoked great controversy on account of the social and political attitudes portrayed. Nevertheless, it would be correct to say that especially after getting the Nobel Prize, Tagore increasingly came to embody an Establishment, a figure towards whom the conservative sections of the reading public naturally gravitated. It was inevitable that his literary successors, when they came into their own, would feel that a 'changing of the Guards' was called for. They chafed at his influence and wished to differentiate their path from his. Quite understandably, they did not wish to be regarded as an inferior generation; they aspired to be path-breakers in their own right. To pick up just one of the points from Sibnarayan Ray's analysis quoted earlier in this paragraph, there had been plenty of 'tormented eroticism' in the young Tagore, but of the 'Romantic Agony' brand, whereas the new sexuality was going to be more Freud-inspired.

In the thirties and early forties a new generation of poets succeeded in establishing themselves. It is to this generation that Bose belongs, along with Jibanananda Das, Amiya Chakravarty, Sudhindranath Datta, Bishnu Dey, Premendra Mitra, Achintyakumar Sengupta, Ajit Datta, Sanjay Bhattacharya, Samar Sen, Subhash Mukhopadhyay, and several others. Bose was the first to gain recognition—for his 1930 collection *Bandir Bandana* (A Prisoner's Songs of Praise), and from Tagore himself, with whom Bose actually had a very good personal relationship. In 1935 Bose founded the poetry quarterly *Kavita* (Poetry), which he edited with loving care for a quarter-century. He did take the help of assistant editors, but the overall charge of the magazine was his. This became the leading Bengali poetry magazine of its time, in which all important poets aspired to be published. To all intents and purposes, this was the first serious Indian magazine exclusively devoted to poetry; a Gujarati magazine devoted to poetry came out from Ahmedabad afterwards, inspired by the Bengali example.[6] *Kavita* was also an extremely important magazine for the discussion and review of poetry. Bose was a superb stylist in critical prose, and some of us have learnt how to write literary criticism using him as our model. It is hard to imagine what Bengali poetry and poetry criticism would have been like without the inspiration and guidance of *Kavita*. Bose also set up for his magazine its very own publishing house, Kavitabhavan, 'The House of Poetry', run on an informal co-operative basis, fellow poets paying for the printing of their collections, and Bose taking on the role of editor-publisher. Both were run from the poet's home. In Bengal it is considered absolutely natural for poets to manage their own magazines and publication imprints with the help of family and friends, and no stigma of 'vanity publication' attaches to such efforts. The first-floor apartment at 202 Rashbehari Avenue in southern Calcutta where Bose lived with his family from 1937 onwards—until he shifted to his new home in the Naktala area of Calcutta in 1966—was the base from which he carried on his literary activities. Affectionately referred to as '202', this apartment home of the poet became an institution in the city's arts world. It was a place where writers, intellectuals, publishers, and their friends dropped in at all hours of the day and late into the night for endless cups of aromatic tea and animated literary conversations. It was a platform and a network of which poets anywhere in the world would be envious. Bose's influence was seminal on younger poets and critics, to whom he was invariably generous and helpful.

By virtue of his magazine and publishing outlet Bose became the central figure in a cluster of poets who came to embody post-Tagore Bengali 'modernism'. Prominent amongst the others were Jibanananda Das (1899–1954), Amiya Chakravarty (1901–1986), Sudhindranath Datta (1901–1960), and Bishnu Dey (1909–1982). By Bose's own count, these four were the most frequently published poets in the first phase of the magazine, with Samar Sen (1916–1987) and Subhash Mukhopadhyay (b. 1919) joining in the second phase.[7] A quick look at the profiles of the first four poets would be rewarding.

Jibanananda Das, whose sensuous, adoring celebration of the landscape of his native Barisal district (now in Bangladesh) has made him a cult figure in both the Bengals, has also commented on urban existence, in each context turning details into crystalline symbols: from mice with silken fur, eyes of lonely fishes, stubble fields with broken shells of birds' eggs and sloughed skins of snakes, to the body of a suicide in a morgue, a leper licking water from a hydrant, or three beggars round three mugs of tea. His poetry evokes the stored presence of the past in the present, engaging with the historical, astronomical, and geological sense of time: Babylon and Assyria, Egypt of old and ancient Indian kingdoms, migratory birds and hunted animals, dead stars and cities drowned under seas glide in and out of our vision as we read him, creating a very special universe. He was known to be a quiet, withdrawn, introverted man in his personal life, and these qualities spill into his poetry. Sibnarayan Ray has commented that Jibanananda's poetry reminds him of some of the paintings of Marc Chagall, adding that the poet was probably not familiar with the work of that painter.[8] There is indeed something Chagallesque about Jibanananda's poetry. Among Jibanananda's unpublished papers were some novels and stories, the posthumous publication of which has also given him the profile of a fiction-writer.

One should note, *en passant,* the efforts that Bose put in to get Jibanananda Das accepted as a modern poet. I have mentioned above that Bose was encouraging to younger poets, but the help he gave to the career of Das, who was a decade older than him, was as impressive as the help he gave to launch the career of a poet like Samar Sen who was eight years junior to him.[9] Samir Sengupta, Bose's biographer, points out that of 162 poems published in collections by Jibanananda Das in his lifetime, Bose published 114: 14 in *Pragati,* 97 in *Kavita,* and 3 in the Kavitabhavan annual *Baishakhi.*[10] *Pragati* was in fact the platform where Bose repeatedly gave Das recognition as a poet when others ridiculed him.

Amiya Chakravarty, who spent a large part of his life teaching in the USA, became the first major poetic voice of the Bengali diaspora. A well-read, well-travelled, exceptionally cosmopolitan poet, he has enriched Bengali poetry by bringing the whole world to it. The sheer geographical span of his first-hand accounts of people and places is staggering. And this poetry of distant places is given in a Bengali idiom that is crisp and colloquial, urbane and sparkling. 'In his poetry,' says Sibnarayan Ray, 'there is a pervasive spirit of quiet detachment, reminiscent of Zen Buddhism, at once compassionate and keen-eyed, untroubled by passion and rhetoric, strong, precise and pure. ... the marvellous bounty which he has found everywhere in people and landscapes is gathered and presented in cameos, highly evocative though sharply outlined.'[11] At home everywhere, Amiya Chakravarty can ask, when in a mountain village in Bavaria: 'did I also have a house here in a previous life? / Did I live once— a son of German-land?' And in a mountain village in Iran he likewise knows he has to 'rest awhile, / for you are HERE: / in this World, your home.'[12]

Also well-read and well-travelled, well-versed in several languages and cosmopolitan to his finger-tips, Sudhindranath Datta, who edited or co-edited the influential magazine *Parichay* from 1931 to 1943, was recognized in his time as a brilliant intellectual. He perfected in his poetry and essays a rich Bengali diction that drew freely on Sanskrit resources, showing how compact and concentrated Bengali could become with appropriately selected Sanskritic words. I have only recently woken up to the fact that Sudhindranath, well-known for his love of life and its social graces, has been regarded by some as a poet of despair. After his death the noted critic Abu Sayeed Ayyub said: '... Sudhin sang of the insignificance of life as no Bengali poet has sung, at least in recent times.'[13] I wonder how many readers of my generation, when growing up in the fifties, thought of Sudhindranath quite in that light? His memorable love poems resounded in our ears: for us, he was as affirmative as a poet needed to be. We were mesmerized by his tightly knit poems, with their elegant gait and richly sonorous movements. Though he used many Sanskritic words, we could see that he was nevertheless clearly modern. Sudhindranath's Sanskritic vocabulary meant that he could say a great deal in a few words. He could be brief yet eloquent, logical and passionate, intellectual and musical at the same time. In his poetry each word is apposite and hits its target like an unerring bullet. The discipline and density of texture achieved are enviable: the poems move and sway like a skilled Bharata Natyam dancer, bejewelled and highly expressive.

Bishnu Dey, the youngest in this set of poets, achieved an impressive universe of discourse in his ambitious poems, in which Indian and non-Indian references were effortlessly dovetailed. Reviewing his collection *Chorabali* (Quicksands, 1937), Sudhindranath Datta commented on poems like 'Ophelia' and 'Cressida': '... I know of no other Bengali poet who is capable of creating anything so very original with material so alien to himself'; he likened the thematic elaboration of 'Ophelia' to that of a five-act drama and noted that in 'Cressida' the poet had created a comprehensive universe where Chaucer, Henryson, and Shakespeare were of equal value.[14] Bishnu Dey, who mediated the influence of T. S. Eliot to many, captivated my generation by his mastery of innovative, jazzy rhythms, by his wit, urbanity, and sense of irony, by his verbal thrusts and parries reminiscent of the art of karate. At the same time, he could be quintessentially Bengali in his simpler lyrics and went through a substantial process of development in his poetic career.[15]

Each of these poets has his own, distinctive voice, and they cannot really be lumped together in a crude fashion. Whilst the shy Jibanananda roamed the world in his imagination, but nevertheless famously said: 'I have seen Bengal's face—therefore I no longer/go seeking earth's beauty',[16] the intrepid explorer Amiya Chakravarty sent poetic despatches from every continent on the earth, not only from diverse locations in Europe, North America, and Asia, but also from the Caribbean, Central and South America, Africa, and Australia; nor was this merely touristic reporting: it was deeply humanistic poetry, taking in the lives of people as well as the beauty of landscapes, and responding to human suffering wherever the poet encountered it, be it amongst Amerindian peoples or in Portuguese Angola. Presumably swayed by his Sanskritic vocabulary, critics readily bestowed on Sudhindranath Datta the tag of 'classical' (*dhrupadi,* the use of which term to signify 'classical' in criticism was Sudhindranath's own invention). Nonsense, said Buddhadeva Bose in his Introduction to Sudhindranath's collected poems, Sudhindranath was at heart a romantic poet, one of the greatest of our Romantics![17] Ayyub, being a trained philosopher, discerned conflicts and paradoxes at the very heart of Sudhindranath's being: a conflict between thought and emotion, between the philosopher and the poet, between the materialist and the idealist, the paradox of a poet whose sentences in poetry seemed meticulously constructed, connected, and laid out as in discursive prose, yet which, on inspection, revealed a manner of composition that was lyrical rather than logical. As a critic, Sudhindranath professed to be a disciple of Mallarmé and to believe that poetry was written with words, not with ideas, but a close look at his poetry convinced Ayyub that Sudhindranath was only a 'theoretical disciple of Mallarmé' and a 'practical renegade from his professed master's teaching':

The poet Sudhindranath wrote in a very different vein. His poetry is heavily charged with meaning, as no other modern Bengali poet's is. And by 'meaning' I do not mean only emotive meaning; I mean truth, philosophical truth, social truth. Sudhindranath's poetry is characterised by an unrivalled potency to express the deepest truths—emotionalised and made oblique no doubt, as the best poetry always is. ... Sudhindranath wrote poetry with ideas (in a broad sense), not with words—which does not mean that he was not a master of words. But the words were the servant of his intuitions. Perhaps his other favourite quotation, 'art is the unity of intuition and expression', better indicated his poetic practice.[18]

In Ayyub's view, the central conflict or contradiction within Sudhindranath was that he was a modern man who wanted to believe in a completely material universe, but who was emotionally hurt and horrified by its indifference to human values: the realization of this unbridgeable chasm brought him suffering.

But what Ayyub, from the perspective of a philosopher, calls a conflict or a contradiction, is simply the existential condition of the modern poet. That, I suspect, is the reason why, in spite of being soaked in Sudhindranath's poetry during my college days, I never thought of him as a particularly pessimistic poet. From the perspective of a student of literature, he seemed a fairly normal modern poet! Sudhindranath's oscillation between materialism and idealism was compared by Ayyub to Bishnu Dey's ambivalent relationship to Marxism:

Perhaps it would be more correct to say that Sudhin loved to be a materialist rather than that he was a materialist—like another superbly gifted poet of Bengal, Bishnu Dey, who loves to be a Marxist though it is doubtful if he is or ever will be a full-blooded one. Bishnu is far too sophisticated—bourgeois to the roots of his being—to be a poet of the proletariat. But that is his *sadhana*. So it was with Sudhin. Deep inside he was an idealist, almost a *bhakta*. But it was his *sadhana* to become a *jadavadi,* a *dehatmavadi*.[19]

The development of Bishnu Dey's thinking, the position of Marxism in it, and the friendship between the two poets Dey and Datta are very interesting topics in themselves and have been studied in some detail by the critic Arun Sen.[20]

Though highly individuated, Bose and his contemporaries did share certain intellectual perspectives and a certain emotional orientation. They were secular and humanistic in their world-views; their lives were not dominated by formal religious belief; but they retained a strong sense of 'the burthen of the mystery' and a faith in the magical and transformative powers of human love. They shared an international outlook which was the hallmark of their generation. They were highly educated and constituted a group that took in the intellectual movements that swept across the world in the inter-war years. They understood the literary experiments that had changed, or were changing, the face of European and American writing. It was mainly through the enthusiasm of this generation (and immediately succeeding generations) that Bengalis became familiar with names as diverse as Yeats, Eliot, Pound, Joyce, Auden, Spender from English-language writing; Mann, Zweig, Hesse, Brecht, Kafka, Rilke, Hölderlin from German-language writing; Baudelaire, Rimbaud, Mallarmé, Valéry, Gide, Proust from French; Lorca and Neruda from Spanish-language writing; Pasternak from Russian, and so on—the whole caboodle that embodied 'Western modernism'. Yet these poets were in no sense imitators. Their curiosity about foreign authors was not merely bookish, but an authentic effort to come to grips with a cultural 'Other' and a desire to understand the big, wide world that was changing around them. They cannot be described as the pampered sons of a ruling oligarchy; they did work for a living; Bose and Das suffered genuine economic hardship. They were not rootless, alienated beings. They never lost their Indian bearings and knew how to mine their own complex traditions and hone their own Bengali styles. Sibnarayan Ray sums up the impressive achievements of this post-Tagore quintet thus:

Their strongest bond of affinity, so I feel now, lies in their conscious and never-flagging dedication to the achievement of authenticity in intuition-expression. The discipline of the spirit which involves the disciplines of the poetic craft—the rigorous avoidance of all that is adventitious, derivative, ornamental, or accretions of bad faith, in language and sentiments,—the pursuit of economy and precision, of the right symbol and the luminous image,—the wrestle with words and meanings,—in these they are all very much modern and major poets. Not so much by opposing Tagore (although that was the conscious starting point with most of them) as by pursuing each his own distinct path, distinct from Tagore and each other, they have extended the bounds of Bengali poetry, widened the ranges of its diction, techniques, forms, and themes, and greatly enriched the Bengali poetic sensibility and the store of its literature.[21]

The relationship of these poets to Tagore was not one of opposition for the sake of opposition: indeed, all were deeply respectful towards him, and Bose, Datta, and Chakravarty enjoyed a close and affectionate personal relationship with him. Bose received a favourable review from his pen in 1931. The very first issue of *Kavita* was duly sent to him, and Tagore wrote Bose a long, appreciative letter with detailed, thoughtful responses, which in turn was published in the magazine,[22] to which Tagore also eventually contributed. Datta and Chakravarty travelled abroad with Tagore and helped him in a secretarial capacity. Chakravarty carried on a remarkable dialogue with Tagore through an exchange of letters, even influencing the elder poet's thoughts and provoking him towards certain tilts in development, encouraging his diversification and modernization.[23]

I shall now try to piece together some biographical information on Bose, the kind that puts some flesh on the bones and helps us to make sense of a poet's work, especially in translation. It is always good to understand the milieu which shapes a poet, especially in the early years, and a few details can only enhance the reader's understanding of the poetry, not interfere with it. I am gleaning this information partly from Bose's own stylishly written memoirs and partly from books written by others. The ambience of his boyhood as given in the memoirs is also confirmed by an autobiographical novel like *Anya Konkhane* (In Which Other Place/Somewhere Else, 1950). My sources are cited at the end, and all quotations from Bengali texts will be in my own translation.

Buddhadeva Bose was born on 30 November 1908 in Comilla, eastern Bengal, now in Bangladesh, the firstborn child of Bhudebchandra Basu and his first wife Binoykumari. (Bose is an 'anglicized' version of the surname, more correctly written as 'Basu', the pronunciation of the full name being something like 'Buddhodeb Boshu'.) Binoykumari, the only child of her parents, and a mother at the age of sixteen, died of post-natal tetanus within twenty-four hours of giving birth to her son. Buddhadeva's father withdrew from domesticity and adopted the life of a wanderer for a year, while the infant Buddhadeva was left in the charge of his maternal grandparents, Chintaharan Sinha and his wife Swarnalata. Bhudebchandra later remarried, while Buddhadeva was brought up by his maternal grandparents, who doted on him and devoted their lives to him. Although left motherless at birth, Buddhadeva never felt the loss. He always addressed his grandmother Swarnalata as 'mother'. To all intents and purposes, Chintaharan, whom Bose has called his 'first teacher, first friend, and first playmate',[24] was the father-figure. According to Bose, his maternal grandfather was a mild-mannered—almost timid—man who, somewhat incongruously, served in the police force, when he would have really made an excellent schoolteacher. Swarnalata, on the other hand, was a woman of strong personality.

Bose's early childhood was spent in the country town of Noakhali on the river Meghna, also in eastern Bengal (now in Bangladesh), where a stupendous tidal wave rushing up the estuary in the middle of the day of new moon in the month of Bhadra (mid-August to mid-September) was the most important annual spectacle. The river was very destructive and every monsoon swallowed a bit more of the town, a sleepy outpost of the Empire, which nevertheless, true to the Raj spirit of the age, possessed a town hall with Doric columns, housing a public library, an indoor sports centre, and an auditorium with a well-equipped stage for cultural activities. Visits to friends and members of the extended family entailed voyages along eastern Bengal's extensive waterways. The landscape and waterscape of the region, as well as the emotional warmth and conviviality of the people among whom he was raised, have left permanent marks on Bose's writings, as I hope will be evident in some of the poems translated in this volume.

Bose was educated at home with great care by his grandfather, who taught him English, in a creative and playful manner, bypassing the aridities of grammar, and also introduced him to Sanskrit. As for teaching his grandson Bengali, Chintaharan did not have to toil at all; Bengali writers themselves were his teachers, Bose has recorded. Wisely, Chintaharan invested in books and magazines for his grandson. Bose became an avid reader in two languages. The very first poem he ever wrote came to him somewhat accidentally in English, a lament on the rented bungalow his family was living in at that time, close to the advancing Meghna. The spacious bungalow, probably erected once upon a time by a Portuguese adventurer, was on a raised plinth under which there used to be a stable in the olden days. In later life Bose recalled the opening lines of this childhood poem thus:

> Adieu, adieu, Deloney House dear,
> We leave you because the sea is near,
> And the sea will swallow you, we fear,
> Adieu, adieu.

Bose has speculated that the effusions were probably triggered by a fat volume bound in red which was his constant companion, entitled *One Thousand and One Gems of English Poetry,* in the pages of which he had first read Wordsworth, Cowper, Gray's 'Elegy', and Ariel's songs. Soon thereafter the young boy started writing torrents of poetry and prose, all in Bengali, and sending off material to magazines for publication, and it was not long before he saw himself in print. He also launched his own hand-written magazine, of which he was the editor, leading writer, and of course the scribe. A somewhat sickly child, short, thin, not good at sports, and who stammered to boot, he overcame his speech problems through organizing amateur theatricals and participating in them. He was acknowledged as the little prodigy of Noakhali.

In 1922 the family moved to Dhaka. In 1923 Bose commenced his formal education, first at Dhaka Collegiate School, to study for two years prior to the Matriculation Examination. Six months before this examination, his beloved grandfather died, after suffering terribly from throat cancer. Bose's very first book, *Marmavani,* containing poems from his juvenilia, was published from Dhaka in October 1924, dedicated to the memory of his grandfather. His education continued at Dhaka Intermediate College, then at Dhaka University, where he read English Literature, obtaining a First in his B. A. Honours in 1930 and a First in his M. A. in 1931. Dhaka was a new well-appointed university founded by the British in 1921 along elegant Oxbridge lines, staffed by well-qualified teachers and vibrant with cultural activities in which both students and teachers participated. Bose had a wonderful time there.

Altogether Bose was a resident of the city of Dhaka for a stretch of nine and a half years, a most tumultuous and formative period in his life. It seemed to him afterwards: 'as if I was there for such a long time, as if many things happened in those Dhaka years, as if I did a lot, as if days, nights, seasons hadn't ever entered my awareness so diversely and profoundly.'[25] These were years of adolescence and early youth, rich in friendships and peer interaction; heady with the discovery and discussion of literature— English books, Bengali books, Tagore's volumes coming hot off the press every year, international titles in English translation; and sweet with the discovery of his own burgeoning creative powers. He saw Tagore when Tagore visited Dhaka. He met Nazrul Islam, organized a reception for him, and entertained him in his own home. He wrote in *Kallol,* started *Pragati,* first in manuscript, then in its printed format, was accused of writing obscenely, sharpened his polemical pen, staged his play in the university campus, published his first novel, his first collection of stories, and his first 'adult' collection of poetry which elicited the admiration of even Tagore. The literary chat sessions he chaired informally at 47 Purana Polton, the corrugated iron cottage his grandmother built after her widowhood, from which he used to trek to the campus on foot, and which was also 'the office' of the magazine *Pragati,* were celebrated in Dhaka.

The seeds of the cosmopolitanism that became a distinguishing feature of Bose's writings were sown not only through voracious reading, but also through correspondence with a relative who was a little senior to him and became a special friend and a mentor. This was Prabhucharan Guhathakurta, later a distinguished intellectual in his own right. Prabhucharan went to study abroad, and kept up a regular correspondence with his young disciple. In his memoirs, Bose recalls this correspondence with exceptional ecstasy:

During Prabhucharan's stay abroad my communication with him was without a break. Ceaselessly I wrote to him, and ceaselessly got his letters. When letters take three months or so to go back and forth, it is not really possible to conduct a proper dialogue; it is only possible for each to describe his present moments, a speaking out through letters in the literal sense. Happily, both parties were extraordinary in their zeal and speed in the matter of composing letters. We were both what is called effusive types of personality, and we did not lack subjects in which we were both equally interested. From Boston, from Los Angeles, from Santa Fé—sometimes from the compartment of a Pullman train—then from London, Rome, Paris, Berlin, Stockholm came letter after letter from him, and with them books from different countries, and monthly and weekly magazines—piles of them—such diversity! From the moment I got one of his letters in my hand, my enjoyment of it began: rows of foreign stamps, paper as crisp as ironed cloth; names of streets and hotels in so many unknown languages—and inside, so many stories, so many items of new information, such affectionate greetings! Books came: Ibsen, Maeterlinck, Gorky, Andreiev, Oscar Wilde, Sean O'Casey, volumes of contemporary American poetry. Illustrated programmes of Moscow Art Theatre's New York season found their way to me. Enclosed with letters, newspaper cuttings came too—on the dancing of Pavlova, the acting of Duse, performances of Chopin's music. Even those items that I didn't entirely follow had something to give me—an intoxicating scent on the bodies of the books, the polish of printing, pictures, and the touch of breezes from far lands. The whole of the Western world, spread from California to Russia, its art, literature, way of life, its living geography, so many rivers, cities, and men and women not seen with my eyes but waxing real in my mind—this it was that Prabhucharan gave me as a gift, from my fourteenth to my sixteenth year, when I was emerging from the ground like a sapling, wanting to lift my thin branches up to the sky that arched over the whole world.[26]

I must confess that two names in the list of these cultural worthies were unknown to me when I encountered them. For the benefit of others in that position let me mention that Leonid Nicolaievich Andreiev (1871–1919) was a Russian writer and dramatist, and Eleonora Duse (1859–1924) an Italian actress. I have quoted at length to underline the intense internationalization of Bose's consciousness during a formative stage of his life. Such a beginning might explain to foreign readers how a poem such as 'Icarus', translated in this volume, could come to be written in a language from South Asia.

Though Bose had a good time in Dhaka as a student, he knew he had to leave the place. His last year in Dhaka was not very happy. *Pragati* had had to be packed up; Bose had burnt his own money—from his scholarship, prize money from an essay competition, gold medals, income from writing—and had used up all his grandmother's funds as well. When the time came to pay the fees for his M. A. examination, a brother of his grandmother, who was a doctor, had to help out. Soon he would have to make a living of some sort, but he wanted to be a writer, to make a career of it somehow. To do that it was essential to get a foothold in Calcutta. So in 1931 Bose bade farewell to Dhaka and came to seek his fortunes in Calcutta.

The times, meanwhile, were getting rougher and rougher. At this point I have to bring into this narrative the political backdrop. I have deliberately avoided doing that until now, because the political backdrop, once brought in, tends to usurp all other perspectives, becomes *the* story, whereas I am more interested in understanding the story of how Bose became a writer.

Politics cannot be kept out of the account of a writer's life in Bengal in the twentieth century; the complicated role it played in the life of the poet Jibanananda Das, a very private man, has been well portrayed by Clinton B. Seely in a literary biography of Das.[27] Luckily for me, Bose's biographer Samir Sengupta in his introduction to *Buddhadeb Basur Jiban* (Buddhadeva Bose's Life) gives a quick reconstruction of the political backcloth against which the young Bose had to forge his literary career. I am gratefully picking the details from his handy run-through.

About the First World War and its fall-out there is nothing much to say: that distant war did not affect the life of Bose's family directly. But among the details Sengupta asks us to remember are these. Bose was born in the year in which terrorist politics began in India. Dhaka, where Bose spent so many formative years, was one of the seats of that politics, and some cell or other of activists did indeed make an abortive attempt to recruit him when he had just arrived in the city from Noakhali, a lad of thirteen.[28] But before that, when he was eleven, the Amritsar massacre happened, and soon thereafter Gandhi launched his non-cooperation movement, the impact of which was felt even in Noakhali. Bose has recorded[29] how under its influence he, among other things, gave up drinking his favourite beverage, tea (condemned as the 'blood of coolies'); wore homespun; even did some spinning at home, producing thick matted knotted yarn; made a bonfire of some of the clothes of the ladies of his own family; read the fiery verses of Nazrul Islam; hung a calendar featuring Mother India, Mahatma Gandhi, and other political leaders; and enviously eyed those lads a little older than himself who managed to get themselves arrested, spent a week in jail, and came out to be lauded and fêted by the townspeople as heroes and mártyrs. He regretted he was too young to join them.

The other events Sengupta asks us to remember are these. When Bose was nine, the Russian Revolution happened; when he was twelve, the Indian Communist Party was formed in Tashkent; when he was seventeen, its waves reached India. When he was twenty-two, a handful of freedom fighters 'liberated' Chittagong for three whole days. The Great Depression set in, with its devastation felt even in India. 'In the midst of all that,' writes Sengupta:

a student with record marks gained at university left Dhaka for Calcutta, his dream city, banking on just a small private tutorship. What for? For doing literature.

To follow that story—how, starting from that spot, this child, whose mother was dead, whose father had abandoned him, became Buddhadeva Bose—is possibly, in the history of twentieth-century Bengali culture, the most thrilling, the most courageous mental adventure.[30]

Bose records how sad and squeezed he felt in his last days in Dhaka, when the terrorist movement simmered; when Hindu-Muslim riots flared again and again, perhaps being even fomented for the sake of 'divide and rule'; when everybody argued about politics, with himself listening and not listening; when well-wishers advised that 'it was better to make lanterns than to write poetry'. He counted the days, waiting for his M. A. results to be out, so that he could at last go to Calcutta, where he felt the atmosphere would favour him, 'where human efforts flowed in many separate channels, where one could mingle anonymously with the street crowds, where life's current was sharp, and where even a writer could choose the company he wished to keep.'[31]

So Bose left Dhaka, his past, and moved to his future in Calcutta, a city which drew him to itself 'with a thousand hands'. In contrast to the university grounds at Ramna in Dhaka which were 'green with the dreams of his youth, lines of song and fragments of poetry stirring in the breezes'—

Calcutta's dominant colour was the grey of its asphalt, its main sound the roar of its traffic; here the speed was intense, there were many conflicts, the restlessness was constant. What we, in those days, used to call 'reality' was more abundant here. ...

A huge and open university—such was Calcutta for me, for the first two or three years after my arrival here.[32]

It was in Calcutta that Bose, constantly fighting for economic survival, fighting against contumely and unpleasantnesses flung at him, through successive acts of stringent self-construction, enormous self-discipline, and dedication to his chosen vocation, finally schooled himself to become a writer of grit. 'Calcutta', included in this volume, written in 1953 when he was temporarily in Mysore in southern India, doing a consultancy for a UNESCO project, is a passionate statement of what Calcutta meant to him—that city to which he came as a young man in search of a literary career after finishing his university education in Dhaka. Halfway through the poem, Bose refers to the difficult times faced by Calcutta in the forties, during the Second World War, with fears of a Japanese invasion, the terrible Bengal famine of 1943 when people converged on the city from the countryside in search of food, literally to die in the streets, the horrendous communal killings of 1946, and finally, what was to change the fate of Bengali-speaking people for ever, the partition of Bengal in 1947, and the flood of uprooted people that began to arrive in the city from the newly created East Pakistan.

While we are considering Bose's special bonding with the city of Calcutta, another poem that is worth a little extra attention is 'One Day: For Ever'.

In the preface to the original edition of the collection in which this poem occurs, Bose wrote thus about the genesis of this poem:

At least twenty years back from now I was returning home from the College Street area on the Gariahat-bound tram. I think it was the month of Chaitra, about three in the afternoon. I remember that the sunshine was bright, the air dry, and the late afternoon rush hour hadn't yet started in the streets. When the tram was turning in the Park Circus roundabout (in my opinion one of the rare beautiful spots of Calcutta—at least so it was twenty years ago), and I was looking out, it suddenly seemed to me that that particular moment belonged to another day. Within the next minute or so, a few sentences composed themselves in my mind, and when I got home, I wrote them down in the corner of a notebook. ... I thought even then that if I could ever turn into a prose poem the fragment that had come to me so spontaneously, I would call it 'One Day: For Ever'. I even decided that should such a poem ever be included in a book, the book itself would have that title as well.[33]

In this poem Bose has deftly created the ambience of a problematic sexual outing, almost of a young man's visit to a brothel in search of sex. 'In reality', as one might say, the visit in the poem is very likely constructed from a much more innocent pilgrimage, albeit charged with all the thrill a young man might associate with his first sexual adventure. There is a quick suture between a memory of boyhood—'Rain through dawn sleep, smell of frying cheera / in the rain'—and a reference to the lane of Potuatola: 'In a sky-craft with a coloured cover / I travel to the lane of Potuatola / and alight.' The sky-craft with a coloured cover is surely a book or a magazine, which could transport the poet to a distant place. The original Bengali word *molat* is most commonly used to mean the cover of a book. Many references in Bose's memoirs indicate that he was exceptionally responsive to the covers of books and magazines. Thus he remembers reading the large-sized magazine *Balak*, with a bright red cover, when he was a very small boy.[34] His childhood companion, *One Thousand and One Gems of English Poetry*, and an Oxford edition of Shelley he was given on his fourteenth birthday also had red covers.[35] He recalls the aristocratic yellow-and-white cover of the magazine *Narayan* and the striking 'rainbow-cover' of the first issue of the magazine *Bichitra*.[36] So he rides the sky on the back of a book or magazine with a coloured cover and makes an imaginative journey to this 'lane of Potuatola'; and where might that be? Actually, there was (and still is) a neighbourhood called Potuatuli in Dhaka ('tuli', meaning dwelling-place, neighbourhood, is just a softer form of 'tola'): the Bangladeshi poet Shamsur Rahman has reminisced how it was in a bookshop on the edge of Dhaka's Potuatuli district that he once bought four collections of poetry at one go, one of them being Bose's *Bandir Bandana*, the volume he enjoyed the most.[37] However, the Potuatola of this particular poem is more likely to be 10/2 Potuatola Lane of Calcutta, which housed the office of the magazine *Kallol,* and was also the lodging of the magazine's editor Dineshranjan Das. Bose has stated categorically that 10/2 Potuatola Lane in Calcutta was pulling him 'like a magnet'.[38] It was in the summer vacation of 1926 that Bose, a college student who hadn't yet seen his eighteenth birthday, paid his first visit to Calcutta, 'that marvellous city, where'—as the young hero of Bose's autobiographical novel *Anya Konkhane* puts it—'all books are printed and from which all magazines are issued'.[39] The young hero's arrival in Calcutta is, interestingly, the climactic end of that novel.

The 1926 visit to Calcutta was Bose's first unescorted trip away from home. He made a beeline for the office of *Kallol,* where he had already published an essay. He met other writers of the *Kallol* group and was persuaded by one of them to submit one of his short stories, 'Rajani Holo Utala' (The Night Became Restless), which was accepted and immediately published, and thrust him at once into the centre of controversy, for he was accused of obscenity, the first in a series of such charges against him in his life. Dyed in the fantasies of a wildly romantic and poetical adolescent, the story was perceived by the author himself to be 'a little morbid'—the English word 'morbid' had just become fashionable, he informs us—but it was anything but obscene. Perhaps the erotic dimension of that story, coupled with the fact that this first visit to Calcutta had for him the aura of a sexual adventure, enabled him to fashion the poem 'One Day: For Ever' out of the various strands of his memories. Indeed all Bose's trips to Calcutta as a student, during vacations, seem to have had the hallmarks of an illicit adventure— with the lads, as it were, the lads being the other young writers who congregated in the office of *Kallol*. Sexy jokes flowed in the gossip sessions there, and it was there that the innocent Bose picked up various 'rude' words censored in polite society. Though the first few lines of this poem were conceived during a tram journey in Calcutta, the poem was finally written years later in Brooklyn, New York, after Bose had resigned from his post at Jadavpur University and was, for a period, working temporarily in various campuses in America. Calcutta was the city which had drawn him like a magnet, and with which he, as a young man, had had his first metaphorical love affair. It was the place where he had aspired to have a literary career, an aspiration which was more than amply fulfilled. It was also a place which from time to time hurt him, thwarted him, humiliated him. He loved it nevertheless, knowing it to be the centre of his existence. I think this poignant relationship is what fuels the powerful existential metaphor at the heart of this poem, which speaks of a great erotic adventure that, because of the conspiracy of trivia, cannot be consummated.[40]

Incidentally, the charge of obscenity was one that Bose would have to face more than once in his life. In the winter of 1932–3 a case was brought by a public prosecutor against four newly published works of fiction, including one of Bose's. The court case was a total farce: the English magistrate could not read any Bengali, and the Bengali barrister who was supposed to be defending him had not bothered to look at the book he was supposed to be defending. Bose had committed the sin of depicting 'love between unmarried men and women', and that was enough. He had to sign a piece of paper declaring that he would not re-publish the book within so many years, and without 'cleansing' it and asking the prior permission of the police. On 14 January 1933 the daily *Anandabazar Patrika* wrote an editorial protesting against the whole sorry business. In 1969, when Bose was an established award-winning writer, a private prosecution was brought against him because of his 1967 novel *Raat Bhorey Brishti* (later translated by Clinton Seely as *Rain Through the Night*). The enormous sense of disbelief that pulsed through me when I heard the news is still with me. The case was eventually thrown out by the High Court, and now when we read this book, it is difficult for us to understand what the fuss was all about, but the reverberations of this court case did linger in Bengali publishing, and in the early eighties the printing of one of my own books was held up for a time, with an editor wishing to cut out two crucial chapters 'in case some nutter decided to bring a similar charge again ...'!

But to return to the subject of politics: it was, of course, impossible to avoid politics altogether in Calcutta. By the 1940s it was no longer the question of whether one was following Tagore, or rebelling against him, that was dividing Bengali writers, but the question of whether or not one had become a Marxist. When in December 1938 the second conference of the All-India Progressive Writers' Association was held in Calcutta, Bose was on the organizing committee and also addressed the conference. At that time the nature of such a politically tinged cultural movement was still broadly humanistic rather than narrowly ideological. Tagore himself sent a written message to this conference. Bose is supposed to have said at this gathering: 'If necessary, let us writers all band together and engage in propaganda work. But let us not say that this is the highest aspect of literature, or even that it is literature at all. For though all art is propaganda in a deep sense, all propaganda is not art.'[41] Two months before giving this speech, he had written in his magazine *Kavita*: 'What is vaguely called progress, whatever else it may be, is not a criterion for assessing poetry or literature. We cannot judge literature by calculating how useful it may be for reforming society. ... Moreover, I do not believe that there can be even a modicum of solution for any of today's problems through the creation of literature ...'[42] In 1942 the All-India Progressive Writers' Association was re-launched as the Anti-Fascist Writers' and Artists' Association, and Bose was still happily and enthusiastically affiliated with it. But slowly, from 1943 onwards, the grip of the Communist Party on the movement hardened. Bose became gradually disillusioned with the movement and disengaged himself from it. There was a price to pay. Some friendships did fade, and some associates disappeared from the convivial gatherings at 202 Rashbehari Avenue. He returned, as Sengupta says, 'to his own dharma, to solitude, to his magic desk, face to face with himself.'[43] See poems such as 'Magic Desk', 'Sonnet of 3 a.m.: 1', 'Sonnet of 3 a.m.: 2', or 'Why', which underline this process. For saying, in 'Sonnet of 3 a.m.: 1', that only the personal was sacred, Bose was denounced by young Marxists as an enemy of the people.[44]

It has to be pointed out that there was something of a paradox in Bose's return to 'his magic desk', for he was, as we have seen, a most generously interactive friend, and someone who thrived on such interaction. But at the same time he could not go against his innermost convictions regarding the function and purpose of literature, and so found, like a woman poet of our own times, that 'To be a poet / You must always be alone.'[45] To be in tune with several poems translated in this volume, it is necessary to understand this situation of the poet vis-à-vis the growing hardening of the arteries of the leftist movement. The third section of Bose's own memoirs clarifies the whole process for us:

The war had then got really going, and in the name of this progressivism, there sprang an association of anti-Fascist writers, in rented rooms in Dharamtala, with some fanfare. I remained affiliated with them, because I hated the Nazis, but not just because of that. I saw that many of my dear friends and favourite poets were travellers on the road of progress, and the principal weakness of my character is attachment to my friends. But as the days passed, and as the current of events turned frothier and frothier, I began to feel a sense of distance between myself and those very friends, as though I couldn't understand everything they said: what little I did understand I did not accept, yet for the sake of old friendship was reluctant even to articulate it. Perhaps they too noticed my unease, my lack of faith. Perhaps deep down they too were disappointed with me. In such a situation, despite the existence of goodwill and efforts on both sides, cracks inevitably developed in friendships, and one by one they slackened—slowly and gently, and sometimes, harshly and suddenly. Our paths separated.

It wasn't happy for me, that complex, twisted politics of wartime Calcutta, of which writing and writers had become one of the tools. In the evening gatherings at Kavitabhavan I had to listen to many arguments which left me cold, to endure much fruitless disturbance, and some nights I went to bed with a bad taste in my mouth. ... Many spoke as if they had found Aladdin's lamp, some all-sustaining talisman that never failed: they were ready with solutions to all problems and answers to all questions. Directly on the opposite side, a few more camps established themselves in the different neighbourhoods, but each against the other—our poets and writers, the well-known and the not so well-known, took shelter under the flags of different colours. What had been conceptually liberal turned into various hardened ideologies: that business of 'progress' became a trademark, an easy means of success for the young and younger writers—the distinction between literature and journalism disappeared. I was at a distance, in the role of an onlooker, sometimes protesting in *Kavita,* and it wasn't as if nobody was listening to me, but those who were dissatisfied by my lack of a declared affiliation were really many more in number. Some of them wanted to persuade me in a soft voice, some ridiculed or rebuked me. ... Through much turmoil, chaos, and conflict, after much squandering of my energies and much frustration of my emotions, slowly I came to the realization that at the end of all motion and progress, and collapse and debate, it was good at last, in some deep of the night, to be immersed within oneself.[46]

It wasn't as if Bose retreated into some apolitical citadel. In the poem 'My Tower', translated in this volume, he gives his answer to those who would accuse him of living in an ivory tower. He could focus well on human beings, but refused to let his sight be clouded by political dust-storms. Poems such as 'Sunday Afternoon', 'The Refugee', and 'A Farewell at Howrah Station' record his acute observation of other human beings. 'The Refugee' is a very credible portrayal of the southern district of Calcutta in the mid-fifties. And indeed, in matters of cultural politics which impinged directly on a writer's concerns, he was very alert, and registered his protests sharply in his magazine, as for instance in 1950 against the rules and regulations of a newly instituted literary award, the 'Rabindra Puraskar'; in 1956, with passion and alarm, against the demotion of India's languages to the status of 'regional languages' and the proposal to merge the states of West Bengal and Bihar; and in 1957, with remarkable foresight, against any forced imposition of Hindi on the speakers of the other languages of India. This last article, entitled 'Bhasha, Kavita o Manushyatva' (Language, Poetry, and Being Human) was subtitled 'A Protest against the Report of the Government's Language Commission'; his biographer has called it 'a classic protest'.[47] In this essay Bose explained why human beings needed the dignity of being able to cultivate their mother tongues, and warned against the consequences of alienating non-Hindi-speaking India. I am presenting this essay in translation in the Appendix, with notes, so that readers of this volume can see for themselves how Bose viewed the relationship between three things of paramount importance to a poet: language, poetry (which he used in the inclusive Indian manner, meaning all of creative literature), and being human. I still remember how deeply this essay of Bose on the language issue affected us when it came out in *Kavita*. Those of us who were at an impressionable age were in many respects shaped by the thinking it embodied. And it certainly deserves dissemination in the pan-Indian context: readers of today may not agree with every single stance in it, but it is a valuable document of its time. It should provoke thought and clarify to the rest of India how a leading Bengali writer and intellectual viewed the language question ten years after India's independence. The discourse was continued in the next issue of Bose's magazine (straddling 1957 and 1958) in an essay entitled 'Ingreji o Matribhasha' (English and the Mother Tongue). His astuteness in all those political matters which affect culture is amply evident in this essay also. Let me quote a few lines to show what I mean:

That Hindi is the language of the Indian masses is an unreal proposition. The phrase 'the masses' is a magical mantra of this age; whatever is done in its name is regarded as benign and correct to such an axiomatic degree that it is not even considered necessary to test if such action has been beneficent or not for the human society to which the term 'the masses' refers. ... just as religion was once the opium of the masses, so the masses today constitute the opium of the intellectual.[48]

A long time back Anton Chekhov said: 'It is our duty not to bring Gogol down to the level of the masses, but to raise the masses up to the level of Gogol.' The modern era has given a strange rejoinder to this directive: by spreading literacy, it has created two rigidly divided sections of readership—the few who are sophisticated, and the many who crave to be entertained. And everything that is being disseminated for the entertainment and benefit of the many—in print or in film, on radio or on television—what has been given the name of 'mass culture' in English, may be horrendous to look at or to listen to, but in the end one has no option but to give it one's support. One has no option because once mass culture becomes strong, the boundary-line between good literature and bad literature—or between literature and non-literature—becomes unmistakably marked out; and even from amongst those who by their social construction are devoted to crime fiction a few readers emerge, who by virtue of their individual talents, in time chance upon the key to good literature. At the end of the day it must surely be that thanks to mass literacy the overall readership for the Gogols of the world is not decreasing, but increasing. In Keats's time it was not possible to read Homer except in rare, expensive editions; today Penguin can make him available in home after home. It is impossible to believe that as a result of this process, a few thousand, a few hundred—or at least a few—new readers, who in a previous age would have remained ignorant of Homer, are not discovering him through their own efforts.[49]

The analyses remain valid in the twenty-first century. As for his own commitment in this respect, it was unmistakably clear: to extend, as best as he could, the frontiers of the readership of good literature, and of good poetry in particular, to create a true community for its reception.

But it is time to turn to other aspects of Bose's life. In 1934 he married Protiva (Ranu) Shome (b. 1915), the great love of his life, whose roots were also in eastern Bengal. A fan of his, in 1933 she had dramatized one of his novels and staged it in Dhaka's Northbrook Hall, this being the first time that men and women acted together in Dhaka. Already, in her teens, a formally trained and acclaimed singer, she sometimes came to Calcutta to record her songs, and thus it was that though the two had met in Dhaka, the courtship really flowered in Calcutta. Protiva became a prolific and popular writer of fiction in her own right, and her literary career has a trajectory of its own. In recent years her memoirs,[50] a rich sourcebook of both family anecdotes and cultural history, have proved to be immensely popular, whilst her canny deconstruction of the Mahabharata, with a heterodox reconstruction of the historical events that might have been behind that epic,[51] has attracted much attention on account of its shrewd insights.

The couple's first child, Meenakshi (Mimi), and the poetry magazine *Kavita* were 'born' on the same day in 1935. The second daughter, Damayanti (Rumi), arrived in 1940, and son Shuddhashil (Pappa) in 1945. All the children of this distinguished couple have had some relationship with the art of writing, as also Meenakshi's husband Jyotirmoy Datta, who launched the magazine *Kolkata,* which had a good run. Damayanti, after a long academic career, has become a publisher in her own right. Kankabati, the daughter of Meenakshi and Jyotirmoy, is also currently pursuing a literary career.

Brought up by his doting grandmother who did everything for him at home, Bose was not a good manager of domestic matters and worldly affairs. Soon Protiva took charge of all that. She stood by him through all his financial struggles, contributed to the family income, shared his enthusiasm for putting on plays, and actively helped him in all theatrical activity. A man of passionate energies and total dedication in his literary life, Bose was also a devoted family man, who did his best to fulfil his familial obligations, including to his grandmother and to his in-laws in their time of need, Protiva's family being one of those families which were truly devastated by the partition of Bengal.

How to combine his writing with earning a livelihood to support his family (and fund activities like running *Kavita*) was a headache for Bose for most of his life, and the grim, sometimes humiliating, struggle to earn a living is often referred to in his poetry. Plagued by financial worries nearly all his life, he nevertheless strove to live for his art in an exemplary fashion. After settling in Calcutta, he wrote furiously. But supporting a family needed a more regular income. In spite of his excellent degrees, in the thirties and the war years Bose was at a disadvantage in the competitive job market of Calcutta, as an 'internal migrant' from Dhaka. For eleven years, from 1934 to 1945, he taught English at Ripon College (now Surendranath College), a job in which he was not happy. Three thousand or so boys packed into a four-storeyed building, in crowded classrooms, without adequate common room or recreational facilities, with disciplinary problems: the scenario was daunting to someone who had been used to the agreeable campus of Dhaka. To add to his misery, initially, as a junior member of staff, he had to teach boys who were re-sitting their exams, whose sole aim was to pass their next exam, and who had no motivation to study literature. For all intents and purposes, the institution operated as a crammer, and it was impossible for Bose to find an outlet for his talents. In 1944 he started doing some freelancing work for *The Statesman* newspaper, and from 1949 took on the task of writing its 'third editorial'. But in 1951 he resigned from this also, finding the demands of this kind of journalism at variance with his needs as a writer.

At a critical juncture of time he was befriended and helped by Humayun Kabir, a distinguished academic and poet who had become a minister in the Delhi Government. Thanks to him, Bose worked for a UNESCO project for a short while, which involved two three-month stays in Delhi and Mysore (where the poem 'Calcutta', included in this volume, was written), then in 1953 went to America on a Fulbright award to teach for a year at the Pennsylvania College for Women in Pittsburgh—his first trip abroad. 'Prayer for a Winter Night', translated in this volume, was written in Pittsburgh.

In 1954, through Humayun Kabir's mediation, Bose was invited to help in the setting up of an Arts Faculty at Jadavpur. Previously dedicated to the training of engineers, the institution was becoming a fully-fledged university. Bose proposed the establishment of a Department of Comparative Literature, and became immersed in all the necessary planning. He set up this

Department, working hard for it, and joined it as Head in 1956. Thus began a happy and rewarding phase in his life—of an appropriate academic career—where his talents were at last put to good use, and where he became a successful teacher, popular with his students. One of his achievements on behalf of this Department was the recruitment of the poet and critic Sudhindranath Datta, who did two stints in it: 1956–57 and 1959–60. Some opposition from conventionally minded people had to be overcome for this appointment, as Datta did not have an M. A. degree, but the battle was fought and won.

In 1961, the year of Tagore's birth centenary, Bose undertook an international tour, lecturing and teaching. This tour took in Japan, the Hawaii, the USA, and Europe. He gave lectures in Osaka, Kobe, and Kyoto. In New York, where he taught for a semester, he met the Beatniks, including Allen Ginsberg, who would later visit Calcutta and have an impact on the young poets there. Bose passed through Britain, then lectured at the Sorbonne in Paris. In 1962 he gave a series of lectures on Tagore at Bombay University.

In early 1963 Bose received an invitation from Indiana University at Bloomington to teach at the Comparative Literature Department there over the fall semester, to cover, as a Visiting Professor, for the Chairman who would be going on sabbatical. Bose discussed the matter with the Rector of Jadavpur University, who agreed with him that such contact with a foreign university would be beneficial for the Jadavpur Comparative Literature Department—which was clearly going from strength to strength—and that the poet Naresh Guha (b. 1924), a close associate of Bose from the inception of the new Department, would be able to look after it during Bose's absence. On receiving oral assurance from the Rector that leave could be arranged, Bose accepted the American offer and made a formal application for leave without pay for six months. Afterwards, however, the Academic Council of Jadavpur University refused him this leave of absence, and Bose was left with the stark choice of either going back on the word given to Indiana, or resigning from his post at Jadavpur. He decided to resign. His wife has recorded in her memoirs how this decision broke his heart. He loved the Department he had founded, he loved his students dearly, and he cared for his colleagues, but he felt that the Academic Council had humiliated him and that he had to go, for the sake of his own honour. It is now openly admitted by members of his family and by his biographers that there was academic politics behind this, that there was an anti-Bose lobby within the university who by their clever machinations deliberately eased him out. The Rector and the Registrar of the university were both very well-disposed towards Bose, but were rendered powerless and were unable to intervene. Those who conspired against Bose clearly knew that given a stark choice between dishonour and resignation, Bose would choose to resign.[52] Circumstances surrounding this unpleasant incident have never been satisfactorily explained. Bose referred to it as 'a deep wound' in his life.[53] Recently, Bose's younger daughter Damayanti has voiced her unease and expressed the opinion that Jadavpur University ought to undertake a full official investigation:

Did they think that if they could get rid of Buddhadeva Bose, they would be able to close down the Department of Comparative Literature itself? What was the real motive behind this personal enmity? Pure jealousy, or a more secretive conspiracy?—Many such questions still disturb us. I think Jadavpur has an obligation to prepare an investigative report and publish the full facts. Who were the people who participated in the machinations behind closed doors, on what grounds was Buddhadeva Bose's leave of absence not sanctioned, what was recorded in the minutes of the various meetings, what did he himself write in his letter of resignation?—for the sake of getting their history right, the public, his readers, his family, and above all, researchers have a right to know these facts.[54]

This call will not seem in any way unreasonable if we remember the fact that Bose was a pioneer in India of the academic discipline of Comparative Literature. He was a man of exceptional integrity, and the Department of Comparative Literature at Jadavpur, which survived any lurking efforts to undermine it, was his brainchild. Setting up and running this Department had absorbed his creative energies and brought out the educationist in him: there is a parallel between his dedication in this respect and Tagore's efforts for his campus at Santiniketan.

Bose was happy at Indiana, where he had the reputation of being the most erudite professor on the campus. It was while he was teaching there, in course of making a comparative study of Greek and Sanskrit epic poetry, that he developed a special interest in the Mahabharata. After his semester at Indiana, since there was no job for him at home to which to rush back, Bose stayed on a little longer in America. He taught at some other campuses: one semester at Brooklyn College, then summer school at Colorado University, then one academic year at the Wesleyan College at Bloomington, Illinois, and finally, summer school at Hawaii University. Altogether he spent a two-year period teaching Indian epics in different American campuses, and some of his important work thereafter, including the play *Tapasvi o Tarangini* (1966), a number of verse dramas based on Mahabharata stories, and a book of essays in exegesis of the Mahabharata[55] could be called the direct result of his preoccupations with epic poetry and myths during this two-year period. Also from this time onwards quite a few of his poems, some of them translated for this volume, reflect his deep immersion in the Indian epics and other subjects drawn from Sanskrit sources. The physical aspects of the North American continent have left their traces on his poetry too.

Bose did not work formally for any other institution in his last years, concentrating on his own writing, though he responded to invitations and gave talks, at home and abroad. In 1966 he gave a series of lectures on Tagore at Calcutta University. In 1968 he undertook a tour in Germany, returning home via Italy. Awards came his way, such as the Sahitya Akademi Award in 1967, a special Ananda Prize in 1972, a posthumous Rabindra Prize in 1974. A major disaster hit the family in the last years of his life. In 1972 Protiva Bose reacted badly to a series of anti-rabies injections she had to take, and was left with her mobility impaired. This devastated Bose, and it is thought that the shock hastened the decline of his health. He suffered what was most likely a mild stroke, but would not give up smoking. In the evening of 17 March 1974 he suffered a major stroke and was taken to hospital, where he died in the early hours of the morning of 18 March.

With his deep roots in eastern Bengal, his equally stubborn love of Calcutta, his wide reading in the literatures of many traditions, his international travels, with the many different kinds of landscapes, and the voyages and flights themselves as storehouses of images and metaphors, Bose brings us a marvellous feast of savours in his poetry. Born of a unique encounter of cultures, and perhaps for that very reason eminently accessible from more than one vantage point, his poetry has great variety, ranging from the romantic ebullience of his youth and the 'taut, dark and introspective' poems of his middle years[56] to the wonderfully sensitive, humanistic story-poems and the meditative philosophical poems of the later years. In my selection I have striven to meet three main objectives: to give readers an idea of his range and variety, to give adequate representation to each important phase in his poetic development, and to make sure that I selected poems which I could reincarnate as poems in English. In the end, as I have experienced before in poetry translation, the poems have tended to choose me.

In the early years poetry came to Bose with the spontaneity and abundance of leaves coming to a healthy tree. 'A Prisoner's Song of Praise', with which this selection begins, written by Bose when he was approaching eighteen, embodies his outspoken youthful rebellion against received wisdom. The collection from which this poem is taken, *Bandir Bandana,* has always epitomized the beginning of a new age in Bengali poetry. Tagore had himself welcomed the advent of a new voice in it.[57] As Samir Sengupta puts it:

For seventy years this slim volume of poetry has been standing as a signpost marking the direction of modern poetry. In truth, it is reasonable to uphold the view that the concept of modernity in Bengali poetry begins from this volume. It is here that we find, for the first time, the announcement that the artist is not an assistant of God, but a rival—an unequal rival; and precisely because he is an unequal rival, precisely because his ultimate defeat is inevitable (because the conflict between what he wishes to do and what he can actually achieve can never really be resolved), he attains the greatness of a tragic hero.[58]

The early Bose is not only a rebel, but also a wonderfully romantic lover. 'Morning in Chilka', written by the newly married poet when he was holidaying with his wife in Orissa, is a universal favourite: it certainly was a great favourite with my generation when we were growing up. It epitomized for us—could it be especially for girls?—every impulse that was fresh, innocent, and beautiful, expressing our need to love and be loved, the desire to embrace the beauty of the natural world and stick it like a rose on the lapel of our human lives. While 'A Prisoner's Song of Praise' embodies the struggle of a male poet in his teens, determined to transform his tormented adolescent sexuality into the human face of love, 'Morning in Chilka' is a 'feminine' poem, showing love triumphant. I would call it a male poet's *écriture féminine*. Bose has himself given us an insight into the creative process behind this much-loved poem: 'Let me give an example of what I mean by poetry of the passing moment. "Morning in Chilka" is a poem which I really and truly wrote sitting beside the Chilka one morning—in a moment of intense joy in my life. It was as if I had caught the moment red-handed, with all its green smell and moisture, not giving it time to dry out, not giving myself time to look back at anything.'[59] Another poem I would call markedly 'feminine' is 'Monsoon Day', also a great favourite of my generation when we were growing up.

At the other end of the scale from the 'spontaneous' poem is the kind of poem Bose often wrote in his mature years, which, by his own admission, gestated within him for anything 'from five to twenty-five years'.[60] 'One Day: For Ever', already discussed in the context of Calcutta, is a fine example. Another example is 'A Poem for Savitri', the last poem in this collection. The story of Savitri occurs in the Mahabharata. Savitri was a woman who chose to marry a particular man, in spite of knowing that he was fated to die after one year, and who brought her husband back from death by holding a dialogue with Yama, the god of death. Bose writes about this poem: 'I had once thought of writing a play about Savitri—I nurtured the idea for a long time—it ended up becoming a long poem, which begins with Rome and the death of Keats, and in which the name of Savitri occurs only in the title.'[61] The evocation of Rome, the Hispanic steps, and the dying Keats is not out of the blue. The poem was written in 1968; that year he was in Germany in October-November and visited Rome and Florence on his way back to India. He certainly visited the celebrated Spanish Steps[62] and must have visited Keats's House next to it.

I have made a special point of including 'Farewell at Midday' and 'Padma', with their images of travel between Dhaka and Calcutta in those days, as poignant poetical records of the lives of people strung between the two parts of Bengal, still unaware of the storm about to burst on their heads. Tucked in these poetical records are leaves from our recent history. These are typical journeys that the poet and his family would have necessarily undertaken, especially as Bose's wife was also a Dhaka girl. In the first poem he seems to be drawing on the experience of leaving her behind in Dhaka and returning to Calcutta. The journey would be by train and steamer via Narayanganj and Goalundo. Eleven miles of a train ride would bring him to Narayanganj, the port of Dhaka, as it were. From there a steamer voyage of several hours' duration would take him to Goalundo Ghat station, about ten miles south of the confluence of the two mighty rivers, the Ganges and the Brahmaputra, where he would board a train again to return to Calcutta. The second poem describes the river voyage from Narayanganj to Goalundo Ghat. Once again, Bose seems to be returning from Dhaka to Calcutta, but this time he is accompanied by his wife. This is a route along which I have travelled myself as a child in the forties, and the memory lives in me. The expanse of water is so vast that it looks like the sea, the shores being hardly visible from midstream.

Those reading the present collection could perhaps view the exquisite poem 'Hilsa' as a companion-piece to the two poems just discussed, as another chapter in the story of the people going to and fro between the two arms of Bengal. The hilsa, a tasty sea-fish of the shad family, comes up the rivers to spawn. Here the poet speaks of hilsa fished in East Bengal waters, then transported to Calcutta by rail. Hilsa cooked in freshly ground mustard-seeds is a delicacy of the Bengali cuisine. As opposed to 'poetry of the passing moment', such as 'Morning in Chilka', this is poetry of recollection. 'The hilsas', Bose recalls, 'I had noticed on the platform of Goalundo; I had got off the steamer at 10 p.m. and was running fast towards the train, and the hilsas, heaped up, were lying in the half-darkness, waiting to be transported. But I had no time to look back; my mind was dominated by one thought, whether I would be able to grab a bit of space to lie down in a third-class compartment.'[63]

'Prayer of A Winter Night', from the collection *Sheeter Prarthana: Basanter Uttar* (Winter's Prayer: Spring's Answer), stands at an important crossroads in Bose's poetic life. At the time of writing this poem he was teaching at Pittsburgh's Pennsylvania College for Women. He was on his own, having left his family behind. Dire financial necessity had forced him to take up this assignment, but he was not really happy there. The place was not rural, but on the other hand lacked that ambience of cosmopolitanism which for Bose was the hallmark of sophisticated urban existence. The college did not have a stimulating literary atmosphere. Social life was also restricted. Even before reaching the USA, this middle period of his life had become a time of crisis when he was feeling hassled and not creative (rather like the author named Satikanto in the poem 'The Refugee', translated in this volume). In an excessive zeal to be self-disciplined in his craft, he had become very harsh to himself and his art, and the poems were no longer coming readily. However, in this meditative poem 'Prayer of A Winter Night' there are signs that a breakthrough was near. Some of his own recollections, vivid, touching, and funny, constitute the best introduction to this poem and the crisis preceding it, and also, incidentally, offer us an insight into what kind of experience goes into the making of our perceptions of alterity:

... having declared a jihad against clichés, I ended up squandering a great deal of my capital. After twenty-five years of a love affair, poetry seemed determined to stand in opposition to me, as if it would not yield even a speck of earth without a fight. And then one day I noticed that I was losing out: I wasn't able to write any kind of poem, good or bad.

*

I was then over forty, and a darkness had descended on my life. My health had broken down, I wasn't earning enough to support my family, my mind was exhausted. Meanwhile my excessive self-consciousness was taking its revenge on me, by making me nearly impotent as a writer. Not that I was writing nothing, but I was writing very wearily, one or two pages of prose a day, overcoming endless reluctance, feeling crushed by an indelible sense of failure. My greatest suffering was due to the fact that poetry had forsaken me: not that my desire to write poetry had died (that would have been a relief, surely!), but that desire was so powerless and fruitless that its pressure only increased my agony and magnified my despair. Occasionally, perhaps, a good moment arrived, flashed in the darkness, then disappeared. And then I sat quietly, pen in hand, my mind dumb, my nerves numbed as it were. I thought lines, I wrote lines, I crossed them out. Some pages of my writing-book showed no fruit except cancellations and alterations. Looking at my writing-desk, at my piles of books and writing-books, at my handwriting on pieces of paper, sometimes I wanted to be sick. Yet my pride forced me to carry on, never allowing me to say, 'I give up, let me go to bed now.' Thus did a whole year pass for me, or perhaps even a greater stretch of time, day after day, very slowly and painfully. But then one day this barren season came to an end for me—suddenly, in an unexpected and adverse moment.

My first visit abroad. I was in Pittsburgh, a city which was friendless and joyless for me. I had no one to speak to, the pressure of work was light too; then, chill and white, the month of December descended. The accommodation I had was of the type that is called 'garret' in English: two rooms on the second floor, one of which was not rectangular—the roof sloped towards the front so much that one could almost touch it with one's hand; the part of the floor that was not carpeted groaned when one trod on it. On the plus side, the front room was sunny by day; before evening the sunset sky hung before my eyes like a coloured canvas. Teaching a little, wandering around a little, sitting at home a little, somehow or other I managed to pass the day, but as soon as the sun-god disappeared, an enemy would attack me. The heating system of the house was so feeble that only small droplets of warmth percolated to the second floor—nothing more than that—while I was a person who minded the cold even in my own country, so every night became a torment for me. In that strange country one had to sit down to one's evening meal at six p.m., whereby the night became even longer. Yet at least the dining-room of the women's college was bright and well-heated; one could see many human faces there, and hear the musical voices of many young women—much laughter, many words, singing in unison, as regulatory, before the meal and in intervals, and my table companions, working-class women [canteen staff], did include me in their conversation. But—perhaps through the fault of my own nature—I could not forget that I was an outsider, it seemed to me that I had come to the wrong place; and when dinner was over, and I began to climb the wooden steps back to my icy den, from that time onwards this thought would haunt me: how would I pass this long cold blood-freezing night? Drinking cups of tea, warming hot-water bottles again and again, rubbing my hands together, pacing up and down, I somehow managed to keep myself mobile, and sailed through many hours by writing letters in all directions. But at some point, one had to go to bed, there was no other way, and as soon as my body touched the bed, I felt that I had plunged into a tank of icy water. Under three blankets the cold kept me awake by means of whiplashes: not even Thomas Mann's story of Joseph could make me forget that suffering. I heard the howling of wolves, the revelry of witches, as if the winds of the North Pole were tearing the world to pieces. And on one such night, from the depths of my loneliness and emptiness, and the tormenting cold, suddenly 'a prayer of a winter night' sprang forth: the last poem of my life that I wrote in one torrential flow, or which wrote itself down under its own steam, so to speak..... Like 'Morning in Chilka', this poem could also be called directly autobiographical; the impressions of my Pittsburgh exile are printed on its long-drawn-out prose rhythms. But here

I didn't just imprison the butterfly of a single moment; within this poem the whole of my mind of that time is working, with all its pain and the yearning born of sentience. From this 'thaw' other poems were not born immediately, but at least my self-confidence was to some extent restored, and—it's good to be able to say this—even before I returned home I seemed to hear an affirmative answer to this 'prayer'.[64]

After his duties ended at Pittsburgh, Bose was free to travel for a while, and went from one coast of the USA to the other. He met many new people, people he liked, and in their company he slowly came to love the country that had at first seemed so alien. He especially enjoyed being in New York, with its art galleries and bookshops, its multiethnic crowds milling in its streets. He could feel life's velocity there, in that city which was used to making foreigners its own people. Hungrily he absorbed all these experiences, till he was once more face to face with himself during his return voyage home. Crossing the Atlantic on a large ship, he kept himself to himself, staying away from all the usual revelry, sitting by himself in a corner of the dining-room, watching the waves, and climbing to the topmost deck at night. He says he could hear a faint stirring within himself, to which he wanted to give way, undistracted by irrelevant socializing. Slowly he wrote what he calls a 'marine poem', and another poem in the London hotel where he halted, and a few weeks later two more on the ship that took him to Bombay. (I have translated three of these four poems: 'To the Sea: Spoken from a Ship', 'The Epiphany', and 'The Surrender'.) These, he sensed, represented a new beginning.[65] Thus began the poems of *Je-Andhar Alor Adhik* (The Darkness that is Greater than Light), regarded as a milestone in his poetic development.

Gradually, says Bose, he found what he had been looking for—a new style, away from saying things simply, closer to saying things obliquely, less of direct statements and more of images: '... instead of saying what I want to say, maybe I should say something different; what I really want to say should be hidden, and yet not hidden. And for this I need a language that will be unburdened, yet not shallow, which can accommodate spare colloquial idioms next to solemn Sanskritic words, which looks good-natured and is nevertheless skilled in acting.'[66] He was plagued by doubts too. Could he really pull it off? Did he have enough of a vocabulary? Or self-discipline? Careful in trying to snare the bird, would he injure it? As soon as he returned to his usual surroundings, the thought of pages with crossings out and cancellations filled him with terror. So he began most carefully, as if he was walking stealthily, composing and correcting mentally, and not committing anything to paper until several lines were ready, to avoid the ghastly sight of things crossed out. He wrote short poems, soon taking refuge in the discipline of the sonnet-form. The sonnet became his salvation. He says that the lessons he learned at this stage proved permanently useful, even when he had moved away to writing poems which looked different.[67] He became a meticulous craftsman, deeply interested in the function of the poet as the artist-craftsman.

Although *Je-Andhar Alor Adhik* is widely regarded as a milestone in Bose's poetic development, I would resist the temptation to put it on a pedestal in a way that would downgrade his other achievements. The tendency to exalt an artist's works of maturity at the expense of the products of his youth is a paternalistic trait, one of the professional hazards of being a critic. A young man can only write like a young man; he cannot write with the mind-set of a middle-aged man before he has arrived at that terrain. I am one of those who believe that every stage in the development of a fine artist is of value and that it tells us something not only about that particular artist but also about the stages of human life and the nature of art itself. Samir Sengupta sees it this way:

One is tempted to call it [*Je-Andhar Alor Adhik*] his greatest poetic opus, but the word 'greatest' is never quite applicable in the discussion of works of art. One can say which work is good, and it is not impossible to indicate why it is good, but one who discusses literature must guard against the danger of pronouncing that *a* is better than *b*. But maybe we can put it this way: after he had written the poems in this volume, there was a noticeable change in his style—in his poetry, fiction, essays, translations. Until this time, the image that the name Buddhadeva Bose conjured before our eyes was the mien of a vivacious young man who believed in the delightful quality of life, who had faith in the struggle of life precisely because he loved to live. But from now on the picture began to change. Gradually it changed and became the portrait of a sad middle-aged man: his staunch love of the positive sides of life was still unflagging, but now the weariness of a loneliness without a name, a sense of loss for flowers that had vanished and songs that had been muted brooded over all his gladness and all his joy, spreading its grey wings. This book is a central joint of Buddhadeva Bose's literary life, standing like a watershed, dividing his work into two clear sections.[68]

The East-West mingling in Bose's poetic corpus, which should be obvious already, deserves to be highlighted. I have already pointed to the early internationalization of his consciousness during his formative adolescent years. In his maturity he became an eloquent proponent of the idea that real intellectual growth is only possible by grappling with what is 'foreign' or 'other'. The essay 'Ingreji o Matribhasha', from which I have quoted before, is an excellent example of this line of thinking. He argues that this kind of growth happened to linguistic cultures in Europe when they connected themselves to the Continent instead of remaining isolated parochial entities: to English after the Norman conquest, to Russian in the time of Pushkin, to German under the aegis of Goethe, to Norwegian in the hands of Ibsen, an artist whose best work was produced while in exile in Italy and Germany.

What the human spirit creates cannot have chemical purity. It is the nature of the spirit to be invasive; it is the nature of creation to synthesize. The mind of no man can develop until many storms—mélanges, movements, invasions—have blown over it. Growing up only within his family, village, or tribe, a man cannot really grow; his development is impaired; his personality goes under a purdah. The same is true of nations. A country that does not have exchanges with foreign countries remains pallid. An extreme example of this is our neighbour Afghanistan. Iran, once a centre of 'Aryan' civilization, has courted immobility and become decrepit.[69]

India's vitality, he argued, was due to its constant contact with the world outside its borders.

Geography favoured it [the contact]; mountain passes in the north and sea passages from three directions allowed foreigners unlimited access to the country. That might have been a misfortune in the worldly sense, but I shall call it a good fortune from the spiritual angle. From age to age foreigners have come and raised storms over this continent; and precisely because of that, through much terror, devastation, and give-and-take, the life of this extremely mixed, great nation has developed.[70]

It follows that we cannot appreciate Bose's poetry unless we are prepared to take his internationalism on board. The poem 'Icarus' is a splendid example of his complete absorption of Western material as though it was his own. He has made this material part of himself, his stock. Written while Bose was teaching summer school in Colorado University, this poem undoubtedly owes something to W. H. Auden's poem *Musée des Beaux Arts* ('About suffering they were never wrong, / The Old Masters ...'); it is quite possible that he had also seen a reproduction of Breughel's *Landscape with the Fall of Icarus* (held in the Musées royaux des Beaux-Arts de Belgique, Brussels), which is the subject of the second stanza of Auden's poem. Auden had drawn our attention to the power of visual art to show the 'human position' of suffering: how, when the most tragic of events is depicted on a canvas, the artist also shows ordinary life going on around it, unconcerned. As if taking his cue from this, Bose goes further: he re-creates the mythical event, imagining all that might have been happening while Icarus fell from the sky and drowned. The old poet in the last stanza, defeated by his poetic labours and lying down to his siesta, 'silently wise', is a very Bosean figure indeed.

At the other end of the scale, 'The Song of a Rusty Nail' is a superb example of the reincarnation of an old Indian story. I have translated the introductory words that the poet has himself supplied at the head of the poem. The seed-story is in both the Ramayana and the Mahabharata. Bose was gripped by it and also fashioned a remarkable play out of it: *Tapasvi o Tarangini* (The Ascetic and Tarangini, 1966). Rishyasringa's psychological development—his weariness in marriage and his yearning for the courtesan who had seduced him—is Bose's own modern interpretation. The attempt to reinterpret traditional stories was, of course, not a new phenomenon. Writers of the Bengal Renaissance including Michael Madhusudan Datta (1824–73), Tagore, and others had done it with great success. Bose was continuing, expanding, and refining an activity that had itself become a modern tradition.

An extraordinary mingling of material occurs in the poem 'A Juncture of Time'. This poem has its origin in a very personal experience, the memory of a lost photograph—perhaps the only photograph Bose ever saw—of his mother, who had died of post-natal tetanus twenty-four hours after giving birth to him, her first-born. Bose's father had had a photograph taken of himself and his dead wife, his arm round her waist, her head resting on his shoulder, eyes closed, hair cascading down her back. Bose recalls in the first volume of his memoirs[71] that the photograph used to be amongst his grandmother's cherished possessions for a long time, that he remembered seeing it even when his widowed grandmother was living with his family in the 202 Rashbehari Avenue apartment in Calcutta. At that time he did not feel any particular curiosity about it, or a sense of bonding with it. He scarcely glanced at it. At some point during the crowded years in that apartment, with books and papers proliferating and children growing up, and space at a premium, the photograph was mislaid and disappeared: he didn't know exactly when. At that stage of his life he felt no particular loss, had no time to think about it even. But in his last years he sometimes remembered the photograph, and even felt a twinge of regret at its loss. He wanted to know what that young woman who had died in giving birth to him had been like, what her likes and dislikes had been, whether she had at all loved books, what character traits he had inherited from her. He felt that she had deserved something from his hands for her labour. This moving poem, written just a few days before his fifty-ninth birthday, is his poetic coming to terms with a loss that had been buried for a lifetime. The third section of the poem leaps suddenly, like a new musical movement, to the visualization of a piece of sculpture. I had at first thought that the sculpture evoked might be Rodin's *The Kiss*. But the details in the poem do not actually match that celebrated sculpture all that closely. In some respects they are closer to Rodin's *The*

Eternal Idol, while in certain other respects they evoke two works by Camille Claudel, *Sakuntala* and *Vertumne et Pomone*. There could well be a composite image here, combining the details of more than one work, either solely from memory, or, as is more likely, aided by reproductions in a book or in picture postcards. It was as if this image had at last made him see the lost photograph of his young parents in Comilla in perspective. An electrical connection had been established between a home memory and a foreign memory/experience. The establishment of this kind of connection between indigenous and overseas material is certainly a characteristic feature of the modernism of Bose's generation and has come to stay in Bengali writing, especially in the work of those of us who are in the diaspora or have been exposed to diverse cultural influences through reading and travel.

Likewise, the mingling of Bengali and foreign landscapes in Bose's poetic corpus, and sometimes within the body of a single poem when there is an interplay between the present moment and a scene or scenes recalled, is an attractive feature of his poetry. Readers will find plenty of examples in the present volume. There is a strange notion sometimes aired, of which I became only recently aware, since embarking on this project, that Bose did not care much for nature. Anybody who reads him without the aid of any reading glasses borrowed from critics will be mystified by this opinion: both his poetry and his prose, rich in exquisitely sensitive descriptions of nature, completely belie it. I was puzzled by it myself when I came across it: what, the poet of 'Still the Koel Calls', 'Morning in Chilka', 'Padma', 'A Day of Asharh', 'Monsoon Day', 'Anuradha' etc. etc. did not care for nature? But since then I have figured out the sources from which this idea has sprung. First, scattered in his poetry of the mature years there are those wry philosophical statements which ask us to see nature for what it is, not to overestimate or idolize it.

> Have I then, accepting the dharma of animals,
> blindly pulled by nature, simply invoked
> my unborn children, when I've written poems?
> My praise of youth—is it merely the adoration
> of procreative power? My verse's rhythm—has it simply been
> another cog in nature's wily machine,
>   and enchanted by Chaitra's moon and summer's champak,
>   and the rain's wildness, and the night's blindness,
> has it just listened to nature's pep talk
> and spread its counsel?—'Swell, seed, swell! Grow, creature, grow!
> More, and more, and more!'
> ('After Death: Before Birth')

> 'Tree', 'flower', 'pond', 'cloudy day': are dry mathematical symbols,
> merely abstract, till you raise the curtain and show that my eyes
> > too are yours.
> ('To Memory: 2')
>
> Winter, summer, spring, rainy day: I have at last
> conquered your grand caprices, and in my heart's gathering evening
> come to know emptiness, who's rid of opportunities, whose
> > fortune's bust,—
> ('In Reply to the Seasons')
>
> Draw the curtain in that window. In that field there's absolutely
> > nothing to see.
> They only want to seduce you—grass, earth, pond, sky.
> Throw away those dolls, flowers, pet birds, pots of precious cacti.
> Sink into ennui that's without pique, ever in the same beat, and
> > doesn't cheat.
> ('For My Forty-eighth Winter: 2')
>
> Nature, so dear to you, is really unconscious matter,
> for ever bound in the iron laws of maths.
> ('The Music of Mortality')

Such wry comments are not necessarily Western-materialistic; indeed they would fit quite well with the ascetic view of nature as wily maya, whose business it is to keep us chained to the endless cycle of samsara, which is certainly an important strand of thought within Hinduism. They link also with the defiant project of improving on God's creation and creating oneself anew that we see in his poetry right from the beginning.

> You gave me desire, as dark as a moonless night:
> from that I've moulded love, mixing it with the honey of my dreams.
> ....
> Upon my own self I have bestowed a new birth.
> Since you are the creator of everything that there is,
> to you I dedicate this my creation with care.
> ....
> I am a poet, and this is my pride—
> I have created this music in exalted delight.
> This is my pride—that your mistakes I have rectified
> with my own dedicated enterprise.
> ('A Prisoner's Song of Praise')

The same theme of human consciousness and creativity going beyond the deceptions of Enchantress Nature, creating values such as beauty and love, and in a profound sense, creating the universe that is perceived, is articulated with total confidence in a poem like 'The Music of Mortality', written when the poet has reached his season of maturity.

> Nature and Time are the cast, but I am the playwright
> and also the audience—until with a final thunderbolt
> they all perish—being, the cosmos, and God.
> ('The Music of Mortality')

Further, the awareness in his mature poetry of decay and disease has a sharp edge to it; it has resonances with the poetry of the Elizabethans, certainly; but again, it is a view very much in consonance with certain strands in traditional Hindu and Buddhist thinking. I suspect what has really triggered the notion that he 'did not care for nature' is what I would call the Baudelaire factor. Ever since his middle years, when Bose became a translator and exegete of Baudelaire, he became associated with Baudelairean qualities: a preference for the urban over the rural, for the artificial over the natural, a morbid preoccupation with angst and ennui, decay and disease, which could not be redeemed by the imagery of rebirth. Such qualities were perceived to be removed from that mature Tagorean vision which could imagine the universe as a benign God-touched place, shimmering with parental tenderness—or if not so, then at least as a vast starlit emptiness within which we could, at least on this earth, somehow create a benign enough niche, with a combination of our human values and some ethereal, dewy, deeply felt blessing from above. Not Shakespeare, not Donne, already very familiar to the Bengali literati since the nineteenth century, but Baudelaire became the epitome of alterity or otherness in the mid-twentieth century. Bose himself jocularly encouraged among his intimates this association between himself and the French poet. Witness his letter to his younger daughter after the shift from Rashbehari Avenue to the less built up Naktala of the mid-sixties:

... Surely you folks didn't expect that I would be thrilled by the move to Naktala—you know I am not a nature-lover, I am an urban man, a fan of Baudelaire. I am in the south-facing room on the ground floor; to your mother's horror, I have permanently sealed the large east-facing door with a book-shelf, and most of the time I keep most of the windows shut too—I don't like too much light and air, I can't concentrate on my work unless the room is a bit dark.[72]

This, from a man who has written enough poems praising golden light and balmy breezes, who adored Tagore and the nature-loving Jibanananda Das, who complained bitterly of his cold, dark, north-facing room in the Rashbehari Avenue apartment—see 'After Death: Before Birth' in this volume—the man who was so utterly miserable in the cold and dark winter nights of Pittsburgh, and who appreciated the sunny aspect of his attic room there—how the sunset sky hung before his eyes like a coloured canvas! We have to realize that some of Bose's statements about being a Baudelaire-loving urbanite are tongue-in-cheek. If Bose did not care for nature, he would not have admired the poetry of Jibanananda Das, nor striven to establish him as a contemporary poet.

There is a good example of Bose's tongue-in-cheek language regarding nature in a letter he wrote to the poet Naresh Guha on 12 September 1963 from Bloomington, Indiana:

We have found lodgings here on the sixth floor, three east-facing rooms side by side, and in all three rooms we have wall-to-wall glass windows, no curtains, and right now no money to buy them either—we are living tormented by the lashings of light and heat. Looking out, one sees no other habitations, just plains undulating up to the horizon, the huge sky always impassive—I am having to swallow nature in big gulps, which is not too desirable for me. On top of that, the power of summer is still predominant; the earth is, as it were, shamelessly uncovered—I somehow feel that these countries have no right to be hot, for they have nothing in their lifestyle that suits summer. In my mind I am waiting for those days when seasonal chastisement will force women to give up dressing themselves in knickers and don garments that hang from their bodies; when clouds, rain, and fog will thicken outside, when there will be nothing out there 'to see', when the domestic interior will acquire an intimate air. By then I will have fixed curtains, acquired a few more items of furniture, and will be able to concentrate under the light of a table lamp: the special delight of staying awake in the winter nights of these lands is not unknown to you.[73]

No statement exists outside a context, and the context here clarifies the meaning. Naresh Guha, an ex-student of Bose's from the forties and an active member of the Kavitabhavan circle, had become a close colleague of his since the Department of Comparative Literature had been set up at Jadavpur. At the time of receiving this letter he was in charge of the Department because of Bose's resignation and departure to the USA. Bose and his wife had arrived at Bloomington, Indiana, but the semester had not yet started. Up there in their perch of rented rooms the fierce sun of a late summer (often known as an 'Indian summer') was beating down on them through uncurtained glass, a most disorienting circumstance. The letter reveals that they were feeling isolated because they were far from both the campus and the downtown area. Bose is really giving a humorous reaction to the total package of a diasporic situation in which he finds himself, almost responding more to the culture than to the landscape around him. Anyone who has gone abroad from India and faced a different climate and living conditions will know exactly what he means, and even an avowed lover of nature could have penned this letter when in a certain mood. This is simply the summer version of a poetic mood of discontent, the wintry version of which we have already seen—in the lines remembering his sojourn in Pittsburgh which I have quoted earlier. Bose goes on to make a few more cheeky comments on the small town ('mofussil') atmosphere and amenities of the neighbourhood, lamenting the lack of a fishmonger and a proper butcher's shop, complaining of tasteless pre-wrapped chilled food and the lack of variety in vegetables; he and his wife were feeling nostalgic not only for Calcutta but also for the human contact available in New York. Nothing that is said here can be taken to mean that he did not care for nature, and indeed he would settle down and enjoy his time in the campus. Naresh Guha comments in his notes that in the conflict between nature and art, Bose was on the side of art, and that in his last years this was where he differed from Tagore, adding: 'Nevertheless, even a few days before his death (March 1974) I saw him gazing with enchanted eyes at a serene late-afternoon natural scene and heard him saying in a hushed voice, "How beautiful is this earth!"—and I can't forget that either.'[74] This perhaps gives us a clue to the real patterning of Bose's thoughts and feelings in the later years, analogous to the pain or *abhiman* which the critic Ayyub detected in Sudhindranath Datta—a hurt feeling at the indifference of the material universe to our human condition.[75] Vis-à-vis the lines from Bose's letter to Naresh Guha quoted above, containing his summer grouch, readers should look at poems like 'Nostalgia' or 'The Constraint of Seasonality', included in this volume, to appreciate the other side of the coin. Guha comments further[76] that in the conflict between town and country Bose was always an urban man and that there is not that much in his writings about rural or country town life; again this has to be set in its proper context. In the memoirs of his visits to Santiniketan during Tagore's lifetime, a unique account first published in 1941, Bose says clearly that inauthenticity in urban life and the parochial narrowness of rustic life were equally detestable to him.[77] What he cherished was the art of living, and without the right kind of company this art of living could not be created or enjoyed. In Santiniketan he found that Tagore had personally created such an ambience, and that is why he called that place *sab-peyechhir desh,* a utopian land where one had everything. The landscape of the district—and there are plenty of nature cameos in that volume of memoirs—became all the more lovable because of this factor. Leaving Tagore's Santiniketan was bidding goodbye to heaven. In the memoirs, too, of his boyhood, written just two years before his death, there are scenes of exquisite beauty recollected in tranquillity; let me offer two such samples from his memories of the country town of Noakhali.

... about four or so rooms round the courtyard, the golden light of the sun glinting through the interstices of the wattle fencing in the early hours of the morning, the middays cool on the earthen floors under the thatched roofs. Right next to this there is a huge orchard, which in sunny days is like a shimmering haze of blue and green. There is so much fruit that the ladies wash their feet in the juice of green coconuts, and the birds peck and peck the jamruls and black jaams, and still can't finish them off. Near by is a church, where on a bed of sleek dense grass large kalavati flowers blossom: yellow petals with red specks. The environment is tidy and tranquil.[78]

My eyes retain the memory of some charming pictures too. An abundance of trees and shrubs; ponds everywhere; the yards of houses enlivened all through the winter with red and yellow marigolds; on road verges flowers of the blood-red hibiscus and the white togor peeping between the leaves; in the grounds of some official building varieties of multicoloured variegated leaves; in the month of Chaitra fiery red flowers of the silk cotton tree burst, releasing small balls of fluff that float in the wind. The iguana wanders over dry leaves that are yellow and bright red; when it meets a human being, it stares with gleaming eyes. There are multitudes of butterflies, creatures of the sun, and when it's dark, clusters of shiny green fire-flies. Brooding moonlight fills the expanse of the sky, and in moonlit winter nights a dense layer of fog turns familiar objects into things of mystery, so that a sudden casual glance suggests a human figure or a human shape.[79]

We just cannot say that a man who could recollect so vividly scenes like these, which had not been before his eyes for several decades, did not have a deep sensitivity to nature. Our sensitivity in this respect is very much shaped by the environments through which we move; one sees this quite clearly in the case of Tagore, who moves from floral allusions drawn from literary sources and the flowers grown in pots on the roof terrace of the Jorasanko house, through the landscape and waterscape of eastern Bengal observed during his houseboat days, on to the trees and flowers of Santiniketan which were planted during his own lifetime. Bose's nature-references too are in consonance with the locations in which his life was lived.

Mixed with the joky element in his 'don't care for nature' comments, there is indeed a tinge of melancholy which becomes discernible in him from middle age. The poetry does show it. As the years advanced, the inevitability of decay and death became an insistent tinnitus in his ears; it was as if he was saying: 'Soon enough light and air will be wiped out from my senses, all that will be left of me are these doodles on paper, so I had better concentrate on making a few more marks on blank paper—in a darkened room, with no distractions from wily nature.' I do not see this as essentially all that different from the defiant gesture with which poets have time and again pitted the 'immortality' of art against the 'mortality' of the life of an organism. We need look no further than English poetry, which had, after all, been a major component of Bose's literary education, and where mutability happens to be a recurrent motif. From Shakespeare's complaint that 'summer's lease hath all too short a date' to the Keatsian knowledge of 'Beauty that must die; / And Joy, whose hand is ever at his lips / Bidding adieu', from Shakespeare's assertion—'My love shall in my verse ever live young'—to Keats's apotheosis of the Grecian urn: the poetical articulation of transience as well as the triumph of art over transience would have been an integral part of Bose's bloodstream. And in his own poetry, too, there is a kind of resolution of the duality—in poetical terms, more than which we neither can, nor should, expect in poetry.

None of this invalidates the sensitivity to nature which is amply evident in his writings and which readers of this volume should be able to check out for themselves without any difficulty. It is what we would expect from a poet who knew his Baudelaire, certainly, but also knew his Kalidasa, Shakespeare, Keats, Tagore, Hölderlin, Yeats, D. H. Lawrence, and many other nature-loving poets. When he is abroad or travelling, Bose responds to landscape with much vibrancy, and he can remember and re-create with clarity a scene which is not before his eyes. He remembers the way the new landscape was different from what he is used to. For a Bengali poet to apply an adjective like 'brilliant' (*ujjval*) to the month of June ('Bloomington, Indiana'), or to speak of spring as 'conspiring, lost, forgotten / in vaporous, white, uncomplicated December' ('Sonnet of 3 a.m.: 2') shows a fine tuning to scenes observed abroad rather than a lack of interest in nature. In the native, tropical context of the Bengali language Western month-names like June and December have other associations, so in effect he invests these names with new meanings. I am personally very sensitive to this issue, for as a diasporic Bengali writer I have to do this all the time, and have probably learnt something from Bose's poetry in an unconscious manner. In 'Welcome and Farewell', a poem about memories, Bose deliberately juxtaposes the Western month-name June and the Bengali month-name Asharh (mid-June to mid-July) to underline the different associations and to evoke two different memories, one of America, the other of his childhood in eastern Bengal:

> I'm in a hotel room. Am used to it now. It's almost my own.
> The season's summer, young and lovely June. At my window
> the sea breeze. June it is, but Asharh is imminent.
> Not evening, but a rain-resonant dawn, the sky blurred above the yard,
> algae rejoicing on the pond, bamboo groves smoky in the rain.

I would ask readers of this volume to approach the poems with minds uncluttered by any pre-conception that there was an element of negativism in Bose's attitude to nature.

Did Bose influence others? Certainly, on many fronts. Through his magazine, which was an enviable platform for poetry, he consolidated a sense of identity amongst the post-Tagore generation, encouraging them to think of themselves as 'the moderns'. Younger poets of succeeding generations too flowered in its shade, beginning their poetic careers in the pages of *Kavita*. The strengthening of prose poetry through experiments was one of the achievements of the early years of the magazine.[80] Through his reviews and essays, he taught many of us how to appreciate poetry as poetry and to convey that appreciation in critical prose. As a translator of poetry, he was a profound influence in the fifties and sixties; I shall touch this subject again in the next chapter. Also very influential was his edition of the anthology *Adhunik Bangla Kavita* (Modern Bengali Poetry). The very first edition of the anthology of this name had appeared in 1940, edited by Abu Sayeed Ayyub and Hirendranath Mukhopadhyay. This edition is now difficult to come by; I remember there used to be a copy in my parents' house. The two editors disagreed so much amongst themselves on grounds of ideology—Ayyub was a philosopher with a theistic faith, while Hirendranath Mukhopadhyay was a 'progressivist' with a Marxist orientation—that they even wrote separate introductory chapters. There was much wrangling on how much space to allocate to this or that poet. The volume was not received badly, but Bose, who had been involved in the launching of the project, who had chosen the two editors, and had even found a publisher for the volume, was less than happy with the results. He later took charge of a completely new edition, which first appeared in 1954; four more editions, each time with additions and alterations, came out in his lifetime. This 'evolving' anthology became a standard anthology of twentieth-century Bengali poetry for our generation and the next, helping to shape our tastes.[81] His focus was on poems as poems, not as examples of a religious belief, a philosophical position, or a political ideology. In his Introduction he pointed to the diversity of the contemporary poetry scene, marked by clashes, eddies, and contradictions, not reducible to a formulaic account. He found in it rebellion and protest, doubt and fatigue, searching and the surge of surprise, the joy of life and faith in the cosmic order, hope and despair, introversion and extroversion, the battles of social existence and the thirst for a spiritual life—and not just in different poets, but sometimes in the same poet at different times. He noted also how poets had continued to be preoccupied with love and nature, extending and diversifying the repertoire of each.[82] His impatience with formulas, theories, and ideologies moulded the mind-set of some of us, whilst from time to time it caused a certain distance to appear between his path and that of others, especially those with Marxist leanings. Inevitably, rifts appeared between himself and some erstwhile *Kavita* colleagues, though courtesy and cordial personal relations were never withdrawn.[83] On the other hand, his catholicism of taste, his capacity to surrender to literature as literature, and to inculcate love of literature amongst his students, made him an influential teacher during his tenure at Jadavpur; and many of his ex-students have made their mark in Bengali writing. At the same time, those who were not directly his students, such as Shamsur Rahman (b. 1929), now the most well-known name in the poetry scene in Bangladesh, have acknowledged him 'as a teacher'.[84]

But what of a direct influence on the poetry of his successors? Younger poets who belonged to the Kavitabhavan circle, such as Arunkumar Sarkar (1921–80) and Naresh Guha (b. 1924), were certainly his *shishyas* in one sense, but according to Bose's biographer Samir Sengupta, they were old enough to wish to avoid any signs of overt discipleship in their poetry and were anxious to retain their separate identities. According to Sengupta, Bose's influence is more visible in those who were born in the thirties, such as Sunil Gangopadhyay (b. 1934) and Shakti Chattopadhyay (1933–95), especially in the latter. Shakti Chattopadhyay began to write poetry in the mid-fifties, when Bose's poems from the *Je-Andhar Alor Adhik* phase and some of his influential poetry translations were coming out in *Kavita*. Sengupta, who has studied Chattopadhyay's poetry closely, traces Bose's influence in Chattopadhyay's love of the sonnet form, attention to metre and rhyme, interest in poetry translation, and even in certain preferences in spelling. He considers that Bose's own sonnets as well as his translations of Baudelaire and Rilke were amongst the earliest inspirations for Chattopadhyay the poet. When Chattopadhyay published his first collection in 1961, a line from a Baudelaire poem translated by Bose was quoted on the dedication page. Other features of his poetry which Sengupta associates with Bose's influence are his many references to the power of words, and writing poetry about poetry itself, something which Sunil Gangopadhyay also has done.[85] 'However much we err, however low we sink, yet in the Bengali literary world we are all like his sons,' wrote Gangopadhyay on 19 March 1974, anxious to affirm his affiliation to the elder poet, in his obituary report on Bose's death and funeral in the daily *Anandabazar Patrika*.[86]

I should add that although as an emerging poet Shakti Chattopadhyay might well have been influenced by various aspects of Bose's activities as a poet in the mid-fifties, he cannot, in my opinion, be really classed as a Bosean poet in a very deep sense. A turn of phrase here or an image there may remind the reader of Bose, yet in temperament and mind-set, poetic voice and accent the two are really very different. Bose is poised, sophisticated, urbane, a maestro of a poet. Chattopadhyay is essentially a poet in the Dionysian style; he has more affinity with the Beat generation and belongs to a new era of turmoil that began in Bengali poetry in the late fifties and early sixties, from which Bose consciously dissociated himself. Chattopadhyay, who was a student of Bose's at Jadavpur, though he did not complete his studies, has thus recalled the time when Bose first told him of his decision to close *Kavita*:

I remember one night—it was well after two in the morning—I phoned him from somewhere, I don't remember from where. I said, 'Sir, I am coming to you right now. I'm dying to see you.'
Guessing the state I was in [i.e. intoxicated], he pleaded repeatedly, 'Please, Shakti, not today, not at all. I am extremely tired. Come first thing in the morning. We can chat all day. Well, shall I expect you tomorrow then?' I was insistent. At some stage I realized that the thing had become ugly. I apologized and put the receiver down. As usual, I didn't manage to go and see him the next day. That night he didn't have a moment's rest. When I met him next, he said, 'You know, it wouldn't have been such a bad idea if you had come that day. Actually, I told you not to come because I wasn't sure how you might make the journey. I've made up my mind about something: I'm going to wrap up the *Kavita* magazine. I can't understand at all what you folks are writing. And I'm not going to print stuff that I don't understand. If Jyoti [Jyotirmoy Datta, Bose's son-in-law] wishes to continue it, he can, and you folks can stay with him. I don't mind.' I was sad to hear this fatal announcement. But I knew that his mind was made up.[87]

One could say that this incident epitomizes a separation of pathways that occurred at this juncture. I remember that when I returned to Calcutta in 1963 after studies at Oxford, Bose had just left for the USA, *Kavita* was no longer coming out, Allen Ginsberg had been and gone, the 'Hungry' movement had been launched, and *Krittibas* was the mouthpiece of the new generation of 'angry young men' in poetry. But Bose was by no means finished as a poet, or as a writer. His last three collections of poetry, well represented in this volume, were yet to come, as indeed were some of his major titles in criticism, drama, and fiction.

Allen Ginsberg (1926–97), who had visited Calcutta in 1962 with his partner Peter Orlovsky, had created a sensation, initiating young local poets into drugs, 'automatic writing', and an unconventional lifestyle. Amongst locals who took a lead in rocking the establishment under his inspiration was Shakti Chattopadhyay.[88] Bose, who had quite liked Ginsberg in New York, and was ready to acknowledge that there was something very authentic within him, was not very impressed by his show of bohemianism in Calcutta: drugs, dirty clothes, and his attraction towards fraudulent holy men and the Soviet regime.[89] To Bose none of this was essential to the business of being a modern poet. In the case of Shakti, a certain flirtation with bohemianism would remain as a permanent trait of his artistic persona and spill over into what he wrote. Not that his poetry is reducible to that dimension in a simplistic sense: it has its own strengths, but they are of a different order from Bose's.

To me the greatest strength of Bose's poetry is its syntactic sinew. Even when exuberant and expansive, as in the early years, or dense and taut, as in the later years, exploring difficult thoughts and emotions, his language never disintegrates, never becomes fluffy. This fibrous strength, linked to his conscientious attention to punctuation, ensures that nothing of what he wants to say disappears, in the name of modernism, into a whirlpool of private imagery from which no shreds can be retrieved by the reader. I am saying that his poetry has some of the *strength* of prose; indeed, in this respect his poetry is of a piece with his prose. This is a feature I personally like very much, where I can really relate to him—a point of affinity between us which has made my task as a translator both manageable and pleasurable. The mature Bose is a very intellectual poet who nevertheless remains engagingly reader-friendly. His deeply humanistic poetry records an impressive diversity of interactions with people. He knows the importance of solitude as well as the pleasures of company. He can be lush, but never loses his self-discipline. He is both infectiously warm and admirably, luminously Apollonian.

It is a fact of life that if someone is a dab hand at doing a number of different things, he may sometimes receive less than his share of credit for one of those activities in which he has really and truly excelled. To understand this phenomenon, we need look no further than the case of Tagore: for those who do not read Bengali his fame as a guru and a prophet has, for the better part of the twentieth century, exceeded an appreciation of his core identity as a poet, and if we grant that this particular form of reception has largely been due to a linguistic barrier, we must also concede that most Bengalis even now respond more to his songs than to that section of his poetry which does not have the assistance of melodies to carry the messages along. For the vast majority everywhere, the aural appeal of songs will probably always overshadow that of poetic texts which demand greater intellectual attention—looking at the printed page and pondering meanings.

In a similar fashion, Bose's unquestionable role as an editor and a publisher, as the leader of a 'modernist' movement in poetry, as someone who befriended other poets and acted as an impresario on their behalf, has for some (who should really know better) tended to take the limelight away from his solid achievements as a poet. His contributions in translation and scholarship have compounded the problem.

Poets with whom we share a temperamental affinity will always have an immediate appeal to us, and in this sense we shall always have some special favourites whilst being able to enjoy the work of many others. To me, personally, Bose's poetry has this special appeal, but I am not enthusiastic about arranging poets in a hierarchical order. The post-Tagore poet who currently enjoys the most popularity is Jibanananda Das. When my generation was growing up, Das was acknowledged to be one of the great post-Tagores, but had not yet become the cult figure he has now become. His recent elevation to an iconic status and the passion with which some of his stylistic mannerisms are imitated in both the Bengals are phenomena which intrigue me; there is something deeply paradoxical about a poet who was known to be reclusive in real life becoming a populist cultural hero in his 'life after death'. I suspect that more than anything else it has to do with his glorification of the Bengali landscape, especially in the posthumously published *Rupasi Bangla* (Beautiful Bengal, 1957) poems. When he boldly asserts that having seen Bengal's face, he no longer goes seeking the earth's beauty, or that he will return again to this Bengal, to the banks of the river Dhansiri, he touches a special nerve-centre and rouses a powerful response, offering the heady wine of patriotic solace to a people who have suffered many ills in the second half of the twentieth century. Poets who do not speak in such an accent, who reveal their cosmopolitan orientation and love and enjoyment of all the world, can never hope to compete in popularity with poets who articulate, with a passionate, parochial, even atavistic intensity, their love of the homeland and its landscape—especially amongst a people who feel deprived or marginalized in some way. One can notice the same tendency in the British Isles, where there is a great cult of the regions in poetry; Wales, the north of England, Scotland, Ireland: each area has its cult poets.

Of Das's gifts and importance as a poet of twentieth-century Bengal there can be no question, yet I would venture to say that without the extra-literary factor I have just indicated, his poetic oeuvre by itself does not justify the current elevation of his status to an almost Himalayan peak which is somehow way above all the other post-Tagore eminences. Looked at without prejudice, Bose's poetic corpus certainly shows a greater range of subject-matter and of human emotions readers can relate to, and a greater span of development. In language too, Bose is much nearer to us than Das, who retained a love of the archaic in his characteristic turns of phrase, a style which is often copied by those who now deliberately imitate his accent. And in human beings one gift, if cultivated with discipline, tends to reinforce another; Bose's versatility—his strengths as a writer of prose, as a dramatist, as an editor, scholar, and translator—certainly fed and enriched his poetry. I began this Introduction with a quotation from Sibnarayan Ray, and will end this discussion by quoting the relevant section in full:

Looking back, it now seems that amongst all these geniuses [i.e. of the post-Tagore generation] Buddhadeva Bose had the most multifaceted genius. In view of the intensive and extensive religious cult that is going on in the two Bengals around Jibanananda, this proposal of mine has a high chance of being rejected without scrutiny. There is no reason to doubt Jibanananda's greatness; indeed, discovering and establishing him as a poet of distinction is one of Buddhadeva's achievements. Jibanananda was an authentic poet; I saw him only once or twice; but reading his works, I think of him as a pool of water in which stars are reflected, where, within the layers of deep darkness, there is the up-and-down motion of many a thought and feeling, but there is no outward flow. On the other hand, Buddhadeva is like a stream issuing from a snowy mountain-peak, cascading down step by step, becoming a river, spreading itself into many branches, and constantly flowing towards the great ocean. I do not see another such genius in the Bengali language after Tagore, as multifaceted and continuously dynamic as Buddhadeva.[90]

The two images capture the two poets admirably. I hope those who love poetry will find something interesting on offer in the following pages. All poems are translated from the collected poems edition edited by Naresh Guha.[91]

End Notes

Enough details are supplied below to identify publications. Where necessary, please consult the Bibliography for fuller details.

1. Sibnarayan Ray, 'Bangla Gadya o Buddhadeb Basu', in *Boidagdhya,* special issue on Buddhadeva Bose, Calcutta, May 1999, p. 10. Unless specified otherwise, all quotations from Bengali originals are given in my translation.
2. Shamsur Rahman, 'Buddhadeb Basu, Tanr Srishtir Tirthe', *Boidagdhya,* issue cited, p. 52.
3. Bose, *Amar Jauban,* M. C. Sarkar & Sons, Calcutta, 1989 reprint, p. 25.
4. Sibnarayan Ray in his Introduction to Ray and Maddern (editors), *I have seen Bengal's face: A selection of modern Bengali poetry in English translation,* Editions Indian, Calcutta, 1974, p. 15.
5. Ibid., p. 14.
6. There might have been one or two attempts in nineteenth-century Bengal, but they did not have much impact. See Samir Sengupta, *Buddhadeb Basur Jiban,* Vikalp, Calcutta, 1998, p. 108.
7. Bose, *Amader Kavitabhavan,* Vikalp, Calcutta, 2001, p. 16.
8. Ray, Introduction to *I have seen Bengal's face,* op. cit., p. 20.
9. Bose's friendship with and patronage of Samar Sen is discussed in detail in a new study by Suman Gun, *Buddhadeb Basu o Samar Sen: Sakhye Samipye,* Vikalp, Calcutta, 2000.
10. Samir Sengupta, *Buddhadeb Basur Jiban,* op. cit., p. 51.
11. Ray, Introduction to *I have seen Bengal's face,* op. cit., p. 19.
12. Quoted from Chakravarty's poems translated and presented in *I have seen Bengal's face,* op. cit., p. 62 (translated by Marian Maddern) and p. 64 (translated by the poet himself).
13. Ayyub, 'Sudhindranath Datta', English article of 1960 appended to Ayyub's collection of essays *Pather Shesh Kothay,* 4th edition, Dey's Publishing, Calcutta, 1992, p. 168.
14. Sudhindranath Datta, 'A Poet of Bengal—Bishnu Dey', quoted from *The World of Twilight,* Oxford University Press, Calcutta, 1970, pp. 212–13; the translation of this essay was mine.
15. See Arun Sen, *Bishnu Dey, E Brotojatray,* Aruna Prakashani, Calcutta, 1983.
16. Quoted from Marian Maddern's translation in *I have seen Bengal's face,* op. cit., p. 37.
17. Bose's Introduction to Datta's *Kavyasangraha,* Navana, 1962, page thirteen of the Introduction.
18. Ayyub, 'Sudhindranath Datta', *Pather Shesh Kothay,* op. cit., p. 170. See also pp. 171–5.
19. Ibid., p. 173.
20. See his *Bishnu Dey, E Brotojatray,* op. cit., and also his *Ei Moitree! Ei Monantor!,* Asha Prakashani, Calcutta, 1977.
21. Ray, Introduction to *I have seen Bengal's face,* op. cit., pp. 20–1.
22. This letter, dated 3 October 1935, has been re-printed in full in Bose, *Amader Kavitabhavan,* op. cit., pp. 13–15.

23. See Naresh Guha's Introduction to *Kavir Chithi Kavike: Rabindranathke Amiya Chakravarty, 1916–41,* Papyrus, Calcutta, 1995; the letters of Chakravarty to Tagore given there; and Tagore's letters to Chakravarty in his *Chithipatra,* Vol. 11. I feel duty-bound to point out that a strangely distorted image of Amiya Chakravarty has recently been projected for the English-reading public by Krishna Dutta and Andrew Robinson in their book *Rabindranath Tagore: The Myriad-Minded Man,* Bloomsbury, London, 1995, pp. 332–3. Chakravarty was not, as they allege, 'a mediocre, pretentious and devious man' who flattered Tagore 'shamelessly', wrote poetry of 'astonishing fatuity', and became 'a counterfeit "world citizen"'; he was, without a doubt, one of our major poets of the twentieth century, and a genuinely cosmopolitan intellectual, a man who had an Oxford doctorate and knew Stephen Spender. Nor was there anything spurious in his relationship with Tagore: it was a genuine friendship which was rewarding for both.
24. Bose, *Amar Chhelebela,* M. C. Sarkar & Sons, Calcutta, reprint of 1989, p. 8.
25. Ibid., p. 74.
26. Ibid., pp. 97–8.
27. Seely, *A Poet Apart,* University of Delaware Press, 1990. Seely also translated Bose's novel *Raat Bhorey Brishti* as *Rain Through the Night,* Delhi, 1973.
28. Bose, *Amar Jauban,* op. cit., pp. 31–2.
29. Bose, *Amar Chhelebela,* op. cit., pp. 69–71.
30. Sengupta, introductory section of *Buddhadeb Basur Jiban,* page twenty-six.
31. Bose, *Amar Jauban,* op. cit., p. 52.
32. Ibid., pp. 63–4.
33. Translated from the notes in Bose's *Kavitasangraha,* Volume 3, ed. by Naresh Guha, Dey's Publishing, 1993, pp. 259–60.
34. Bose, *Amar Chhelebela,* op. cit., p. 19.
35. Ibid., p. 34, p. 95.
36. Ibid., p. 47; also Bose, *Amar Jauban,* op. cit., p. 19.
37. Shamsur Rahman, 'Buddhadeb Basu, Tanr Srishtir Tirthe', *Boidagdhya,* issue cited, p. 51.
38. Bose, *Amar Chhelebela,* op. cit., p. 110.
39. Bose, *Anya Konkhane,* New Age Publishers Ltd, Calcutta, 1950, p. 49.
40. The details regarding Bose's trips to Calcutta in the student days are taken from his *Amar Chhelebela,* op. cit., p. 110, *Amar Jauban,* op. cit., pp. 35–7, and Samir Sengupta, *Buddhadeb Basur Jiban,* op. cit., pp. 36–43.
41. Quoted in Sengupta, op. cit., p. 144 and p. 176.
42. Quoted in Sengupta, op. cit., p. 176.
43. Sengupta, op. cit., p. 177.
44. Samir Sengupta, 'Je-Andhar Alor Adhik', essay in *Boidagdhya,* issue cited, p. 140.
45. Anne Stevenson, 'To Be a Poet', *Enough of Green,* Oxford University Press, Oxford etc, 1977.

46. Bose, *Amader Kavitabhavan,* originally published in the Puja issue of *Desh,* 1974, quoted in Sengupta, pp. 177–8. This is the source I followed when I translated this extract. Since then *Amader Kavitabhavan* has been published as a separate book (Vikalp, 2001), and the relevant passages may be found on pp. 30–32: the word *jorbahul* at the top of p. 31 in the book looks like a misprint. I have followed Sengupta's reading of *morbahul,* which makes more sense.
47. Sengupta, *Buddhadeb Basur Jiban,* p. 282.
48. Bose, 'Ingreji o Matribhasha', *Kavita,* Year 22, No. 2, Poush 1364, pp. 114–15.
49. Ibid., pp. 118–19.
50. Protiva Bose, *Jibaner Jalchhabi,* Ananda Publishers, Calcutta, first published in 1993.
51. Protiva Bose, *Mahabharater Maharanye,* Vikalp, Calcutta, 1997.
52. Protiva Bose, *Jibaner Jalchhabi,* reprint of 1996, p. 235; Sudakshina Ghosh, *Buddhadeb Basu,* Paschimbanga Bangla Akademi, Calcutta, 1997, pp. 59–61; Sengupta, *Buddhadeb Basur Jiban,* pp. 320–4; Damayanti Basu Singh, chapter entitled 'Samyojan' in her edition of Bose, *Amader Kavitabhavan,* 2001, pp. 93–4.
53. Letter to Naresh Guha, 6 November 1964, quoted in Sengupta, *Buddhadeb Basur Jiban,* p. 334.
54. Damayanti Basu Singh, chapter entitled 'Samyojan' in her edition of Bose, *Amader Kavitabhavan,* 2001, p. 94.
55. Bose, *Mahabharater Katha,* M. C. Sarkar & Sons, Calcutta, first published posthumously in 1974.
56. Sibnarayan Ray, *I have seen Bengal's face,* op. cit., p. 17.
57. Tagore's discussion appeared in *Bichitra,* Kartik 1338 (1931). See the notes in Bose's *Kavitasangraha,* ed. by Guha, Vol. 1, pp. 390–1.
58. Samir Sengupta, 'Je Andhar Alor Adhik', *Boidagdhya,* issue cited, p. 134.
59. Bose, *Kavitar Shatru o Mitra,* M. C. Sarkar and Sons, Calcutta, reprint of 1997, p. 32.
60. Ibid., p. 43.
61. Ibid., p. 44.
62. Bose, *Amar Jauban,* op. cit., p. 59.
63. Bose, *Kavitar Shatru o Mitra,* op. cit., p. 32.
64. Ibid., pp. 34–6.
65. Ibid., pp. 36–7.
66. Ibid., p. 38.
67. Ibid., pp. 38–9.
68. Samir Sengupta, 'Je Andhar Alor Adhik', *Boidagdhya,* issue cited, pp. 139–40.
69. Bose, 'Ingreji o Matribhasha', *Kavita,* Year 22, No. 2, Poush 1364, p. 110.
70. Ibid., p. 111.
71. Bose, *Amar Chhelebela,* op. cit., pp. 14–15.
72. Letter to Damayanti, dated 27.6.66, quoted in Sengupta, *Buddhadeb Basur Jiban,* p. 346.

73. Quoted in Naresh Guha, 'Buddhadeb Basur Chithi', *Boidagdhya,* issue cited, p. 42.
74. Guha, 'Buddhadeb Basur Chithi', *Boidagdhya,* issue cited, p. 44.
75. Ayyub, essay cited, *Pather Shesh Kothay,* op. cit., p. 177.
76. Guha, essay cited, *Boidagdhya,* issue cited, p. 44.
77. Bose, *Sab-Peyechhir Deshe,* Vikalp edition, Calcutta, 1998, p. 41.
78. Bose, *Amar Chhelebela,* op. cit., p. 18.
79. Ibid., pp. 27–8.
80. Prabhat Kumar Das, 'Tarun Kabider Abhibhabak', *Boidagdhya,* issue cited, pp. 253–4.
81. Further details are available in Bose, *Amader Kavitabhavan,* op. cit., and Sengupta, *Buddhadeb Basur Jiban,* op. cit.
82. Bose, *Adhunik Bangla Kavita,* 1963 edition, Introduction.
83. For instance, in the late fifties an interesting gap opened up between him and Amiya Chakravarty over the evaluation of Pasternak's *Doctor Zhivago.* At first (December 1958) Chakravarty expressed a high opinion of the book, but by April 1959 he had changed his mind quite drastically. He now regretted that Pasternak's hero could not see the truth that beneath all the disasters a new age was being created in Russia. Bose, a great admirer of the book, held the opinion that whether Pasternak had done justice to the Russian Revolution or not was not really a relevant issue, for literature did not have to hold a brief for objective truth: the creative writer's task was simply to make his readers *feel* subjective truth, greater than which there were no truths in literature. See Sengupta, *Buddhadeb Basur Jiban,* op. cit., pp. 290–6.
84. Shamsur Rahman, essay cited, *Boidagdhya,* issue cited, p. 54.
85. Sengupta, personal communication to me, 7 June 2002.
86. Quoted in Sengupta, *Buddhadeb Basur Jiban,* op. cit., p. 395.
87. Shakti Chattopadhyay, 'Gadyer Garhasthye', *Gadyasangraha,* Volume 1, Dey's Publishing, Calcutta, 1996, page fifteen of the introductory section.
88. Samir Sengupta, 'Shaktir Kavitay Rabindranath', *Prasanga: Shakti Chattopadhyay,* ed. by Sunil Gangopadhyay and Sounak Chacraverti, Vikalp, 2000, p. 82.
89. Letter to Damayanti, 7 December 1962, quoted in Sengupta, *Buddhadeb Basur Jiban,* p. 318.
90. Sibnarayan Ray, 'Bangla Gadya o Buddhadeb Basu', in *Boidagdhya,* issue cited, p. 10.
91. From the first three volumes of Bose's *Kavitasangraha,* in five volumes, Dey's Publishing, Calcutta. Volumes 4 and 5 house his translated poetry.

Translator's Testament

Readers of this volume need to know that several post-Tagore Bengali poets took a special interest in poetry translation. Sudhindranath Datta, Bishnu Dey, Bose himself, the somewhat younger Loknath Bhattacharya (1927–2001) were all distinguished poet-translators. The impact on us of their translations was profound. I remember clearly how from the fifties onwards we were transformed by these translations, which added new horizons to our poetry. Bose believed passionately in the viability of poetry translation:

Whether the translation of poetry is possible or not is a big meaningless debate which I want to skip, and I want to say at once that translating poetry is also a living, infectious, valuable literary activity, and sometimes—if the translator is a poet in his own language—it can attain the status of creative work. ... Those of us who do not know languages like Russian, German, Latin, Greek, or Chinese, can get close to the poetry written in those languages if we compare two or three translations; we get to know the poet's mind, what he wanted to say, maybe even a modicum of his manner; certainly much of the charm of the original may be lost, but if that poet had not just vended words, if he had also *said* something, then we do on the whole get something precious out of it, the like of which is not available in the literature of our mother tongue, and acquaintance with which increases the chance of enrichment for our literature.[1]

Good translation too, he granted, depended on some kind of inspiration, but on the other hand, because in translation someone else was providing the thought, the translating poet could convert it to an almost technical project, relying heavily on his skills in language and capacity for hard work. Every poet, he pointed out, faced lean times, when he did not have that much to say; at such times translating other poets was better than repeating oneself, for translation work provided excellent limbering up exercise, its discipline kept one fit, and the added expertise gained thereby could be invested in the next poetic project one might oneself undertake.[2] This theory of translation as an act which is at once creative and technical is something that I find quite irresistible: it is both liberating and realistic.

Bose's translations from Kalidasa, Baudelaire, Hölderlin, and Rilke enriched his own creativity and leavened the poetic style of his middle years. They also effected a sea-change in the sensibility of those who were beginning their poetic careers in the fifties and sixties. His well-written prefaces and scholarly notes to the translations enabled us to see the material in its cultural context. His introduction to his translation of Kalidasa's *Meghaduta* made us look at Sanskrit poetry with new eyes. Master of the long line that he already was, did he not learn how to perfect it even further through the exercise of translating this Sanskrit poem? The fascination that the long line held for him can also be seen in a poem re-creating verses from Shankaracharya's *Anandalahari*. Such exercises link with Bose's own poetic reinterpretations of old stories from India's classical hoard, his desire to give them a new lease of life and reintegrate them with the present.

Through his sensitive renderings and brilliant introductions Baudelaire, Hölderlin, and Rilke ceased to be 'foreign poets' and became our own kinsmen. Shakti Chattopadhyay is known to have quoted a line from Baudelaire in Bose's rendering on the dedication page of his first collection of poems. Funnily enough, in the exercise book in which I used to preserve 'fair copies' of my poems from the fifties onwards, the very first page, otherwise blank, sports two separate quotations from two sources as mottoes, and one of these is a line from Baudelaire in Bose's translation. I did have a little reading knowledge of French and was actually reading Baudelaire in the original at that time; yet I have no hesitation in saying that it was Bose's Bengali renderings that enabled me to see that the French poet could belong as much to me as to any French reader. In my teen years I was so much under the spell of Charles Baudelaire *à la* Buddhadeva Bose that I actually painted a watercolour to illustrate the Bengali version of the poem 'A une dame créole'. When I was the editor of a wall-magazine at Presidency College, Calcutta, I published there a fine poem written by a fellow student which was entitled 'Rilker Kavita Porey' (On Reading Rilke's Poetry), several lines of which are still etched on my mind. It is no exaggeration to say that just as Keats had discovered Homer through Chapman, our generation discovered poets like Baudelaire, Hölderlin, and Rilke through Bose. As a tribute to Bose the poetry translator, I have included in this volume his own poem on the poetic genius of Hölderlin. This interest in translating 'foreign' poetry links with Bose's cosmopolitanism. Besides his more well-known translations, there are also many less known ones, fragments from British and American poets, and even from Russian (Pasternak), Swedish, Chinese, and Japanese—done via English, of course, but nonetheless an index of his intellectual curiosity. The Lebanese-

American poet Khalil Gibran (1883–1931) was discovered by Bose in his student days in Dhaka, long before Gibran's popularity in the West in the sixties, and his translation of an English poem of Gibran's was published in *Kallol* in 1926. Even in the case of French and German, Bose acknowledged readily that he had no formal training in these languages, but he worked hard to get at the heart of the original poems with the help of bilingual editions and by comparing different English translations of the same poems. The English translations were what opened his eyes to such poems in the first place, acting as windows on the poetry world.

Apart from the fact that in the fifties and sixties we were undoubtedly in a suitably receptive frame of mind, with heightened responses, the secret of Bose's success as a poetry translator—the reason why, despite his lack of formal training in French and German, his renderings moved an entire generation so profoundly—was his power to make the new poems work as poems in Bengali. In his 'Translator's Statement' prefacing his renderings of Hölderlin, he says explicitly: '... I have constantly striven so that the translations become readable as poems in the Bengali language, because I believe that the most important obligation for a translated poem is to become a poem.'[3] When it comes to poetry translation, I belong to the same school of thinking. To make the translated text work like a poem is my goal too, because I believe that if a translated poem is flat, wooden, prosaic, readers of poetry fall asleep, then wake up at the end without having taken anything in, saying 'Hey, what happened?'

Translation can, of course, have various aims. We may wish to get as close as possible to the meanings of certain original texts, such as legal or religious documents. Or we may wish to persuade an examiner in a language examination that we have understood every twist in the syntax of an original sentence. But to convey the *rasa* of literature, literary translation has to be a creative art, a genre of writing in its own right. To be a good literary translator one needs to be a good writer: the same kind of linguistic skills are required. My primary purpose in an undertaking like the present one is to win new readers for the poetry I am translating. Of course, I am always striving to capture the contents as faithfully as I can, but my overriding aim is to recruit a new readership for the poet I am translating, and for the translated texts qua poetry, so that they produce sympathetic vibes in the community of those to whom poetry matters. The only way to achieve this is to become a co-creator along with the original poet, to use words in the target language creatively and daringly, sometimes unconventionally and experimentally, exactly as a poet in it would, to use language with gusto, confidence, and panache. I want the translated poem to speak to the reader as a poem in the new language, while suggesting, from time to time, as and when necessary, and in the manner of a musical counterpoint, the slight alterity or 'otherness' of the complex linguistic-conceptual-cultural system encoded in the original source. Theorists of translation, following the either/or logic so dear to contemporary savants, are often polarized between those who support 'fluency' and those who believe in offering 'resistance' to that tendency, but those of us who practise the art know that we need an approach that includes both. I wish to achieve as much fluency as I can in the new texts, but I do also wish to retain a close relationship to the originals, as close as I can manage, resisting the temptation to yield to wholesale 'domestication', and combining the two is necessarily a balancing act. Excessive 'resistance' delivers a wooden text from which little literary pleasure can be obtained. A total obsession with fluency, on the other hand, robs the text of that fitful light of 'otherness' which we prize in a text translated from another culture. Good translation is a craft skill that 'finds' solutions and strikes a balance.

In keeping with this aim, I have tried not to clutter the text with too many italics: names of flora and fauna which are not aliens in the context of the poems and words of Indian origin which would be instantly recognized within India or have entered English dictionaries either in the past or in recent years have been left in roman in the vast majority of cases, so that they do not attract more attention than the poems themselves, but can alert foreign readers to the slight otherness of the setting in a gentle, unobtrusive manner. In the Notes section, though, I have tried to provide fuller notes than might be strictly necessary in the Indian context; this is hopefully to make the book more reader-friendly outside India. In the spelling of Bengali words and names, I have trodden a pragmatic middle ground, giving occasional tilts towards the Bengali mode of pronunciation, but retaining romanized forms which have a pan-Indian currency. As things are today, a certain amount of inconsistency in this respect is unavoidable. In deference to Bose's own practice, *Kavita* and 'Kavitabhavan' are spelt with a *v* rather than with a *b*, though the latter is nearer to Bengali pronunciation, and to avoid confusion the spellings *kavita* and *kavya* have been adopted elsewhere as well, for instance, in the Bibliography. To simplify printing, diacritical marks for romanized Sanskrit have been avoided in this book, except on two occasions: once to clarify the identity of a tree in the Notes to the poems, and once in the essay in the Appendix, when quoting directly from the Sanskrit.

While on this subject, let me also clarify that while writing in English I am utterly unable to change the habit of a lifetime and write 'Kolkata' instead of

'Calcutta'. I could, of course, issue a 'universal command' to my computer, asking it to change the spelling mechanically throughout the text. That, to me, would be a gesture of inauthenticity, a concession to political correctness, not an act of my own volition. If the idea is that by writing 'Kolkata' we move closer to the Bengali pronunciation, then I must point out that even 'Kolkata' is only an approximation, as in the case of my own first name. To someone who does not speak Bengali neither the vowel *a* nor the consonant *t* in either 'Ketaki' or in 'Kolkata' can indicate the original pronunciation unambiguously. 'Calcutta' is the English version of the city's name, with a very long history. I do not see the point of changing a form which has been established for so many years and by which the whole world instantly recognizes the city's identity. 'Calcutta' is also historically more appropriate in the context of Bose.

A degree of literalism, something like a literary equivalent of so-called 'fundamentalism', can sometimes bedevil the critical jargon surrounding translation. In the case of literary translation, and especially in poetry translation, this approach is self-defeating. It is so easy to keep to the letter—in respect of *either* meaning *or* form—and betray the poetry. When we ask: 'Is this new text working as a poem?', our query has to be in the context of the target language, not the source language. Our notion of a good translation needs to be broad and accommodating rather than narrow and rigid. First and foremost, the quality of literary vitality and vibrancy has to be conveyed. When building a bridge between two languages of such different provenance as Bengali and English, our attitude to form needs to be flexible. True, Bengali has come under the influence of English from the nineteenth century onwards, yet for the major part of their histories the two languages have evolved in different habitats—natural, cultural, intellectual—and carry the marks on their bodies. It is the differences that make the bridge-building such an exciting and challenging task of practical engineering. Words and phrases in different languages, even though rough lexical equivalents, are never exact equivalents in the geometrical sense of congruent triangles: they may look very similar as explained by the relevant dictionaries, but may still have different resonances in the different linguistic contexts. This means that there is no room for mechanical consistency in literary translation: the same word or phrase may have to be rendered in one way in one poem, and in a slightly different way in another poem. We have to eschew rigidity, trust our 'instincts', and learn to oscillate. Constant accommodation and innovation are necessary, and we cannot move forward without numerous 'micro-decisions' or 'local fixes'.

One interesting point that emerged for me during the present project was the extent to which, in poetry translation, we have to be sensitive even to the graphic aspects of the two languages we are dealing with. Bose's passion for the long line, derived from a tradition where calligraphy and the handwritten format still retain their primacy, and strengthened by his emulation of a Sanskrit metre such as the *mandakranta,* and possibly also by his familiarity with the poetry of D. H. Lawrence and Walt Whitman, both fond of the long line, brought this issue to the fore for me. As long as I was producing printouts in the standard (A-4 size) format, I did not run into problems, because this size could accommodate even his extra-long lines, but the book itself was going to be a demi-octavo and was not going to give me A-4 width! Alarm bells had already begun to ring in my mind when a couple of British magazines which published two of the poems with exceptionally long lines had to reduce the font in those pages to a very small size to accommodate them. Though magazines often do change font-size to suit individual poems, I knew that this was not usually done in a book! As soon as I began to experiment with the narrower page-width myself, many a long line began to spill words into the next line. Yet the original poems, printed in the same demi-octavo size, managed to avoid too much of such spillage, and the font was still readable. Why? Because English 'expands', and while this does not matter in the translation of prose, it does matter in the case of poetry because of the requirements of formatting: not only does one accumulate all those definite and indefinite articles without which English cannot move, and which are unnecessary in Bengali, and those prepositions, the functions of which may be expressed in Bengali by means of inflectional word-endings, but also, the roman script itself is more 'rotund' than the Bengali script, which, with its vowel-signs and conjuncts, is 'slimmer'. Take a word like 'dharma'; it requires six separate characters side by side to represent it in the roman script, which gives this word of two syllables some girth. In Bengali (and other scripts of the same family) the job will be done by two principal characters, the vowels in this case being included in the consonants, and the *ref* sign going on the head of the last consonant will indicate the conjunct *rm*, giving the sign height, but not adding to its girth. The nature of the script, in combination with the nature of the language, means that long lines of poetry can be more easily accommodated in Bengali printing. I began to look at my 'spillages' minutely and critically. Sometimes they were unavoidable, because the number of lines to a stanza indicated a pattern that had to be respected and clearly indicated in the translation. In such cases I have had to accept them: readers of the present volume will notice them.

Other instances, where conformity to the 'shape' of the original poem was less critical, offered possibilities of 're-construction': either altering some of the line-breaks—needless to say, in consonance with the rhythms of spoken English—or making tiny editorial alterations to the language itself—again, without moving away from the original meanings, or a combination of both strategies. As I did the necessary chiselling here and there, I was struck by the many alternative ways in which the same line or lines could so often be rendered. There is really no *one* way to translate a poem. And at every step I was made aware of the need to negotiate between 'fluency' and 'resistance'.

The question of mistakes in translation is complex. Some mistakes may be of the straightforward kind (say, a word or phrase inadvertently missed out, or a word misunderstood) regarding which we can reach an immediate agreement with others; with other mistakes, it may be necessary to have quite a long discussion before any such consensus can be reached; and sometimes slightly different interpretations are entirely possible, so that translators (and scholars) will have to agree to differ. A problem which every translator faces in a task of any great size is the sheer physical difficulty of maintaining intense concentration on two texts: the original text, which is fixed, and the new one, which is being generated step by step. Eyes have to move constantly from the one to the other, back and forth, and after some time the eye muscles get fatigued. That is when a word or phrase slips out in translation. It happens to everyone. You can ask another person to go over the same ground again, but he or she will face exactly the same problem. Such chores are extremely labour-intensive, and hardly any literary translation project carries even a fraction of the kind of funding that would enable either translators or their assistants to receive adequate remuneration for their time and labour. So a few mistakes are inevitable, but I do not think they invalidate the whole work.

I personally believe that slight shifts of meaning are in a sense inevitable when a text moves from the terrain of one language to that of another. Some critics get terribly agitated if such a shift occurs, complaining that we have moved away from the nuances or associations of the original word, phrase, or line; but reading a poem is in any case a complex subjective process. As soon as five different people have read the same poem, five slightly variant mental images of it have been generated in five different minds. Add to it the fact that a concept which looks roughly the same in two languages may actually have different resonances in the two languages. And further, translating poetry, like writing an original poem, means juggling several balls at the same time. The translator, like the original poet, is trying not just to capture meanings, but also to create a rich pattern of sounds within which the meanings can be danced, because that is how poetry operates. If the translator's goal is first and foremost to make the new text work as a poem, then slight shifts of meaning hardly matter. If the reader's goal is to understand the original meanings and nuances as fully and accurately as possible, then shortcuts are not feasible, and he or she must really take the trouble of learning the original language and perusing the original texts. In my model of poetry translation we engage in a dance of approximation: we try to transport what is transportable by touching the substratum of common humanity in readers and by activating their poetic receptors, and this isn't as simple as opening a bottle of milk and pouring it into another jug, but we have to try our best without getting wound up about it.

Take the very first poem in this selection, 'A Prisoner's Song of Praise', written before the poet had reached his eighteenth birthday, a veritable embodiment of youthful rebellion. How do we convey the defiant and boisterous mood of the original? We can't, unless we are prepared to re-create its colourful, rhetorical, richly alliterative style, unless we can write con brio and surprise the reader of the English version with some 'fine excess'. We have to go for bold, racy expressions rather than dull, bland ones. We have to be rhythmic and rhetorical, creating evocative clusters of sounds within which images and emotions can cavort, making every use of alliteration, assonance, internal rime, and other echoic devices. Playing safe and being precious are not going to deliver; we have to be brash and over-the-top, let rip, spitting the sounds. We have to be *creative* rather than *faithful in an academic sense*.

What about the tightly structured poems of *Je-Andhar Alor Adhik*? Initially I had deep misgivings about whether I would be able to tackle the translation of any of these. Almost like the poet writing the original poems, I proceeded stealthily, hardly admitting to myself what I was trying to do, until I found I could achieve what I have elsewhere called the construction of a parallel or corresponding structure, using all the sonic devices available in English. I have not pursued the will-o'-the-wisp of trying to match a rhyme-scheme exactly, because the images in these poems are very important, and I did not wish to distort the images for the sake of rhymes. In each poem I relied on a series of gentle negotiations. Rhyme-words are not abundant in modern English, but much can be achieved by other devices. So in my translations rhyme-schemes may not match with those of the original poems, but in each case I have tried to create an attractive sonic design within which the tension of the poem can be contained. I find what rhymes I can, thankful for every serendipity. In the end, the effort was actually less arduous than I had initially imagined it might be. I would say that overall it was pleasantly challenging. I am so glad I did not shy away from these poems; until we try, we do not know what we are capable of doing.

Translating the 'prose poems' of *Ekdin: Chirodin o Anyanyo Kavita* (One Day: For Ever, and Other Poems) was a very different experience again. It was great fun, more like sailing with the wind, writing con amore. For these poems I decided to create a rhythm of speech, with line-breaks decided by me. Appropriate skills in translation, I believe, can be sharpened through workshops, where by focusing on small details we can raise our awareness of the practical issues involved in the craft of literary translation.[4]

This is an appropriate point at which to introduce the subject of my personal connection to this translation project. Acts of literary translation do not happen out of the blue. It is good to understand the process—who gets translated, who translates whom, and why. I have not come to this task along an academic corridor, but as a practising poet who happens to write poetry in two languages. Insofar as I am a Bengali-language author, I would consider myself an *uttarasuri* or successor to the heritage of Bose's generation. When Bose's younger daughter Damayanti Basu Singh asked me to undertake this task, I knew immediately that I had no option but to take it on, not only as a personal challenge, but also because I felt I owed it to his memory to make his poetry known to those who could not read him in Bengali.

Speaking about poetry translation just a year before his death, Bose said: '... I think it too is creative work; it too requires inspiration, originating in a love felt for the original poet, and sometimes in a sense of affinity with him; it too gives us the same kind of delight as we get when we write something of our own; and it too makes us work very hard, demanding all our intellectual faculties and concentration.'[5] I could not agree more, and I would not have agreed to prepare a volume like this if I did not love Bose's poetry and did not feel a deep sense of kinship with him. He has been a mentor in my own life as a writer, and I feel I must acknowledge this debt.

There was a friendship between him and my father through their common roots in Dhaka. I am not sure exactly when they met: I regret I did not quiz my father about this when he was still alive. But I imagine they must have met in their university days, for my father was also a graduate of Dhaka, albeit in economics, and two years Bose's junior. I grew up hearing tales of the get-togethers in Purana Polton, the green beauty of Ramna, the delights of the Dhaka campus, the fame of the young Ranu Shome (Bose's wife) as a singer, and so on. As a child I too made a few journeys to and from Dhaka along the route described in Bose's poems, via Goalundo. I come from the same subculture as Bose, sharing a common sense of humour and a common cuisine. Bose and my father also had common friends in the economist Parimal Ray, who had married a cousin of my mother, and in the poet Samar Sen, whose paternal grandfather and my mother's maternal grandfather were cousins.[6]

As far as I can recall, I was always aware of the existence of Buddhadeva Bose and of the fact that he was an important poet. I knew that Tagore was dead, that he was a classic. But this other poet—he was alive, a man with whom my father corresponded from his various postings in country towns, to whom he sent my childhood poems for comment, from whom there always came some encouraging feedback. Indeed I was first 'published' in a 'manuscript magazine' edited by the poet's two daughters. This poet, I knew, was also the editor of the printed magazine for grown-ups called *Kavita*, to which my father subscribed. Although he had read economics, and was a civil servant, literature was my father's great love, and he read widely. Somewhat later my father had the volumes of this magazine bound, and was always urging me to read them. The bound volumes of *Kavita* were an essential part of my literary education, from which I learned something I did not learn at school or college: how to relate to contemporary poetry. Bose also became an important model for me in critical prose. About the impact of his poetry translations I have spoken already. And then there was his great novel *Tithidore* (1949),[7] a family saga which was like a mirror held to our eyes, in which we recognized the culture within which we were embedded.

After India's independence my father was posted to Calcutta. We came to live in Rashbehari Avenue, the very street in which Bose lived, and later in another street near by. Bose valued my father as an intellectual friend, especially as my father had taught himself French and German, and read a lot of French and German literature in the original. Thus it came about that I had the privilege of entry to Kavitabhavan, 'The House of Poetry' at 202 Rashbehari Avenue, from childhood onwards. I remember meeting many luminaries of Calcutta's intellectual world in that living-room—in the fifties, before I came to Oxford. They included writers and editors, naturally, but also the renowned physicist Satyendranath Bose, the Bose of bosons.

In due course I received encouragement from Buddhadeva Bose as a fledgeling poet. When I started to write poetry seriously, he gave me some valuable advice. In 1959 I reviewed *Je-Andhar Alor Adhik*, at that time his latest collection of poetry, in the *Presidency College Patrika,* of which I was the editor that year. How to write a book review had been learnt from his magazine in the first place! Regrettably I never had the chance to be published in his magazine. He did choose some of my poems—I had already come to study at Oxford at that time—but soon thereafter he chose to cease the publication of *Kavita.*

    I have always regretted not being able to interact directly with Bose during his last years. I never actually saw him in the sixties and seventies. When I returned from Oxford in 1963 he had just embarked on his important two-year period in the USA. When I taught briefly in the English Department of Jadavpur University, I had no idea whatsoever of the circumstances in which he had just left the Comparative Literature Department. In 1964 I married and left for England again, and Bose was still in America. In the sixties we often published in the same magazine, the weekly *Desh*—so many of his poems are familiar to me from my first reading of them in either *Kavita* or *Desh*—and I felt proud to think that he must be noticing my work, now that I was at last coming of age. Indeed he was—he was following my career with an avuncular interest—and though I did not know it then, he even wondered if living in England, with an English-speaking family, I would be able to continue writing poetry in Bengali. I know for sure that the tenacity with which I have continued to write in Bengali as a diasporic author owes a debt to the two ideals which I imbibed from Bose and internalized at a formative stage of my life: an artist's vocation and that of service to the mother tongue, in both of which he passionately believed. I took my cue from the coexistence in him of a wholehearted loyalty to the mother tongue and an equally committed cosmopolitanism. I also know for a fact that it was his example and the example of the other poet-translators of his generation that encouraged me to render Anglo-Saxon poetry into alliterative Bengali half-lines. I did the first batch of that work in early 1967. From the example of his life I always knew that one had to make do with less cash in hand and little or no institutional support if one wished to follow difficult ideals. But since beginning this project I have learnt further lessons from a closer study of his life and writings. Faced with false accusations in the media, based on misquotation and misrepresentation, or the contumely of critics and academics, to what extent should a writer fight back, when should one withdraw from battle, when should one ignore such things? In the biographical information on him given in the previous chapter I have not included the details of a baseless and ignoble attack on him in 1961 in certain sections of the Calcutta press. I knew nothing about this episode in his life until I started this project, and reading about it in sources such as Sengupta's biography of Bose or the memoirs of Mrs Bose has certainly made me see some of my own experiences of a similar nature in perspective. The pain of such experiences certainly shows in a poet's work. It shows in Bose's work, and I know it shows in mine.

I have developed some of my own ideas by sharpening them against his. Some of his opinions and statements became springboards and points of departure for me. His essay 'Ingrejitey Rabindranath' (Rabindranath in English) in *Kabi Rabindranath* (1966) is a seminal paper on the translation of Tagore, which I re-read when I came to translate Tagore's poetry. Bose thought that Tagore would have to wait until a Roy Campbell or a Michael Hamburger was born to translate him. He never thought that the shy girl in plaits who came to visit him in the forties and fifties might try to tackle the job one day! If I have had any success in that job, it owes something to what I learnt from him about poetry translation. When my translations of Tagore's poetry received the Poetry Book Society's Recommendation, when I was interviewed on BBC's Radio 3 in the same series as Michael Hamburger, the little girl in me so much wanted to tell Bose where she had got to, but by then he had been dead for seventeen years. My latest publication on Tagore is a book embodying interdisciplinary research in which three other scholars have collaborated with me. It explores the consequences of Tagore's protanopic vision on his writings and visual art. The book begins by taking some comments of Bose's as points of departure. Bose had noted certain peculiarities in Tagore's imagery which he had realized were somewhat strange but which he had been at a loss to explain. He didn't know that Tagore had a partial colour vision deficiency of the genetically inherited kind. I wanted to put our 800-page tome in his hands, but he had been gone for twenty-three years.

It has bothered me—this not having met him in his last years, especially as I have 'grown up' and become properly aware of my intellectual debt to him. Only once might a meeting with him have been possible, in the winter of 1970–1 when, six years after leaving Calcutta in 1964, I re-visited my family for six weeks, with two small infants. But Calcutta was then still in the throes of the Naxalite movement; one had to move about carefully; and I was more anxious about securing a bibliography for the doctoral research I had started than anything else, though I managed to place my first batch of translations from Anglo-Saxon poetry with a magazine. The days slipped, I returned to England, and became re-immersed in my work—the thesis, the children. Meanwhile in the subcontinent there was the war for the liberation of Bangladesh, and while I was completing my thesis, one day I heard from my parents the news that Bose was no longer in this world.

When we are young, we absorb influences and lessons from our elders in an unconscious manner. Those things are their gifts to us, and we receive them as happily as chocolates at a birthday, as though it was our right to get them. It is only much later that we realize the extent of what we have been given. And it is then that a wish to give something back begins to surface in us. It was because of this unfinished business in my literary life that when Damayanti asked me to translate her father's poetry into English, I knew at once that I could not say 'no'. I wanted to do it so that those who could not read Bengali but could read English could have some idea of his poetry. From my childhood on I have always known that he was an important author, one of our very important authors, and if he is that, does he not also belong to all of India and also to the world? Unlike some other Bengali writers of my generation or a few years older than me, I was never directly a student of his. I did not read Comparative Literature at Jadavpur; I read English at Presidency College, then went to Oxford—a different trajectory. Yet in so many ways I am who I am because I was shaped by Bose and other Bengali writers of his generation. That is another reason why I have chosen to translate Bose's 1957 essay 'Language, Poetry, and Being Human' for the Appendix. This essay with its fierce loyalty to the mother tongue is in the nature of a manifesto, and this kind of material left a lasting impression on me. Loyalty to the mother tongue has certainly been *the* deciding factor in shaping my life as a diasporic writer. At the end of the seventies, finding it difficult to launch an academic career in Britain, and sensing also, in academic and literary circles here, a general indifference to the culture of the place where my roots were, I swiftly decided that whatever else I did, continuing to develop myself as a Bengali writer ought to be my priority, that this was far more important to me than any other 'career goal'. This decision points to the profound influence of Buddhadeva Bose at the core of my life, and explains something which often mystifies my British, American, and even some Indian friends: how come, having studied at Oxford, I did not become a 'post-colonial writer in English', like some other Indian or Indian-born writers. These friends do not know how Bose and his contemporaries have helped to shape me. In the end, undertaking this translation project became linked to the identity question— I was doing it to explain myself. It became a box of chocolates that I myself wanted to wave to the English-reading world.

In his various discussions of poetry translation Bose of course envisages the poet translating from a 'foreign' tongue to his own. This is the classic model, and rests on the assumption that it is a creative art, and that one can be creative in only one tongue. I have a few thoughts to offer on this.

First, we have to take on board the reality that as in other activities, so in linguistic culture, we are an evolving species: what seemed impossible even in the near past may become viable along that path of evolution. Linguistic landscapes change, sometimes beyond recognition, with social and political changes and the passing of generations. Languages spoken by small human groups are dying all the time. In his essay 'Ingreji o Matribhasha' (English and the Mother Tongue), written in 1957, to which I have already referred a few times, Bose argued strongly for the retention of English in Indian education, not as a medium of instruction, but as one of the subjects to be taught, as a door to the world outside India. What is interesting in this well-argued essay is his touching faith that English could somehow be contained in a benign role. He was genuinely worried about the hegemony of Hindi in a land of diverse tongues (as the essay I am presenting in the Appendix will amply show), but he seemed to think that unlike Hindi, English could operate with a degree of neutrality in the pan-Indian context; '... with respect to our mother tongue, English will never be a competitor,' he argued, 'but as in the past, so too in the future, will enrich the mother tongue ...'[8] This stance shows us that in human affairs it is never possible to predict the future with a hundred per cent accuracy. Bose did not foresee the passion with which the middle classes of urban India, including the speakers of Bengali, would embrace English-medium education in the coming decades, how it would come to pass that English would indeed become an aggressive competitor for the hearts and minds of the young, and how in his beloved city of Calcutta, Bengali would be caught in the pincers of two hegemonies, the Hindi of pan-Indian mass culture (Bollywood and prime time television) and English, the language of the pan-Indian elite. The decline of the visibility of the Bengali script in the cityscape is now very noticeable; nowadays it is only in certain restricted areas of the city that we can see a shop sign in Bengali. I have often wondered what Bose would have said about the situation.

To return to poetry translation, I believe that to translate poetry effectively you have to understand poetic craftsmanship in the target language, whether that is your 'mother tongue' or one that you have 'acquired', but this understanding itself is no static thing. It too can grow. Ideally, the translator should be a practising poet in the target language, but the truth is that some people are dormant or suppressed poets, who may not have written much poetry beyond their student years, but whose poetic creativity is spurred and maintained by the exercise of translation. They begin to thrive on it. The German writer, scholar, and translator Martin Kämpchen, who translates from Bengali into his native German, is one such example personally known to me. Similarly, the distinction between 'first language' and 'second language' becomes blurred when, because of the force of their life-circumstances, some individuals may become so bilingual (or even trilingual) that they can claim to have more than one 'mother tongue'. In a sense Bose is right when he says that poetry and other creative literature can only be written in the mother tongue. But perhaps a re-definition of 'mother tongue' is called for in the contemporary context? Indians writing creatively in English no doubt feel that English *is* effectively a mother tongue for them. Yet someone like Sujata Bhatt can at the same time lament the loss of the original mother tongue, in her case Gujarati.[9] This lament indicates that at least for some Indians writing in English the language question is not a simple but a complex issue. It is true that in the process of acquiring an intimate knowledge of English many Indian writers of today seem to lose their capacity for articulate discourse in their original mother tongue, or to be realistic, do not acquire it in the first place. Personally, I think this is a serious problem, because it has intellectual and spiritual consequences for such a writer, but just because one is acquiring finesse in another language, loss of the mother tongue does not *have to* happen: it is not *intrinsic* to the process of linguistic acquisition; it happens because the subject has acquiesced in a certain kind of educational and societal processing. Others who have not so acquiesced are able to hang on to both their languages. I think there are enough examples in the Indian subcontinent. I myself, living in England for most of the time, but going back and forth between England and India, have managed to become a bilingual writer. As I have mentioned, Bose worried if I would be able to continue writing poetry in Bengali. I managed, partly indeed through the fermenting, in my life, of that very principle of loyalty to the mother tongue which I imbibed from his writings. But whereas Bose believed that one could be truly creative only in one language, namely, the mother tongue, I was able to branch out a little in writing poetry in English also. Among the creative genres, it is only poetry that I write in two languages; my fiction and drama to date have been written in Bengali. There is no space here to go into the details of the reasons of my choice of languages as a writer: I have written about it in other places, in most detail in the Preface to my translation of my first play, and those interested may look it up.[10] Here I just want to say that I write poetry in two languages because the lines come in both—they seem to spring from the depths of the inner 'I'—and I do not block them. Whether we are disciples of Marshall McLuhan or not, there is no denying that the medium does to some extent shape the message. Poetry tends to come encoded in language, sprouting from the rhizome of language, and whichever of the two rhizomes it springs from, I nourish the shoot, and that is that. So I would say that I have effectively two mother tongues. The process whereby an individual could acquire two 'mother tongues'—both so good as to make no real difference to the business of writing—had not been clearly visualized by members of Bose's generation. Changing times and circumstances have shown us that if there is exposure to the appropriate environments, and to that is added some intelligent application, this diversification is not impossible. Just as a musician can learn more than one musical instrument, so a poet can also, in the right circumstances, pick up poetic skills in more than one tongue. With her neural pathways accommodating two mother tongues, a bilingual poet may be able to translate poetry in both directions. If translating from 'an acquired language' to the mother tongue is called 'translating in', and translating from one's first language to a second (or third) language is called 'translating out', some of us may be in a position to translate 'both in and out'. How successful we shall be is for others to judge; all we can do is try our best.

But here I must add a proviso for the benefit of Indian readers of this volume. Of the two mother tongues I am claiming, the first is obviously Bengali, in which I continue to write in almost every genre, and arguably I now write a 'diasporic' Bengali, about which some critics of my metropolis may have their own reservations, but diasporic writing and writers in Bengali are now indisputable facts, and as long as I continue to be publishable in the metropolis, and as long as editors from there continue to ask me to send contributions to their magazines, I can legitimately maintain that insofar as I am a writer, Bengali continues to be a fully functioning mother tongue for me. After all, expatriates and exiles all over the world have always been able to write in their mother tongues decade after decade: they have proved that it can be done. The language that I am claiming as my second mother tongue, though, may not quite correspond to 'Indian English' as the term is currently understood, because in the circumstances of my life I have not had the chance to acquire it. I have been domiciled in England for a very long time, and British English is the language of my marital home and the variety of English I hear on a daily basis. I started writing poetry in English only after living some years in England, in the context of my life here. When translating poetry into poetry, in order that the new poem can work as a poem too, one has to fine-tune one's ears to the speech-rhythms and current poetic idioms of the target language. When I work in English, it is impossible for me to do so except within the overall framework of British English. That is the only dialect of English in which I can work comfortably, stretching and tweaking it as best I can. Several of the translations in this volume have been presented and discussed in the poetry workshop I attend locally. I hope in these days of the 'global village' my translations will be acceptable both within and outside India, just as I am accepted as a Bengali writer within India and Bangladesh, as well as amongst diasporic Bengalis.

To speak the truth, I am myself not very happy about the position of English as the privileged language of translation within India, and have voiced my unease in several articles and seminar papers. The quickest way to explain what I mean would be to quote from one such article. Reviewing a recently published collection of short stories by contemporary Bengali women, this is how I put it:

> This collection belongs to the recent surge of expansion in India's internal market for English translations from the many modern languages of the subcontinent. That expansion is in direct response to a perceived need for improved communication between the different language groups, combined with a widening pool of skilled people who can translate with confidence from their mother tongues into English. It is clear from Malini Bhattacharya's Foreword that this 'intercommunication' is an important target of this project; she hopes that the voices in this anthology 'will find reverberations in other regional languages'. 'To evoke such reverberations,' she says, 'is the most important function this anthology may be expected to perform.' If by 'intercommunication' one means better information, more mutual knowledge, I agree entirely, but if 'reverberation in other regional languages' includes meaningful literary cross-fertilization, then I am less sure that translation into English is the best means for achieving that. It is natural that we want to translate from our mother tongues into what is both India's and the world's link language par excellence; and while we pursue this goal, we must of course do it as professionally as possible; but while this is better than no translations at all, within India this still remains very much an elite-to-elite transaction. Stories such as these would attain a much greater resonance and kindling power in the Indian context if they were translated directly into the other Indian languages, reaching those social classes from which many of today's creative writers in the modern Indian languages are recruited and not just those who have the advantage of an English-medium education. Creative sparks would then flow more effectively from one language into another. It was along such a route that Bengali writers like Bankimchandra and Saratchandra fertilized other Indian literatures in an earlier period. This is not happening enough today, because of the sheer dominance of English and the reluctance of modern Indians to learn one another's languages. Translating from the other languages into the mother tongue needs to be a long-term goal; that would surely be a more effective way of resisting what Malini herself calls 'the persistent hegemonic position of English'.[11]

If a poet like Bose is translated into English, he reaches an English-reading audience, but I would have also liked to see his poetry make a direct impact on those writing in the other languages of India, through those very languages, exactly as when he himself rained on our consciousness Bengali versions of Kalidasa, Baudelaire, Hölderlin, Rilke, and many others. Translating between the Indian languages must also be slightly easier from the point of view of some of the cultural material, local habitat, references to Indian myths and legends, and so on, whereas translating into English is more clearly trans-cultural. But could it be that translators in my situation have a modest role to play in disseminating Indian writing beyond the frontiers of India, something that also needs to be done?

One thing we know for sure: for the translation of the South Asian literatures, there are simply not enough outsiders with the necessary linguistic skills, so if the insiders themselves and insider-outsiders like myself did not co-operate, even less would be translated than what gets done. Bose himself translated, and competently, some of his own poems; I have seen a few samples.[12] However, at Damayanti Basu Singh's explicit request the present anthology consists only of new translations done by me. Though he did not write poetry in English, Bose was a fine prose stylist in English. Henry Miller was impressed and wrote to him: 'I must tell you that of all the letters I receive in English, yours are the most fluid, spontaneous, natural and sensitive. What an accomplishment for one not born to the language! But if one is a poet, he is poet in all tongues, is it not so?'[13]

I have often reflected how ironical it is that in these so-called 'post-colonial' times the names of those who mediated 'modernism' to us are almost totally unknown in the West. For my generation, Tagore was a received classic, while Bose and his contemporaries were the really tumultuous 'moderns' who were daily shaping us. These poets first came into prominence not yesterday but long ago: in the thirties of the twentieth century, when India was still formally a part of the British Empire; and since then, in the succeeding decades, waves of able poets have joined their ranks. By now at least the poets of this first wave of modernism could have gained some recognition—in their own right, as major poets of twentieth-century South Asia. But in Britain, the nation that had first ferried concepts of Western-style 'modernity' to India in the 'colonial' days, the names I have been discussing are, to all intents and purposes, unknown names. Well, of course, the names have been *uttered* from time to time; what I am saying is that they have not been *heard*. When *Kavita* was launched, a copy was actually forwarded to E. J. Thompson, one of the handful of Englishmen who cultivated Bengali at that time, and was duly noticed by him in the *Times Literary Supplement*.[14] And in our own times articles are written and special issues of magazines published—after the publication of my Tagore *Selected Poems* I was myself asked by *Poetry Review* to write a short article on Bengali poetry after Tagore, which I did, hoping to generate some interest in the subject[15]—but the odd article, the odd special issue of a magazine, the odd seminar directed at academics does not seem to change 'mainstream' consciousness. If we leave out a few scattered specialists, usually from academia, the modern Indian author is almost always understood to be someone who writes prose in English. The swathes of creative people who have been writing in the indigenous languages of modern India throughout the twentieth century, in all the genres, are not in the picture. For an expatriate like me this gap in the map means that I cannot give a proper account of myself in the ambience in which I live, that people with whom I must socially or professionally interact—at least to some extent—have difficulty seeing me in my true context, which in turn restricts my opportunities-to-act as a writer and translator.

At this point one little anecdote will not be amiss. As I heard some wits declare at a luncheon party in Buenos Aires, when I was there doing my researches on Tagore's relationship with Victoria Ocampo, one little anecdote can sometimes go to 'el corazón de las cosas' (the heart of things), when long, learned discourses cannot. While engaged in the present translation project, I had occasion, in the year 2000, to have dinner once in my old Oxford college and was placed, at the 'High Table', next to another occasional guest, and in the course of normal dinner-time conversation I discovered that this gentleman had never heard of Rabindranath Tagore. No, he was not a specialist in business management or information technology; he was by profession a teacher of literature in one of the European languages, in a school in Cambridge, as far as I can recall, and as soon as I had explained that this poet named Tagore was to my language what Goethe was to German, he became acutely embarrassed, and very apologetic about his ignorance. I am not suggesting for a moment that his lack of knowledge on this front immediately made him uneducated in my eyes; I could see that he knew his own stuff, and heaven knows we all carry enormous rucksacks of ignorance on our backs as we trudge through life; but it did make it difficult for me to explain where I was coming from, what my project was all about. If you are talking to someone who has never heard the name of Tagore, the information that you are translating a post-Tagore poet has little content. The context is entirely missing, and everything needs to be explained from scratch. Yet my presence at that dinner-table that evening was directly to do with my involvement in the present project! I was mildly intrigued that I had been placed next to this man, because I was under the impression that place allocations at such formal 'guest night' dinners were done carefully, so that conversations could flow smoothly. I could see a chain: someone else also had not quite understood where I was coming from. No matter how fast our world shrinks, areas of mutual ignorance will remain, but it is the context that shapes our perception of scale in any activity. The context in this case was the colonial nexus, the long historical connection between Britain and India: this is perforce the enveloping space whenever I engage in an intellectual interaction with a native-born British person. So returning to my dinner-table neighbour, an equivalent lack of information in a university-educated Indian might be never having heard the name of Shakespeare, which I think would have certainly surprised a British guest at a dinner party. If we regard history as important, only then are we entitled to say that the gap in knowledge is serious enough to raise eyebrows. If history is not important, then it does not matter, in which case there is no need to make a song and dance about 'post-colonial studies' either.

And in the Indian context this is the point that needs to be made: these days when so many children of the urban elite in India are being raised more or less exclusively on a diet of English-language writing, it is of utmost importance that India's potential writers from these powerful strata of society acquire a mental map of the rich vein of writing in the modern Indic languages, that they do not construct a narrowed history based on their own limited education and then project and pass on that distorted image to the outside world. Young readers of the socially privileged classes in the different regions should surely get to know each other's literary hoard and perceive it as their common heritage. Such knowledge cannot grow except with the help of translations. Fortunately, as we know, India's internal market for translations is expanding. More departments of comparative literary studies in the different Indian languages, with study modules in translation, are needed to create a pool of translators between languages. And in Britain too, notwithstanding the existing problems, it would be correct to say that in recent years there has been a certain rehabilitation of Tagore in literary circles through a new wave of translations, and a revival of interest in Tagore has happened in the continent of Europe also. It is surely time to introduce the profiles of those who came after him. Some of the values we desperately need for our survival as sane human communities in the twenty-first century are encoded in poetry; hopefully these poems from the twentieth century can give us a measure of the needed sanity.

End Notes

Enough details are supplied below to identify publications. Where necessary, please consult the Bibliography for fuller details.
1. Bose, 'Kavitar Anubad o Sudhindranath Datta' (The Translation of Poetry and

Sudhindranath Datta), *Kavita,* Asharh 1361 [1954], quoted in Sengupta, *Buddhadeb Basur Jiban,* Vikalp, Calcutta, 1998, pp. 280–1.
2. As before, quoted in Sengupta, op. cit., p. 281.
3. Bose, *Kavitasangraha,* Vol. 5, p. 19.
4. Readers who are interested in such issues might wish to check out an extremely detailed article of mine entitled: 'On the Wings of Hummingbirds, Rabindranath Tagore's Little Poems. An Invitation to a Review-cum-Workshop', discussing William Radice's translations of Tagore's *Particles, Jottings, Sparks, The Collected Brief Poems* (Angel Books, London, 2001), in the Internet magazine *Parabaas* (www.parabaas.com/translation or www.parabaas.com/rabindranath).
5. Bose, *Kavitar Shatru o Mitra,* M. C. Sarkar & Sons, Calcutta, reprint of 1997, p. 42.
6. In Suman Gun's *Buddhadeb Basu o Samar Sen* (Vikalp, Calcutta, 2000) there is an Abanibabu referred to more than once in Samar Sen's letters to Bose written from Contai in 1940. Though in his notes Gun does not say who this person might be, I am quite sure that this is my father.
7. *Tithidore* is an interesting compound word, probably made up by Tagore, and occurs in one of his songs. A word of multiple nuances, it is the title of one of the poems translated in the present volume, where I have translated it as 'The Constraint of Seasonality', in the context of the poem itself and of the Tagore song to which it seems to hark back. Please see the note on this in the Notes to the Poems section of this volume. In the context of the novel, the word could be translated in a number of other ways.
8. Bose, 'Ingreji o Matribhasha', *Kavita,* Year 22, No. 2, Poush 1364, p. 120.
9. Sujata Bhatt, 'Search For My Tongue', *Point No Point, Selected Poems,* Carcanet, Manchester, 1997.
10. Ketaki Kushari Dyson, 'Translator's Prologue', *Night's Sunlight,* Virgilio Libro, Kidlington, Oxon., 2000.
11. Ketaki Kushari Dyson, review published in: *In Other Words, The Journal for Literary Translators,* London and Norwich, Winter 2001, No. 18, pp. 80–1, of *The Stream Within: Short Stories by Contemporary Bengali Women,* translated and with an introduction by Swati Ganguly and Sarmistha Dutta Gupta, foreword by Malini Bhattacharya, Stree, Calcutta, 1999.
12. In the anthology *I have seen Bengal's face,* ed. Sibnarayan Ray and Marian Maddern, Editions Indian, Calcutta, 1974.
13. Quoted in Sengupta, *Buddhadeb Basur Jiban,* op. cit., p. 252.
14. Bose, *Amader Kavitabhavan,* Vikalp, Calcutta, 2001, p. 15.
15. Dyson, 'Calcutta Gemütlichkeit', *Poetry Review,* London, Vol. 83, No. 1, Spring 1993, pp. 26–8.

From
Bandir Bandana (1930)

A Prisoner's Song of Praise

A perpetual prisoner in the instincts' inescapable cage —
that's how you've made me, my ruthless creator!
And this is merely your delight — without rhyme or reason!
I fancy — I shall be free; I won't leave anywhere
a single sign that betokens bondage for me.
Dressed as a rough pirate, I begin to laugh and ride
the swelling streams of my self-will. Millions of midget thorns
made by the world, by society — I ignore their cruel jabs.
And convention, that darling child of serfdom — on its breast I launch
sharp pointed jagged jibes, harsh scornful taunts.
I imagine freedom sliding closer to me,
the sky's vault rippling with streams of deathless beauty.

Then one day I cast an astonished glance —
freedom! — where's it gone?
Day and night they hem me in — a thousand unseen shackles —
the more I try to escape them, the more they fetter my feet,
obstructing my life's mobility.
Along with me walk my constraints, in life's eternal tryst,
towards beauty's tabernacle.
They keep me immersed in muck up to my chin,
poison the air I breathe
with the microbes of a million agonies,
turning my red blood blue.
No release for a moment. In the work I do
and within my innermost being,

in each dream, every waking,
you've kept me tied with the hot damned snaky coils
of a million diurnal desires and expectations
ever since that first dawn of creation –
my creator, so indifferent to me!
My freedom's a mirage, a dream of sweet lies.
You've made me a perpetual prisoner to myself.

In longing's heartland my hungry youth weeps and wails,
its ache, irrepressible, dying to open itself.
Lusts, starved for a lakh of years, in blood's bashful blushing
daily seek the grace of defeat in the coital war,
and must deal with the terrible turmoil of being cheated.
There's the gaze of ruthless self-interest. And greed, dirty and stupid.
And the lowly snake of malice hides in love's golden chalice.
Desire's ugly tooth-marks scar the body vibrant with gladness,
and the lust to kill exists as well, with its hideous perversity.
Constantly they come, interrupting my visions of beauty,
wringing from me tears – of humiliation, hurt, embarrassment.
I want to forget them, and do so in snatches, drowning in surges of
                                                    loveliness –
but alas I can't blot them out.
Mistakes every minute, slipping and falling at every step,
forgetting oneself – beauty's daily dishonour.
Creator of the cosmos, if you've created me so powerless,
may you redeem yourself by forgiving me!

Refulgent one, from my prison bereft of light
I sing your praise today.
Neither covetous of heaven, nor stocked up with holy deeds,
with my tormented desires I fashion this offering for you:
the grisliness of my bloody wounds – on my breast injured in a
                                                      ceaseless war –
accept it, please, with my salutation, you who are beautiful for ever!

Creator, you don't know how immeasurable is my thirst
for immortality!
Maybe I am sunk in a worm-thick sea of slime,
yet in my secret innermost spirit I am dry,

From *Bandir Bandana* (1930)

thirsty for the elixir of eternity.
Maybe you've kept me captive; yet know – that my little chained hands
are keen to fly in the firmament's upper bands
and clasp the boundless blue in their eager grasp.
In the still midnight my eyes remain alert,
taking their own seats in the sleepless hall of stars,
or on an enchanted chariot, roaming in the clear white Milky Way
in sheer ecstasy.
You gave me desire, as dark as a moonless night:
from that I've moulded love, mixing it with the honey of my dreams.
Hence when my body goes wandering like a beggar –
thin, famished, all bones –
all my spirit, even then, bursts into song
bearing a lasting message world without end.
In the infinite's ears it whispers these secret words –
'Yet I love, yet right now I love!'
Wine foams in my blood, where the god of the fish-signed flag flies his
                                                                pennant;
in my veins shudder a hundred reptilian forms;
greedy appetite absent-mindedly slobbers.
Yet I am a seeker of the immortal –
and in that quest I love, I only love.
I love – that is all.
O artist, he whom you created is not me –
he is your grotesque nightmare.
Gathering the universe's sweetness drop by drop,
I have fashioned myself. And during that act
of great creation where were you lying, doped? – You alone know that!

Upon my own self I have bestowed a new birth.
Since you are the creator of everything that there is,
to you I dedicate this my creation with care.
This new creation of mine – why, it's a living song of your praise,
the unified choir of all that is without beginning.
I am a poet, and this is my pride –
I have created this music in exalted delight.
This is my pride – that your mistakes I have rectified
with my own dedicated enterprise.

So then this humiliated prisoner, in a rush of joy without chains,
goes flinging the cruellest mockery athwart your way
in the guise of a hymn of praise.

> 1926 [9 Ashwin 1333], night

No Other Wishes

No other wishes. Not for me, I know, the crown of fame, the victor's
> floral wreath.
Where the world's poets shine as stars — on night's deep-blue sheath —
no place for me there. Songs in my praise won't rise in the remote
> heavens,
nor my hands feel the touch of cool leaf-offerings, adoration-drenched.
No home for me where men's minds are pilgrims. My ultimate fate —
death's bitter venom. No twenty-first century girl, seventeen years of
> age,
will read my poem, I know, by a window which the moon bathes.
Pipedream too — to be an aromatic memory in the lotus-hearts of
> classmates.

Yet the fact that ripples of music stir today in the heart's chill lake
is only because of you. That I had you in all of me — body, mind, heart,
> spirit,
in the throbbing darkness of being alone, in sleepless togetherness —
is something I want to tell the sky, the wind, the waking night.
This burden of fullness within me on my own I cannot carry,
so I deal myself amongst thousands in a million melodies.

> 1928 [Rewritten from memory, 1963]

Love and Life

1.
As a poor boy standing in front of a theatre's gates,
one foot on the street, the other on marble steps,

with sad eyes of longing stares at the lovely palace
and curses his own indigence under his breath:
the hours pass, the auditorium's plunged in darkness,
the stage is lit, the air throbs with poetry and music –
through his eager ears the melodies reach his spirit
like a dream overture, and his mind's in joy's high tide: –

even so, love, all I've had so far in life
is just a glimpse of you, your finger's touch!
Yet already the earth's at my feet, the firmament's my finger's ring,
and amazed, I think: that thing whose faintest hint
brings births and deaths in instants, and in tears raises seas –
its complete revelation – what a miracle that must be!

3 February 1929, night

6.
You are of this life, yet you are more than life.
Life's misery's sandbank – girt with the sea of sleep –
on its sand your teeming footprints you leave
and with those marks life's insignia you inscribe.
Where all is transient, unreal – you are the pole star's light.
Those who, in the cave of death, have discovered God,
whose fragile lives hang on the insupportable, on roots of hope –
you, steady and stable, are the truth on their rostrum of lies.

A lump of flesh is man – a pot of slime, a pile of primal urges,
until you come and charge him up, make him quiver;
it's when you pour your wine that his crystal form appears –
all over the rim of life's cup that wine fizzes.
Foamy madness – waste without compare –
till at last in blood's darkness heaven sparks, and a fire blazes.

27 March 1929, morning

From
Kankabati (1937)

One Hand

Clouds in the sky; the street deserted;
    all is quiet; it is the depth of night.
The city sleeps; the houses are dark
    on either side.

All alone I walk home,
    my limbs weary, my eyes heavy with sleep.
Soon it will rain; so I force myself
    to walk with speed.

At the turn of the street I suddenly notice a house
    in whose ground-floor window
there is electric light casting
    a pale-blue glow.

Only this window is lit,
    the rest is in darkness.
But as I come nearer and glance at it,
    – the window closes.

In that second I take in
    one white hand –
and the shutters are closed from each side
    that very instant.

One white hand, its fingers,
    glint of a diamond ring,
a thin gold band round the wrist, the pale-blue light
    – all over in a blink.

The earth is dark again
    and sleep fills my eyes:
– without knowing whose hand it was
    I'm going to die.

I'm in my room, and the rain comes down as well,
    I can hear the wind's clamour.
If tomorrow I see the face that owns that hand,
    I won't know her.

I'm lying down, sleep has abandoned me;
    who knows where the clock-hands stand;
Should I ever touch that hand, I wouldn't know
    that it was the same hand.

                                                    5 May 1930

This Is All

Eyes meet eyes once in an open window –
much delight and a touch of surprise,
    a leap of wild hope:
then the day wanes, burnt by the fierce sun,
and mists of dream gather in the mind's skies.
    – Nothing more.

The faces of many stars, a slice of the moon,
time to sleep when one has finished one's chores –
    the dew of peace:
Pleasure and pain, a few words, desire and sorrow,
then death's night, its darkness.
    – Nothing more.

                                                    8 May 1930

From
Natun Pata (1940)

This Winter

If I could die
this winter,
as a tree dies,
as a snake stays dead
all through the long winter!

At winter's end the tree renews itself.
Fresh sap rises upwards from its roots.
It flourishes, with glossy green leaves
and abundant arrogant flowers.

And the snake sheds its sheath,
its new skin crafted like a conch:
its tongue dashes out like the flame
of a fire that knows no fear.

For they stay dead
all through the long winter,
knowing how to die.

If I too could stay dead —
if I could become totally empty,
sink into bottomless sleep, without memory, without dreams —
then I wouldn't have to die every minute
in this effort to stay alive,

trying to be happy, to give happiness,
to write well, to love.

There Isn't Time

I could have waited for you —
days as long and brilliant as swords, nights like trees
murmuring with branches, leaves, and the colonies
    of a thousand invisible birds.
I could have waited, season after season turning,
through the ever-revolving wheel of the rainbow years.
If the sun was in the south, and days were short,
I would have thought of you
    through the fragrance of my dozings;
if the sun was in the north, I would have let my thoughts fly
    towards the sunset sky
as if they were a flock of white pigeons —
their wings' wind the melodies of poetry.

In this manner
one day the time of our union would arrive.
Like the wild monsoon wind the smell of your hair
would dash on my breast,
and my song's humming would become a full moon,
stupefied upon your eternal face.

But there isn't time.
Night after night the moon thins. The moon decays. And we —
we too decay by living through every day, every night.
Tonight is a night of the moon's waning phase.
The moon will rise late. The stars in the dark sky
are like tears of separation.
But I know that one day, looking at the western sky, I shall surely see
the burning flame of the young moon.
The moon will return, will fill out.
Evening after evening a renewal, an unfolding without compare.
We, on the other hand, burn like candles;
our bodies are fuel to life's fire.

We burn and are extinguished. We are used up.
Nothing remains.

So now, while there's still time,
I'm calling you.
Am calling you, standing where time's narrow lane turns,
both sides packed with walls of death. Don't delay,
don't delay any longer. All the time we might waste,
being shy, being hurt, deceiving ourselves, –
does death deserve it? Is death such an important friend of ours
that we should give him such a special present?

2 February 1934, night

Gods are Two

1.

Maya,
this world's maya –
the Hindu seers used to say, so that it didn't hurt,
but in so doing they tore up joy also, with its roots.

If indeed it's maya,
what was the point of it in the first place?
Couldn't it just as well not have existed?
Couldn't the Brahman have stayed alone, in his timeless lotus posture?
Why did this egg have to be, which he broods for all eternity?

It would be better if we were brave and accepted suffering.
If we were not afraid to drink suffering's cold, blue stream,
then joy too would blossom one day like a red lotus,
its stem issuing from our navel, its face upon our heart.

Maya! Maya!
These merciless tears choking my voice – is this maya?
And my body burning like a flame, joyfully –
that too is maya?

Must we only fear God's puissant thunder
and not remember his glittering festival?

Must we, from fear of the God of thunder, stay blind
and say with all our might, 'All that's nothing, just maya! Mere maya!'

But God flowers again in the clusters of springtime,
in the festival's mirth,
in love's hot kisses:
how can we call these maya?
For they are good, in them are loveliness and well-being,
they are nothing but life's perennial source.
If we don't accept them, it's death:
even God's thunder doesn't deliver such a total death.

But if we don't accept the God of thunder,
we have to lose the God of spring as well;
hence we have to accept both.
We need both,
we need both in life.

Not extinction – but fullness.

8 February 1934, night

New Day

Today the earth has come and stood at my door
with all its sweetness.

All its sweetness, all its softness –
as if the breeze of this young spring were its body.

And something is breaking within me,
as rock crumbles under the pressure of the terrible fire
hidden inside the earth.

And something is waxing within me, is collecting within me,
just as the green mangoes will begin to redden within days
under the sun's fierce kiss.

What a strange death!
What a strange new birth!

A new music has invaded my life.
Blood is burning in both my hands, like red fire,
because you touched them.

I had forgotten that life had so much sweetness,
so much softness.
My mind was full of fear – hard, discoloured fear.
Whom was I about to hit with my ridicule?
Whom was I about to bash in my cruelty?
– I'd wanted to pluck out my heart
with my own hands.

You touched those very hands.
Never again will they have permission to become snake-hoods.
From now on, they'll have to be sweet,
they'll have to be alive with the warmth of blood,
because from now on these hands are yours.

Today I'm beginning to understand
that invisible darkness whence our lives spring;
and the tiny leaves of the sacred basil
on my window-ledge
are filling with all life's sweetness.
And this night dances in my blood
like a burning star traversing the sky.

12 February 1934, night

Still the Koel Calls

2.

Still the koel calls.
Though I'm being encircled by death, by death's darkness,
though a salt breeze is blowing from the black bottomless sea,
though the waves of a catastrophe are breaking over my chest,
sweeping me away, dashing me in the tumult
of vortex after murderous vortex;
though today I'm defeated, exhausted, out of breath,

split in two by the cruelty of the world's
diabolical powers –
still the koel calls.

In the middle of the day
the wind outside becomes oppressively hot,
the rainless sky is bleached of every colour.
I lie quietly, and within my breast
a thousand hungry dogs yelp, making a dreadful racket.
Hatred, resentment, fear, anxiety, disgust,
and intolerable, intolerable rage,
self-pity, tongue-lolling thirst for revenge:
a thousand maddened dogs, finding nothing else,
want to tear me instead
and cut up and eat my nerves.
And outside the koel calls;
suddenly a reassurance rings like a bell in my breast:
all the diabolical powers of the world
haven't been able to destroy me yet.

At night, my sleep disturbed,
I keep waking in shock from nightmares.
Suddenly the koel's call pierces the darkness, lands upon my breast.
My sleep vanishes. I open my eyes and stare into the darkness.
I lie and listen.

I listen, and it seems to come back to me –
what I'd seen in the past – when was it? – the red glow
on a pubescent girl's cheeks: such a lot of gold scattered there!
And the soft green of grass, and the glowing desire
on a lover's moist eyes.

Now
I can bear everything –
this death of mine,
the suicidal bitterness of despair and resentment –
because the koel still calls.

12 March 1934, night

Rain and Storm

Rain and storm, rain and storm, night and day.
The day grey, barren, dark. No light, no
shadows either. Just the rain's haze, the obscurity of clouds,
and the groan of trams, the rumble of traffic.

In the sky — a muted crying. In the wind — long-drawn sighs.
Long, long day. How much longer to night?
The hour weary, the moment sluggish. The rattling of time's chains
unending, unwearied.

Night. Emptiness within doors, darkness without.
Rain and storm, rain and storm.
Empty, empty heart. Failed, failed night.
Just the furious city's sleepless snarl.

Emptiness in the heart, moans in the city, darkness in the sky.
Shadows, gusts of wind, voices,
murmurs, angry choked voices, elongated sighs
in the city, in the empty room, in the rain-dripping darkness,
in the clanking of time's chains — all night, all day.

The day empty, quiet as a stagnant pool. The night mute too. There's
nothing. Absolutely nothing. Creation's face
is covered with rain's grey sheet, with the windy city's
tormented voice. There's nothing. I am alone. All alone.

Captive like a blind fly on time's enormous wheel. The window
to the universe closed. The day like a stagnant pool,
dark, stifled. The night
like the bottom of an old forgotten well. And loneliness, interminable.

In the streets — crowds, bustle, madness. In offices, parks, restaurants —
work, play, getting drunk; gambling, gin, siestas
after a bone-breaking week: all indistinct, cramped.
The city numb. Rain, rain. In the streets
the jostling of shadows, the boneless procession of nightmares.

Shadowy Calcutta, without a body, without a skeleton:
irresponsible, wayward

like a dream. Myself a shadow too, trembling at the touch of a breeze
upon the wall, behind the curtain. Within my breast swing
rain and storm, rain and storm, night and day.

1939

Sea-bathing

1.
Why not see what the sea does to you? —
this blue salt water and whiplike wind!

As these waves paint for a thousand years
conches and glistening mother-of-pearl
in so many colours, such diverse patterns,
brown and violet and exquisitely smooth,
and curving wavy lines —
let them fashion your body in the same way,
your conch-smooth body!

Why not give yourself to the sea just once? —
then see what it does with you!

Let the waves scour you
with the commotion of white foam.
Let the sea play with you,
with your smooth clean body.
Let its sand-brown water embrace you from all sides:
as it has fashioned the gleaming white conch for a thousand years,
so let it fashion you, your smooth brown body.

Don't, don't be afraid of the sea.
It has endless affection.

Plunge right within
the bosom of this foamy tumult.
Go dancing with the waves. Leap up to their peaks
like a mermaid.

The sea is infinite. The sea is terrifying.
But the sea loves to play with you:
it has affection without end.

7 November 1934
Puri [Orissa]

Peace by the Lake

Here, by this green lake,
I seem to have rediscovered a long-lost friend —
I'm not quite sure who it is.

I'm not quite sure.
Good — isn't it? — that I'm not quite sure!
Just a hazy delight, an obscure fear —
as if a newly wed wife was getting undressed
in the night's darkness, her bangles jingling,
and I was sitting, listening.

Wonder what I had lost, and what I have regained.
Is it this stillness,
after the roar of Calcutta's traffic and the roar of the sea,
this living, tactile stillness?
Is it this star-thatched sky,
or the new moon's curved line,
or the horizon-beckoning
of that rail-track that curves, skirting the hillside?

Only this I know — that all my heart is full
here, by this lake.
I gaze, and can scarcely blink —
such an array of stars fills the sky!

Soon the train from Madras will arrive,
sweeping stillness before it with its wheels;
early tomorrow morning it reaches Calcutta.
But Calcutta is so far away now:

even Calcutta is so far away now!
How far away is the clang of battle that's only just ended!

10 November 1934
Chilka [Orissa]

Morning in Chilka

Ah, how very happy I have felt this morning —
    how can I say it!

How spotlessly blue is this sky, how unbearably beautiful,
like a master singer's raga variations spreading unrestrained
    from horizon to horizon!

Ah, how good I've felt gazing at this sky —
green hills curving all around, hazy in the mist,
    Chilka glinting in the middle.

You came over, sat by me awhile, then strolled to the other side
to see the train that had come and stopped at the station.
The train left. — How much I love you —
    how can I say it!

The sun floods the sky, dazzles the eyes.
The cows graze with total attention — how tranquil!
— Had you ever thought — coming here, beside this lake we would find
    what we hadn't found so long?

The silvery water lies dreaming, while all the sky
streams on its bosom in a flow of blue
with the sun's kisses. — That here a gorgeous rainbow would blaze
circling the ocean of your blood and mine —
    had you ever imagined it?

Yesterday sailing on the Chilka we had seen
two butterflies coming along — flying over the water
for such a long distance. — How bold! You'd laughed,
    and how I had loved

that wonderful, radiant happiness of yours! See, see
how blue this sky is. — And in your eyes tremble
so many skies, deaths, new births —
   how can I say it!

11 November 1934
Chilka [Orissa]

Everest

They came. They went back. Miserable death
summoned this one, kept that one. In groups they go
away, come back. On avalanches,
on the spotless sky's walls reverberate
my loud laughter, scaring them. I watch quietly.

Far, far below the wild spring burns.
There — water, the flood of floral hues, the turning of the season-cycle.
Here seasonal ways are useless. No mad spring. Time is without end.
Still — you people?

Only snow-storms, crashing avalanches, blinding light, and creation-
blotting darkness. Night and day sans youth or ageing. Time stupefied.
There's neither gold nor coal. The possibility of an empire is zero.
Still — you people?

Miserable death will summon someone. I summon none.
It's death who will hang on to someone. But I hang on to none.
Then one day they will climb the last peak, plant a flag, and return.
Still — me.

The flag of their victorious clamour will fly. Not here, though.
More will come at the century's end, maybe after a blood bath.
Markets will open in remote areas, pleasure-gardens in terrifying
forests. — Not here, not here.

Markets bazaars shops ports factories military parades,
flowers birds springtimes, birth death love transformed
by time's oblique passage. Earth's rebirth at the century's end.
I watch quietly. For here there is no time.

Century after century as unending as snow-spray.
Only me.

Not mine: memories, the ways of seasons, changes of motion.
Memory is time's skeleton, and I am timeless. Let them come
repeatedly – in fearless amazement, joyous triumph, the fertile
overflow of brains. Still – me.

Intellect imagination amazement desire – nothing's mine.
I'm ever-barren, ever-lonely.
They will know the end of mystery, yet mystery is endless.
In so many summers they will circumambulate me in amazement.
I have no summer, no winter, no spring. Timeless, without youth
or old age, there's only me.

Here – only the blustering wind, like snow of invisible motion.
Only my loud laughter that echoes on crashing avalanches.
No horizon, no path. – Is this for ever? Is this a dream?
Only me.

And you who, perched on a mound eight and a half thousand high,
watch me today – me stuck between two peaks, resembling a white
giant's thumb (or is it a shy new bride, her face lowered?) –
some of you poets, some trembling with greed, with cameras open –
if you knew, if you heard, if you understood,
you would be afraid, you would quietly hide your faces
in the green plains.

11 October 1938

Sunrise on Tiger Hill

The auditorium is ready.
The moon's weary at the end of perambulation.
In the sky dawn's breath trembles in the stars.
Wrapped in various winter garments, some one hundred and fifty
or two hundred men and women are today's audience.
Pushing and shoving,
words spoken in different languages and intonations.
Only the picture-wallahs
wait in ambush in silence, their secret eyes open.

On no account will they allow the right moment to slip,
instantly they'll imprison it in the chambers of their cameras.

Like the stillness of an exhausted bird
above a blue-black cloud
a red line appeared long since.
How much longer? How much longer?
The viewers are restless.
Is there a trickery? A deception? Where is
the sun? Was it for this I came here in this wretched cold?
Just wait, you'll see it soon.
Keep an eye behind you, can you see Everest?
How *grand* is Kanchenjunga!
But is it worth while, after all? —
A Bengali lady sprinkles Feringhee English,
make-up on her face, eyebrows pencil-drawn.

Waiting and paying money,
sleep wrecked and climbing the chest-busting mountain
were not all in vain.
The sun rose.
Even after a thousand nights the viewers were just as eager —
so brilliant was the actor.
Putting on the same performance for a thousand nights,
he was tired, but expert and faultless.
So even today, on 8 October 1938,
from behind the blue mountain
galloping like a horse of fire
the sun came up.

Click click click,
murmured the forest of cameras,
and the audience praised.
Cries of delight in sharps and flats:
look, look, did you see!
Oh how lovely! Really wonderful! —
rolled the Feringhee English.
Nothing was omitted:
fire on all the snow-peaks from the north to the west,
rainbow colours on the cloud's blue-black body,

the money recovered, the trouble worth it.
The face with make-up cadaverous in the clear light of day.

> ... Sun-god, did you have to rise in spite of everything,
> did you have to rise even today?
> Is the law of the universe so merciless, so unerring?
> There can be no exception in any way
> even for one day?
> O sun, O snowy ranges, peacock-necked clouds in the valley,
> prisoners, as you are, of nature's iron laws,
> are you slaves of man's accolades too?
> Or are you really very distant,
> truly complete and free of desires,
> for ever on your own in time's nursery?
> This forest of people, talkative, bristling with cameras,
> never really gets to know you?

10 October 1938

Moon

I was sitting all alone in the darkness
when all of a sudden there was someone in the room –

Who? Who's it?
The quick breathing of sudden amazement leaped
over the steps of a few moments arranged one after another.
And someone who had been climbing for so many days, so many nights
up, up the thousands of invisible steps
twisting and turning inside my breast
seemed suddenly to arrive – this very instant.

This very instant the moon is gazing at my face –
what a big moon!
How complete, how beautiful, how incredibly completely beautiful!

But how much more beautiful is this little patch of moonlight
that has come and fallen on my floor
like the trembling water of some blue fairy-tale sea –

as if some exquisite, exquisite girl, borne
on the flood-waters of her own loveliness
had just landed in my room.

The flood of loveliness in the sky will sweep the moon away.
When it leans to the west like a tired flag, the city sleeping beneath it,
I won't see it.
When high in the sky, burning like clumps of snow in spring,
it melts in soft petals of moonlight,
even then I won't see it.
Yet that exquisite, exquisite girl
will perhaps twine around my sleep tonight
like a dream,
will clasp it like memory –
maybe, maybe.

To My Poems

2.

O poems, my poems,
chaotic tossing waves
    in the flood-tides of my youthful days,
      shy eccentric youths free of shackles
        on the high road of the world's commercial swelling
    and imperial expansion,
        what will you do? Where will you go?
        Whom will you visit? And what will you say?

If you go to the doors of the rich, you won't be allowed to enter,
or you might get two rupees of tips, simply standing outside.
If you go to the dwellings of the poor, they will gape at you –
they've become stupid from continuous starvation.

You may go to the houses of the middle classes,
who have only themselves, love themselves, and are pleased
with themselves. They are good folk, cultivate the arts,
though that always escalates their expenses, and they'll say,
'Ah, two rupees have to be thrown away! OK, let's see.'

In truth, they find your tattered clothes distasteful, and do not like
your family name. ... Had it been one of those upper-class names
with a high price-tag, riding cars, dominating conferences, then at least
one could have decorated one's drawing-room with it. ...
They want to go up, up –
    falling, dying, they want to climb, climb, climb, climb.

O poems, my poems,
    shy eccentric youths,
        your days pass in wandering from one turn of the road to the next –
        where will you stop and stand?

> *Young men crowd in cinema halls*
>   *and in sports grounds.*
> *Young women are busy putting make-up on their faces –*
>   *it's got to be perfect.*
> *Adult males go out to hunt for money,*
>   *females economize.*
> *Old men pant and die,*
>   *and children shout.*

Where, where will you go, my poems,
    you shy eccentric youths free of shackles
    on the smoky hazy twisted streets of this world's
        pursuit of self-interest and self-increase,
        poverty and violent death,
        struggle for a living and the killing of life?
    What will you do here? Where will you stand?
    Whom will you visit? And what will you say?

                                                23 June 1937

3.
Ah, had I been a chemist or a philologist,
    an astronomer or an expert in machines,
    a painter or a singer,
or a mechanic, a cobbler, a tailor, a potter,
a barber, a carpenter, or whatever,
    anything else besides a writer,
    how much better it would have been, something truly respectable!

Nowadays no one can, just because he fancies, become,
> just like that, a chemist or a physicist,
>> or a singer or a painter,
>> or even a mechanic or a cobbler, a barber or a tailor.
>>> For all jobs have to be learnt,
>>> especially jobs like a mechanic's or a cobbler's.
In no sphere is there room
for a stupid ignoramus without skill, expertise or training,
> none at all before the door of a mechanic or a tailor.

Anybody, but anybody, who has learnt to write his alphabet
> and has turned the pages of a few books
> can now suddenly, if he wishes,
>> become a full-scale writer.
>> Someone who couldn't have opened his mouth if he had to sing,
>> would have been in tears if he had to paint,
who hasn't got the qualifications to be either
a mechanic or a cobbler, a tailor or a potter, a barber or a carpenter,
can suddenly, if he so wishes, become
> a very great writer.

Alas, this work of writing that I do! This profession of writing,
> troubled, tormented, bruised by uneducated hands,
> humiliated by barbarian greed, bloodied by vulgar bludgeoning!

What a source of happiness and honour it would have been,
> had I been a physicist or an anthropologist,
>> a psychologist or a philologist,
> a mountaineer or a seafarer,
>> a sculptor or a painter,
>> or an illiterate singer,
>> a cobbler, a mechanic, a carpenter,
>> a tailor, a barber, a potter,
anything except a writer –
how much happiness and honour that would have brought!
For in no other sphere of work is there room
for unskilled inexpert untrained stupid ineptitude.

25 June 1937

New Leaves

I am getting out a new book of poems.
Perhaps you people will read it.
My critic friend will say: 'Was it really necessary to make up a volume
with these pieces? Why throw pebbles into the ocean of time?'

This book
is what I've dreamt about for many days.
How many nights I've spent without sleep, thinking about it!
And along with that, I've remembered someone who had once
emerged from the billows of my blood like white Aphrodite,
on whose feet all my mind had once flung itself
like the sea on a full-moon night.
Seeing her, my language had become sonorous, like an incantation –
that's what poetry is.
That's the book that's out today.
You people are saying, 'This is not touched by that perennial melody
which could have pulled it along time's current, from wave to wave,
   from one century to the next;
here we notice many imperfections, many parts that are bitty,
much fragmented imagination, expression that's stiff.
Can you stand with this at the door of poetry's palace,
which is for ever radiant?'
... You people are saying all these things – and I,
I don't even have the time to sit down for a little while
and turn the pages of this book, to have a look at it.

I've lots to do.
Words swirl around me.
Life, dragged in daily dust,
is down like a defeated army's tattered flag.
From one minute to the next the warp and weft of necessities
weave a veil over my soul
so that I scarcely recognize myself.
No time, in the midst of all this,
to pick up my book of poems and look at it.

You're saying, 'This book won't last.
It'll disappear in the ocean of time after drawing a few tattoos on it.

Why then —.' But precisely that's why.
Precisely that's why I can endure this life,
this exhaustion, this filth, this unremitting unrelenting effort
    to string a garland with scraps of thread.
Precisely that's why — when the words emerge from my pen's tip
like a long procession of small black insects,
blocking the sky's light from my eyes —
I don't object.
That nothing will remain is indeed the last hope, the chance of peace.
Could I have survived with these lumps of words and piles of work
had I not known that one day all would vanish
into the final oblivion, the ultimate end,
had I not known that time was merciless and terrifying,
scattering the seeds of oblivion with both hands,
distributing death's sweetness with both hands,
that nothing remains?
At the end of all vain efforts and broken dreams,
after tearing oneself to bits and handing them over to the daily grind,
that indeed is the joy —
that nothing remains.

Yet be quiet, you people, for today.
Allow me to be a little quiet.
Let me read my poems, alone in my room,
in the fading light of the late afternoon.
Let that day return for a moment, let the air carry
the fragrance of her hair.
She at whose feet I had once flung myself
with the abandon of the sea on a full-moon night —
let her return for a moment from the massed foam of my poems.

If Rebirth Were Really True

If rebirth were really true,
I would hope for at least the following. —
I wouldn't be too brainy. And my scholarly skills should be such
that I can sign my name in two and a half minutes flat.

However, I would be good in reckoning,
especially in reckoning my own profit.

At the crossroads
where people change trams,
where from dawn to midnight
the flow of people doesn't stop —
there on a pavement
I would have a stall for selling papers.
Yes, a stall to sell papers is what I'd have.
Then, sitting all day on a piece of gunny,
I'd be able to clank my money:
513 quarters, 270 half-rupees, and annas, double annas, pices in plenty
would always be stashed under my gunny.
So when the greatest poet of that time
comes to place his verse-pamphlet in my stall,
I'd be able to tell him with a solemn face:
'Not much point in stocking that. Not a single copy will sell.'
And if the greatest fiction-writer of that time
wants to stand and browse through the magazines,
well — why, then I'd be kind and allow him to browse,
I wouldn't stop him.

4 August 1936

From
Ek Paisay Ekti (1942)

Thoughts on a Day of Bhadra

Post-rains peering through my debt-crushed threadbare life
    can't bring me delight.
Srabon's blackness will soon dissolve into light.
In the blue released by the end of the rains will burn
    torn clouds, those gangs of vagabonds.
I sit and wonder with what funds my home will run.

What a mingling of moist and bright, dark and white –
    enough to get you high!
Such a day is simply too much for my wan life:
though covered in debt, yet it won't increase debt's pile
    to you, post-rains.
In a furtive, private nexus they won't be enchained –
    the torn verses of my tattered soul.
They too will melt in light and burn in gold.

16 August 1941

The Rains Come To Santiniketan

Tawny beast-herds come running. In the north-west
the sky-line stirs with the haze of whirling dust.
What reddish yellow frenzy shakes the sky's
dance-floor, as layers of the atmosphere pulse!

Joyful trees, arms raised, raise a din
in sudden gusts of keen, cool, wild wind.
Come, thirst's water, smash summer's pride. With your dance's pace
bring revolution's beauty, bloom in terror's grace.

Ah, the sultry heat bursts at last, it seems.
And who comes out? The new rain, a steady drip
of lyricism. Withered Birbhum, opening weary lips,
drinks the life-flow. Santiniketan hurls songs
at Rabindranath's mind in pain's silent seeping,
in rain-ceased sunset glow, recalling some other evening.

30 May 1941
Santiniketan

Farewell at Midday

In Narayanganj station at midday
how many times have I gone through these arrivals and departures!
The railway whistle goes, the steamer's horn blows,
the sun glitters in the river.
Dust blows in the gusty wind, boat sails swell,
little boats toss in the waves made by the steamer.
The ice-wallah shouts, the porters chirp and chatter,
a barrage of East Bengal speech besieges you.

From the Narayanganj steamer at midday
your face receded in the distance.
Tears blurred the orange-coloured sari,
the red tin roofs of the jute godowns came forward.
With the chug-chug rhythm of the steamer's engine throbbed
a sky-vast heart being tugged away from its love.
In the water's slurping speech, in the roar of the wind and the waves
East Bengal's dialects in husky voices dyed my heart and soul
on the Narayanganj steamer at midday.

1941

From
Baishe Srabon (1942)

For Rabindranath

I remember you today – in these times of total terror –
O friend, most beloved! Civilization lies on its funeral sheet
and an epidemic spreads to man's bone-marrow, to his inner spirit.
Life's grace is banished. Flying on a chariot that brings death,
Beauty pierced on his arrogant gore-drinking spear,
a barbaric demon shouts, 'I am the biggest, I am the greatest!'
In land after land, in shore after shore, trembles
life's golden deer in a furious predator's mouth.

Life stifled. Song silenced. On India's gentle coast
greed's saliva dribbles. So much suffering, such intolerable disdain –
could I have endured this hell at all, my friend,
had not to my blood seeped, to my innermost core penetrated
your imperishable message? Your words have I received within me,
and that's why I'm not afraid, and know that life will win.

May 1942 [25 Baishakh 1349]

From
Damayanti (1943)

O Africa, Covered in Shadows

O Africa, covered in shadows,
    white civilization's sun
        has today sucked dry your last meagre shadow.
        Hail, hail the victory:
            the dense darkness is torn,
            the cloud-coloured girdle has fallen down –
                and there comes your lover, the merchant-warrior,
    quickly to make your naked virginity
        bring forth the child called civilization.
Your burst heart's blood is the dowry of that match.

    O Africa, become pregnant.
Bring, bring quickly to your lap
    commerce's bastard.
        Let time reach its plenitude.
Let pot-bellied tongue-lolling greed,
blood-swollen commerce's seed
        reach its plenitude.
            Hail too
your deformed genderless child, paralyzed, infirm of limb:
        wish him victory.
Furious eunuch, mad with desire – whose self-defence is self-killing.

O Africa,

       on exhausted merchandising's lurking death
              lightning will flash
and time's crooked gait will make a skeleton pregnant.
O Africa, whore-continent,
       one day the clumped darknesses of the centuries
       of your ruptured equatorial line
       will wake to the keenest labour-agonies.
              So hail,
              hail the victory:
churning death, comes new birth, all a-quiver.

                                          November 1937

Padma

The whole day has gone aboard the steamer.

The rain falls in gusts,
 suddenly stops. Sunshine through broken clouds
glitters in the fast-flowing waters.
Again it descends,
clusters of black clouds pile,
someone builds in the sky from time to time –
hills, royal palaces, tall minarets.
Shadows spread in the black breeze, the steamer's propellers
churn up rows of waves
of white froth, which pierce the black river's heart, frisk and eddy.
Soon those hills and royal palaces crumble again, and the tall minarets
disappear without a trace. What fanciful frolicking this is!
Half of the river under a black shadow, the other half gleaming
in the sun,
and for a moment the huge river burning like silver
below the blue heavens.
The sun breaks into a hundred thousand splinters on the wave-edges,
dazzling the eyes;
the sky comes down in a torrent of light. In another minute
clouds swish their wings, shading distant villages;
rows of waves twine like a black braid, tremble, roll on to the shore,

while the rain comes down in gusts, blurring the sky-line. —
Watching this endless whimsical play
of light and shade, I've spent the whole day
on the steamer.

The red tin roofs of Narayanganj disappeared first.
The slow freight vessels like herds of tame elephants
and the little ferry-boats briskly moving about
like slim young women
were no longer visible. Now there was only water.
Water lurching on three sides, blue water on the sky-line,
far off the dark green shore fading in a curved line,
sometimes blue, sometimes silver-white,
sometimes the colour of soft mud, soothing the eyes.
Water — brown or aubergine, or tracts of desert grey —
below the sky another sky rushing on,
wave-swung, gambolling with tints.
In this wildness of Asharh, the waters of River Padma
spread across Bengal's heart — arrogant, exuberant.

A massive river is this Padma, like a sea:
with two arms she embraces Dhaka and Faridpur,
then becomes cloud-coloured Meghna, to merge with the sea.

The blue horizon's lost; before me comes
a shore painted with green trees and paddy fields.
A slim canal, curved like a half-moon, falls
laughingly on the laps
of five villages,
as if the river's full bosom's love's flood-tide
was overflowing because of its own pull, spreading life
in Bengal's corners every moment.
Eight tin sheds of the railway station on the canal bank —
even those are beautiful in afternoon's oblique light.
On one side of the steamer is the shore, on the other a sandbank.

Sandbank of the monsoon river, half above water, half below,
like a sliver of the moon in a black night.
And right on that, surrounded by tall rice plants,
a few tiny tin huts.

Beyond the sandbank the massive river, no shore in sight,
such intimacy between the colours of cloud and mud! –
the colour of the red soil leaching into the desert-grey waters,
swift currents tossing on the sky-line.

Really how beautiful
is a sandbank on the Padma of an afternoon!
You said, this would be just the right home for us:
ever-restless gestures of love filling the sky above,
and wherever we look, River Padma, our companion day and night.
Cool breezes, fresh hilsa, soft and tranquil soil;
the only snag – there's no electricity!

Really, it is quite delightful sitting comfy on the steamer,
knowing there's no doubt we'll reach Calcutta in the morning,
gazing at the solitude, the verdancy of sandbanks,
this luxuriance of River Padma in Asharh,
thinking to ourselves – ah, couldn't we come and live here!
Such sky-filling light, the wind so free and bracing, the soil
so soft and kind,
the waters of the Padma on three sides, touching the horizon,
voluptuous in its liquid beauty;
on the other side villages with green rice plants,
a tiny railway station on the bank of a canal
that's curved like a half-moon.
Away with trendy gear, following fashions, doing things
to avoid embarrassment!
We'll put on weight as much as we please, on a diet of milk and fish!
Where shall we go, leaving such a paradise? What's there in Calcutta!

Meanwhile the steamer's propellers turn again.
We've done enough poetizing, now let's have some tea.
When we are sipping our tea and nibbling our snacks,
suddenly I notice
the steamer's passing close, very close to the bank.
The water's being churned up
quite violently; curious women and girls, leaving their chores,
are watching what the steamer is up to, perhaps hoping
their huts would be spared this rainy season. How much earth
has Padma swallowed, burst how many thousands of dwellings,

caused how many royal palaces to sink,
and still the demoness knows no peace!
Propelled by the steamer's motion, huge noisy waves, one after
another, are hitting the bank, breaking in white foam.
You said it reminded you of Puri:
didn't I remember the tremendous surf there, so similar?
Look, just look at those little black boys there – in their loin-cloths, –
standing with their feet in the water, not a care in their heads;
a wave will hit them any minute, – watch it, there it comes, –
a row of waves is running breathlessly,
chasing whom, one wonders! Dinghies kept upside down flounder –
pull, pull them to the high ground – and there it comes,
sweeps away with a mighty whoosh
six little black heads – goodness me, how bold those kids are!
Even in such waves they are flinging their arms and legs,
playing with Padma herself!
They hurl themselves in the waves, wrap their arms
round the water's neck –
into one wild thing six little wild imps dive –
where have they gone now? – Ah, there they are,
on the bank, a little way off,
shouting at the steamer at the top of their voices,
the slippery light gleaming on their wet shining bodies –
but hang on now, what a disaster! – there goes a boy, swept off
like a straw on a wave.
He sinks, rises, – another wave leaps on him like a tiger, –
and where has it taken him? Alas, alas, he's gone under:
all the people are standing on the bank, gaping.
Is that boy going to drown in front of so many eyes – oh dear!
Where's the captain, call him, let them stop the steamer!
How extraordinary, nobody is saying anything at all!
And you too are a fine one – going on crunching your fried peanuts!
What's this! There bobs up
a little black head like the bottom of a round cooking-pot,
a hand stretches out, grabs the stem of a jute plant.
Holding on to it, he pulls himself to the jute field's mud, lies on it,
then in a minute leaps up and runs home –
well done, lad!

As we proceed, the eddying waters round the steamer lose their shores,
a void of open waters rushes on to the horizon.
Tin huts, rows of trees, curious women and girls — all are lost.
In the evening in sunset's *abir* tint
the light dinghies fling themselves
into a short-lived sport of round-cheeked red-orange sails.
We pull chairs on to the deck, sit down,
and speak in low tones,
and then in the river's waters burning with gold
the sun dips his lurid red neck.
In the sky the clouds catch fire,
spreading in the west the colours of a bridal night,
cloud upon cloud — yellow, Holi-red, pink, violet —
haven't seen such a display for a long time!

Huge, massive is this river — Padma of many tints —
scattering her colours in the light and shade of day and night,
giving life to fifty-two parganas of Bengal.

Then night descends.
Shadows hug one another in the river's waters, under the sky.
Waves rise, the wind races on. Stars, scentless kunda flowers, open.
Still three more hours to Goalundo.
Lost in the darkness: the blue edges of vegetation,
those staircases of clouds, royal palaces and tall minarets.
The murmur of black waters puts you to sleep. Dinnertime now.

The night grows older.
Black Padma races on, cleaving the heart of the vast night,
herself pierced by the keen arrow of a search-light.
Waves roll, foam swells, both shores are totally lost in blackness.
The vast night, veiled in a darkness without a sky-line,
is being kept out by the little cabin's electric light.
Only the chug-chug rhythm of the steamer vibrates.
Time lies heavy on our hands. When will Goalundo come!

1940

From *Damayanti* (1943)

A Day of Asharh

Been a long day today.   The sun's tremendous circuit
along the sky's track – long, radiant, semi-circular –
is almost over. The day is over. A prolonged evening. In the evening's
coital moments the night trembles, like a wife on her first night.

Day, long day!   Time's procession –
like a horseman, flag-bearer, victor, warrior, king –
clamour, grandeur!
                    Dawn arrives, tearing night's
womb of darkness   in ebullient delight,   warm current
of a golden flood.   Midday, long, incandescent: a diamond mountain,
the sun's palace,   ineffable
Gaurisringa,   blinding
high peak of light.   Vast afternoon:
cascade of still light,
all-flooding, wine-dripping,   brimful
floodtide:
                how resplendent
the sky's colours,   always on the go!
A wild forest of colours spreads
to marble-smooth clouds;   the restlessness of a mobile architecture
wraps the sun
in cheeky delirium.   The sun's body trembles under
the pressure of a golden flood,   at the beauty of the golden evening.
In sunset's burning jungle   a feral golden tiger
licks his paws.
                The battered west bursts,
birthing the night.   Day, the long day
is almost over.   The day is over.   The blinding, high-peaked
diamond mountain collapses;   the fierce soundless cascade
– the uncontrolled sylvan   delirium of colours –
blends, fades in the copperish west.   Dispersed
from the horizon's burst heart,
one long red line cuts in half
the greying sky's long semi-circle.   Even now, even now issues
– oh memory's undying   secret murmur! –
from a chink in the sombre dark wall of

night's fortress,   difficult of access:
still, solitary,
yet colourful, unabashed of speech:
the day.

June 1938

Hilsa

Asharh's in the heavens, and Bengal's monsoon-drunk.
Rows of coconuts on cloud-coloured Meghna's shores
are hazy in the rain. On Padma's brink, a palace, a century old,
expecting the worst, stands like a painted scene, unconcerned.

Midnight. Cloud-clotted darkness. The river treacherous
with wicked wild eddies. Swift as arrows, the little darting boats.
Those who, half-naked, furiously cast the nets, haul the ropes,
are famished themselves, but are food's pipeline for others.

Night ends in Goalundo, filling the blind black wagons
with heaps of hilsa corpses, the water's lucent harvest,
hillocks of death for the river's deepest delight.
Then in Calcutta's homes, in a bleary morning, leached of colour and
                                                                light,
the rising smell of frying hilsa, the clerk's wife's kitchen
tangy with mustard. The monsoon's here, and with it the hilsa-fest.

June 1938

From
Rupantar (1944)

Transformation

My days are pallid with the hard pummelling of work,
    my nights are incandescent with waking dreams.
Arise from the clash of metals, O beautiful one, white fire-flame,
    may the mass of matter become wind, the moon become woman,
        may the flowers of the earth become the stars of the sky.
Arise, O sacred lotus, rise from the spirit's stalk,
    free the eternal in the unfading forgiveness of the moment,
        make the momentary eternal.
May the body become mind, the mind become spirit, the spirit unite
                                    with death,
    may death become body, spirit, mind.

                                                          February 1944

From
Draupadir Sari (1948)

Magic Desk

Then brighten the lamp, and at the magic desk
drown yourself in the narrow pool of that light
whose seed engenders woman's beauty, whose song makes the ocean's
blue
tremulous, whose chemise of shimmering dreams beneath the moon
guides the world-conquering ship to dash it on ancient rock.
Then brighten the lamp, the lamp that casts the shade
which on a wondrous endless cloth of grass, trees, sun
gives the earth form, the form which the wind shakes
for ever with a lakh of hands, — yet the cry of that leaf-fall
is vanquished, stilled, given a rhythmic pace by its art.
Then brighten the lamp, pledge yourself to that light
which says goodbye to youth, wipes off life,
pierces with colour's undulations the core of the hot, dense mine,
and in veins of metals, in flames of lotuses of stone,
kindles unending, unerring, cruel diamonds of eyes.

November 1947, revised

Afternoon

Tree's green and sun's yellow on each other's neck pressed;
speech stirs in leaves, urged by the wind's sudden unrest;

shy poetry's slender buds peer within my breast —
    Ah, afternoon! Golden afternoon!

For someone pent in his room, stretched on his sickbed,
it leaves a message in a glistening ink — tender, compassionate;
buds of colour ripple in the sky — winter's withered breast.
    — Ah, afternoon! Short-lived afternoon!

29 November 1944

Sunday Afternoon

How happy they look — the people who pass in the street —
the very mobility of life's unthinking waves!
Their bodies drip bliss, their merest gestures speak,
eyes brimming over with desire's unreasoned excess.
Today, sadness seems to have forgotten dark forebodings.

The bright sky appears to open hope's floodgates.
Sitting indoors, I see some of it, hear somewhat less:
three young women have just walked to a tree's shade, whence
pouring into the sun's manhood a show of girlish tints —
              red, blue, yellow, aubergine —
they get on a tram, and away they go laughingly.

I see a middle-aged couple walking side by side, their faces satisfied;
a young girl conceals behind her sari youth's round pots.
In shops, friends' houses, cinema halls, and elsewhere
fun's froth swells the city, and within its veins, —
diverse, irritable, dense, — circulate the Sunday afternoon crowds.

I stare and think — how happy these people must be —
but when the fun's over, and they return home, who knows what might
                                          happen.
Trivial words may stir up a tempestuous argument,
ruin a poet's draft by the mere stroke of a pen,
leaving just a page of despair's blind doodlings.

20 October 1944

The Refugee

Those who walk by the side of the Lake at dawn
    are all either elderly or dyspeptic –
        this is what some people think
            for whom dawn means eight in the morning.
But the reality is different.
    All kinds of people go there.
Minimally clad exercisers, well-wrapped pensioners,
    sightless runners, children gathering flowers –
        even if these categories are put to one side
            those who remain are by no means small in number.
At least Satikanto, who has been in Calcutta since his birth,
    and in spite of having lived in Ballygunge for a decade
        is walking by the Lake for the first time today,
            is somewhat bemused by the human variety.
A plump Bhatia merchant gets off the car with his family,
    waddling happily like an overweight boy,
is overtaken by a Punjabi as tall as a sal tree, with his wife,
    and a robust Bengali sahib of fierce mien
in thigh-displaying shorts, a leather-bound walking-stick in his hand.
    A Madras clerk sits and reads a book beneath a tree,
    perhaps studying for a departmental exam.
A proud tight-lipped lady
    with a huge Alsatian and her own past behind her
        turns the corner,
and immediately from the opposite direction three slim young women
    approach, raising waves of their light, slender, new youth
        in rich tinkling laughter, and walk away.
        One solemn group is genuinely anxious
            about the state of the country –
some of them are professors, others do editorial work in newspapers.
    A fragment of their conversation makes two bald ageing
    slow-moving people fall silent and stare,
        then shaking their heads they resume
            the story of Durga Puja in Rasuipur in the year '17
                in the authentic dialect of Comilla District.
A dark young man with a thin line of moustache
    sits on a stone bench by the water,

wrapped in a shawl, glasses on his eyes, ever so quiet,
>   as if he was having his picture taken.
Some days you may even see a female college student
>   on some other bench, alone.
It would seem representatives of all sections of people come here,
>   except one group –
>   young married couples.
For so far nature has reserved for them some possibilities
>   more delicious than traipsing round the Lake of a wintry dawn.

People move, speak, wander around,
>   turn corners again and again. Some turn homewards.
Some lucky guy in a long white racing-boat
>   shoots off into the milky mist like a beautiful arrow.
Meanwhile beyond the rail-line
>   golden light glints on the mop-heads of coconuts;
>   >   a red flower blossoms in the cool sky;
>   >   >   its petals fall into the bluish water a few at a time.
Then behind the Buddha temple, tearing asunder
>   the darkness of shrubs and trees,
upon this landscape strewn with human beings
>   the sun-god with his sacred smile
>   >   appears, like a hero on a superhuman stage.
And gazing at that red, soft, throbbing sun,
>   a man in a threadbare sweater and dirty sandals,
>   >   his palms together, still on his breast,
>   >   >   mutters Sanskrit mantras –
>   >   no doubt he's somewhat deranged,
maybe from grief, or his trespasses, or 'cause he read too many books.

Every day Satikanto sees all this,
>   that half-crazy chap, and all those who will never go mad –
the lady carrying her past, the young women slender as bamboo stems,
the heroes of exercise and oratory, the blessed good folk of this world –
>   and the pale water, the tinted clouds, the sunrise.
He sees, and thinks –
>   well, not about anything else, just about himself,
>   >   about his suffering, which he cannot bear, cannot talk about,
>   >   >   a burden which has truly exhausted him.

His suffering is not the kind that makes tears flow,
>   pushes the chin onto the breast,
>   destroys appetite, makes the eyes sunken,
>   or robs one of sleep at night.
It's a dumb suffering, suffocating his chest: no relief from it
>   even for a minute.
>   Everything's fine from the outside, but no relief even for a minute
>   from this thing which is eating him, making him hollow inside.

The truth is that Satikanto is a writer.
>   He has written many books, and many more are in his head,
>   or at least he had thought so.
But for some days now something's the matter with him —
>   he can't write anything.
His pen doesn't move, nor his mind; his spirit's extinguished —
>   you blow on the coal a thousand times, yet no sparks flash.
>   He's been in this state for days now, for months.
Then why not give up writing? That would bring some peace, surely?
>   No way!
>   He's got to write, got to sit at his desk,
>   even if he can't put one letter down, yet he must stare for hours
>   at that blank, white paper.
>   A terrible torment this, hideously unfair;
but to whom can he complain? —
>   for his slavery is simply to himself.

Satikanto has thought things through.
>   What exactly is the matter with him?
Has he nothing more to say? Or is it his language that's bankrupt?
>   No, he does have things to say, nor has he forgotten
>   how to express his thoughts,
>   but as soon as he sits down to write, things cool off.
>   He feels he's no longer alive in a real sense,
>   has somehow slipped out of the frontiers of life,
>   has no claims anywhere; nothing seems to be meant for him.
But if that's what it's really like, then surely
>   suicide is the only way out.
>   With all his might Satikanto is resisting
>   this deadly line of thought.

From *Draupadir Sari* (1948)   45

His protests are like a mother-bird's dire, feeble wing-beatings
    when a snake visits her nest.
Perhaps something's wrong with his physical health:
    perhaps it's rest that his mind needs
        and what his body needs is exercise.
To achieve those two objectives together
    he's getting up early these days and taking strolls by the Lake.
Not that he minds taking strolls,
    but it wouldn't be correct to say that he enjoys them either.
As he walks, he looks at the different kinds of faces,
    tries to overhear what they are saying,
        at times feels restless –
            just for a moment.
The face recedes with its unseen history –
    in the expectation of another artist.
The words fade within his ears –
    the tuning for their reception is somewhere else.
    No melody, no pulsation.
        'With all my flesh and blood I'm floating like a shadow' –
            so he thinks, and as he does he recognizes
                his self-deception.
This walking – tell me truly! – what does it really mean?
    The pleasure of moving the limbs?
        Health from fresh air?
            The sunshine full of ultra-violet rays?
                Or the urge to observe snapshots of moving life?
                    – None of these!
It means killing time – just passing the time –
    nothing could be more dreadful than that.
Coming home to a shave and a shower, a cup of tea and a newspaper,
    and thus resisting, postponing
        that one irresistible, undeniable moment –
            when with an empty mind, a broken string
                he must sit at that very desk
where even the other day – not so long ago – there was stashed for him
        his sunshine, breezes, health, pleasure, happiness, fulfilment.

It was bitterly cold.
    Not many people by the Lake.

        Or rather, it was hard to see if there were any or not.
   A thick veil of fog had lowered itself,
as happens in Calcutta in the month of Magh, suddenly on some days,
        before the koel's first cry is heard.
The water was indistinguishable from the ground, the sky was overcast:
all around one there was this layer of bluish white, intangible stillness.
      In the gaps one could make out one or two people walking,
          indistinct, almost unreal, like black shadows,
            like visible embodiments of Satikanto's sick soul.
Satikanto rather liked this state of affairs,
      this covering, the earth acting as though it was receding.
Fog too could be handy at times,
     sometimes to draw a curtain of decency
        when a great sage, with the brashness of greatness,
          covets a fisherman's daughter
              on the bosom of the river, on the boat, that very instant;
and sometimes to conceal the misery, embarrassment, humiliation
   of someone who's been hurt in the soul, to make him forget it all.
When he thought of that, Satikanto had an odd sense of consolation,
    and feigning some enthusiasm to his own self,
       made a longer tour than on other days –
keeping the swimming-club to his right, skirting the railway line,
     where the air was hazier with mature, massive trees,
he went right up to the Japanese garden in the most deserted street.
Didn't sit down or stop anywhere, but started to walk back homewards
   along the same route, trying to be brave, with a heroic gesture.
'If emptiness is what I deserve, I must face that too. This failure too
   won't be altogether in vain – everything is grist to my mill.'
But as home drew nearer, his heart began to sink again;
   his body felt drained, his confidence evaporated.
Not possible to hide any more. The light appeared. The fog trembled,
about to disappear in a glittering haze, after scattering particles of gold.
   And there it was! Day again, shining day,
     day with its heartless demands.
Trying to look that day in the eye, Satikanto bowed his head,
   then suddenly stopped, as if he had stumbled. –
It was nothing to do with himself, he'd noticed something else.

At the turn of Manoharpukur
   where Hindusthan Park begins – or ends – abruptly,

From *Draupadir Sari* (1948)

someone was lying on the pavement –
    it must be said, a human being, a woman –
        since there was no other name.
It could not be called a very original scene in Calcutta,
    but even in that context this was something special to catch the eye.
She was lying in a tidy pose, as though she had made up her mind,
    as animals select a spot in the jungle
        to eat, to sleep, to die.
She had wrapped herself in some jute sacking
    and even had a piece of tattered quilting beneath her.
By her head was a cooking pot, its brim broken, and a ragged towel.
    One hand was uncovered on one side,
    and near that hand was a long slender bamboo branch.
On the other side through an opening in the quilting
    a tiny head, a longish forehead, dirty hair
        betokened another existence.
The baby seemed to be sleeping cosily
    nestling against the smell of the mother's body.
The woman was lying stretched, taut.
    The colour of her face and hands was muddy.
    Her hair was like coconut fibres; her eyes were wide open.
She had no expression on her face, in her eyes,
    neither of pain, nor of prayer, nor of protest.
Just staring stupidly with still eyes –
    a human being, the wife of a human being, the mother of a child,
when around her in houses with gardens
    people were not yet fully awake,
kitchens smoked, cows grazed quietly on the pavement's grass verge,
    and from the translucent sky dripped
        the warm, soft, indolent sunshine of a Magh morning.

Soon a few more people gathered there,
    among them an elderly milkmaid.
        The elderly woman gazed for a while, then asked,
            'You spent the night here then?'
Satikanto did not expect to hear a reply,
    but was amazed by the voice that rang out.
        Dry, sharp, shrill, like a stage actress's.
As if the body's last remaining store of energy
    had concentrated itself in the voice,

as if on the outermost edge of powerlessness
    the power of words had resurrected itself
        in order to vanish like an arrow into the bosom of nothingness.
       'Would a jackal eat me? Haven't I got this stick!
I could do a robbery with this stick – yes, a robbery!
Come midday I'm going to the Congress – everyone knows me there.'
    The milkmaid bent down and said, 'Where was your home?'
        The woman paused for a while, then spoke again,
in a high pitch as before, drawing out the words in a histrionic style –
    'Auntie – will you take my daughter –?'
As she spoke, her eyes moved, made a huge round circuit –
    unmeaning eyes – yellow, bewildered.
Satikanto watched, fascinated. Yes, this too was a sort of fascination –
    never before had he seen such bleary eyes on a human face.
He remembered Dante's *Inferno,*
    where a father in prison, with his two sons, was dying of starvation.
        One day the younger boy wailed, 'Father, I can't see anything!'
Those who die from lack of food have apparently
    this symptom in the last stage –
        their eyesight fails.
– The same might have happened to these eyes. Unable to see,
    they were just staring.
Maybe she wasn't hearing well, and was therefore speaking so loudly.

'From where has this one come? Didn't see her on our way out.
    Doesn't seem like a refugee from East Bengal either,
        speaks with a Twenty-four Parganas accent.
            The famine's long over. If even now –'
                So saying two other gentlemen returning from the Lake
                started homewards.
Satikanto waited a little.
    Once, unknown to himself, his hand reached out to his pocket.
        Immediately he was ashamed of himself.
        No – that would lower her dignity.
Was there anything at all that he could do?
    Nothing – nothing that would not lower her dignity.
    Let none of the do-gooders, duteous and arrogant,
        get to know of this.
            Let human beings move off, let nature give her honour.

From *Draupadir Sari* (1948) 49

Casting one last glance,
    Satikanto resumed walking, slowly,
        his heart fluttering a little, a spot of warmth within it.
           It seemed to him
                that somehow
                    in an obscure manner
            it had happened to him – a little relating to another –
                the compassion of a touch,
                    a re-connection with life.

                        1954 [From the 1963 joint revised edition,
                          Damayanti: Draupadir Sari o Anyanyo Kavita.]

From
Sheeter Prarthana: Basantar Uttar (1955)

After Death: Before Birth

This is not a day for songs. On the year's shortest day
sunlight and warmth, minimal, and the moon, its radiance fog-dimmed,
pop hope-against-hope in the coffin, mingle hope with despair.
Yet it is in winter that hope, even hope against hope, pauses once more;
pauses, dying, dead, at the news of the day that's a day only in name.
The grave of the year's shortest day gives birth
to the very next day, in brevity the second-best of the year.
Shrinking daily, the days bring the shortest day;
thereafter day by day the days grow bigger, longer,
with more light, more heat,
more!
Get longer, day, get longer!
This song — if you call this a song, as I would —
is sung by crow, blackbird, sparrow
in sharp tones, conch-shell tones,
when at night's end, day's fingers, from under the horizon,
pulls night's tail, and darkness flutters
just like their own wings —
the wings of those birds I mean! When evening comes,
they sing again the same song —
    More day, more! —
Thus sing crow, blackbird, sparrow — as soon as from the highest,
lightweight, green plaits of the tree-branches above the pavement
sunlight's golden comb slips off, and darkness

covers the earth with the colour of their own wings —
the wings of those birds I mean!

     Then why do you say there's no song?
Birds do sing. Be they crow, blackbird, sparrow,
they are still birds, and it's still song.

      Some say more.
They say, this is a season for fun. In Bengal the winter's mild,
and it's in these two months that the body can have a good time.
Just for a few days this sharp piercing cold, the sky a soft blue,
the sunshine burnished yet mellow; so in the healthy north wind
 just go ahead and fulfil
a little freely any of the year's wishes:
have a go, have a go!
Give everything, take everything too!
You might not get this wish back next year, or be able to return to it.
(The winter in which the clamour of another group of girls
will perhaps send a call to the merry din of another group of youths
is near — quite near.)
If today you have nothing else, at least you have your wish;
and if you have only your wish, and nothing else, in that case
still take, take, ask for it and you might get it,
try asking, go!
Christmas in Calcutta, thrill in Delhi, and in Santiniketan
the fair, fun and games, all day — how quickly the day goes!

      — Let it go.
The day has indeed gone. My day certainly has. When you are an oldie
a volatile mind doesn't suit you, gusty winds of wishes don't suit you:
you should just listen, and accept. So
I have really accepted this cold room, facing the north,
noise in the street till midnight,
and from huddled neighbours
the noose of their coal-smoke, the overpowering smell
that billows when they cook rotten fish.
I am an old guy now, well, as good as old. So
I spend all day sitting on a chair.
If I can't write, I read. I read books,
and if the light seems not enough — as my eyesight isn't

what it used to be —
I sit quietly and think. Yes, I think,
and when I am too tired even to think,
I look out of the window, at the street, or at night
I lie down and stare at the wall,
so very familiar and yet unknown.

                        Perhaps now you'll admit
that winter's not a happy time, at least not for me.
Winter ... is winter.
My hand touches the desk's cold wood, my feet touch the cold floor,
the cold wind pierces my back. Cold, dark, closed
is this north room.
The day is shorter, and the light less, in this room.
My notebook remains open, books remain shelved. —
What's this,
morning delayed so much, and evening arrives so early,
where's the time to do things!
No day, no light, not the right mood, no time
for anything, except for sleep. Yet
I keep sitting on my chair, because the bed is even colder.
Since nothing is achieved by sitting
I get early to bed, curling up
like an animal in the shelter of the quilt.
And as the bed begins to warm up
I think —
what? What do I think?
I, an old guy, as good as old, what have I got,
what have I got to think about
apart from a few sharp memories,
sharp, bitter, intoxicated memories?

                        Songs in this winter?

Songs in this winter. No songs in this winter, unless I shape them,
for the calls of crow, blackbird, sparrow
aren't songs — though they may sound so in my ears.
Birds weren't given songs, they were given just cries.
I was given songs, so I invoke them.
I invoke winter, enduring winter's enmity, on pallid, meagre days,

From *Sheeter Prarthana: Basanter Uttar* (1955)

during intolerable blood-sucking evenings.
Sitting all day in the dark cold room,
I, an old guy, as good as old, call out – Increase,
songs, increase! Not finished yet, there are more –
more songs! More days!
Waning daily, then bringing us the shortest day,
the day waxes again – every day. In the interim
Tropic of Capricorn's sun
breathes a little freely, leans on the sky's convexity, face turned north.
Once more there'll be the keen-edged path, steep staircase, Phalgun
of gentle breezes. After that, Baishakh's pinnacles of happiness.
Before that he takes a break, looks back, looks far, sheds the fatigue
of his trek, does the northbound sun.
                        Therefore songs, songs even now. Because I too
look back, look far, lay down the fatigue of my trek
in my fleshless winter's body. For though
my youth's over, yet there's some way to go
before I win the freedom of fleshless winter for ever.
I am not impatient, yet my veins' ropes are still tied
to life's demands; so I, sitting on the steps of my allotted days,
hear behind me memory's waterfall –
a turbulent babble! – And before me I see my road's lines –
rough, vertical, steep, as curved and lonely as they are steep; so
finishing one incarnation, and before commencing the next –
I do just this – nothing but this – I arrange and spread
my thoughts on day's desk, and under night's quilt. And at night's end
when I wake up in the dark that covers my face, stifles my breast,
I feel: No! – there's nothing! – nothing exists at all –
except this load,
just this load
of my own thoughts.
                    Hence songs,
songs I must shape, to return to reality's well-being.
But which songs?

                    When I was young, I sang in praise of
youth. When youth was going, was nearly gone, then again
I sang in its praise, for life
loves youth – nature's way it is.

Who has youth loves it, who hasn't loves it too.
The father basks in the sun of his offspring's youth;
Grandma toasts her hands in her youthful granddaughter's warmth;
old men who hate each other's guts
see their own infirmity writ large
each on the other's face, and afraid, become supplicants
even to youth's arrogance. And that's why old men are so lonely
and why old age is
so cruel, so terrible.

                         Have I then, accepting the dharma of animals,
blindly pulled by nature, simply invoked
my unborn children, when I've written poems?
My praise of youth — is it merely the adoration
of procreative power? My verse's rhythm — has it simply been
another cog in nature's wily machine,
    and enchanted by Chaitra's moon and summer's champak,
    and the rain's wildness, and the night's blindness,
has it just listened to nature's pep talk
and spread its counsel? — 'Swell, seed, swell! Grow, creature, grow!
More, and more, and more!'

                         Indeed, if that was so,
then today, after twenty-five years of writing poetry,
    I would have let my poems go
floating on the waters, or be merged with dust,
be killed by the wind that makes leaves fall to the earth.
For if I have nothing more to say than echo, re-echo
phrases that nature makes a crore of voices repeat,
then surely it would be better if the poet kept mum.

              I believe, though I've hymned unremittingly
youth, rebellion, life's blind delights,
or their tumultuous memories, yet I've never stooped
to mere flattery. In my worship there was
no idolatrous lust. I could fashion the image in colour and beauty
for there was rhythm in my spirit, craftsmanship in my hands,
yet even when marvellously happy in that art,
I never forgot that the original — of which I was
making an image, breaking and re-making it again and again —

was nothing but the love dwelling within my soul,
my ecstatic love in which I lost myself –
nothing but that.

       Therefore I say,
whatever I've written – be it the hymn of youth,
 or the praise of blind creaturely delights –
whatever I've written is love poetry – all of it.
Weaving phrases, stringing metres, churning words,
what I've done most intensely, madly, truly is loving – I've just loved.
– It's the same today! Even now, sitting in this cold room,
shivering, rubbing my hands to keep warm, racking my brains
all through the dark day, I fetch and weave phrases, churn words;
for that way I love most,
most truly – even to this day.

      But whom? Whom do I love?
Is it a woman? Any particular woman? The unending nectar,
 ineffable, unforgettable,
of the lovely face of an eternal seductress?
Or is it poetry? Its burning imagination, metre's maddening
 intoxication, the fire of speech
in all one's limbs, pores, blood-cells?
If I think – didn't think like this before – but now when I think,
woman and speech seem the same. It seems that the poetry,
the love of poetry that there was in my body's threads and seams –
out of that stuff's white flames I opened the lotus,
making woman its imaginary stalk. It seems I have loved woman
 because poetry has arisen, has been sparked off
by her eyes – without her grasping how it happened.
She has not herself grasped how by loving her I have
loved even more my metre's magic, the hypnosis of words,
and by loving poetry more I have loved her even more
until within my heart love has become
poetry, and poetry in turn has
become love.

      But surely, surely this is old hat, familiar stuff,
what all the earth's poets rave about. The old and the new,
 those forgotten and those still unheard:

all poets speak like that. ... Besides,
your woman's body no longer drugs,
the sari's undulations no longer sing,
eyes don't speak to eyes,
hands' trembling touch lacks poetry's warmth.
Still, who once more ferries back your hand –
in a cold room, throughout the dark day –
across the sharp teeth of the cold
to poetry's heat,
intoxicated, intense,
to the heat of intense, intoxicated waiting?
                                            Waiting for what?
For love. And who waits? That's love too.
No veins of imagination left in woman's body, no wine of poetry left
    in the flood-flow of veins; but there is love, there is still love –
    not love of poetry or of woman: just love.
Never thought like this before – nor thought, nor realized
I would have to think thus –
but now I see that I must reflect on this, must understand
who it is that holding my hand has brought me so far, to my life-span's
steps of winter; and who again, ferrying me across winter's teeth,
guides my hand under steep, vertical, heart-breaking
poetry's pressure. ... What shall I call you
    if not
love? If I think – well, the more I think, the more it seems to me now
that love and what I love are one and the same.
It seems I love *love itself*, no one else.
Not in woman's body, which is like fresh cream, does that love dwell,
not in a name that sings like waves, a name like a thousand waves:
indeed, not in poetry,   not in the rhythm of words,
    not in the hypnosis of metres:
the dwelling of that love is just within my heart –
my ardent, drunken heart! My ecstatic heart! –
Yet age brings cold to the heart – still that love knows no winter;
yet that heart drains away in the dark – still that love knows no end.
As for example, right now. Already now,
having sat on my own in this cold room, all through the dark day,
my mind seems to merge with the wind's killing act. Already now
I wish I could return to dark mother night's womb, and then
    to the unborn soul's extinction without a thought.

I seem to want to destroy with my own hands
the dwelling that's destined to crumble, let my heart drip away,
murdered by the wind that causes leaves to fall.
  It seems, seems even today
that this could be the winter when poetry's hand
will no longer touch my breast, poetry's warmth
  will no longer return to my hand;
sitting alone in the dark, in this cold room, rubbing my hands,
no longer will I, in love with poetry, say, 'I love',
in the unending lipless dark,
in the bitter spermicidal cold.
So I go to bed early. Like a dog that has been chased I hide, curl up
under the quilt's warmth.
Until the bed gets warm, sleep seems to be
the secret lair of an infirm animal, barricading, with its lesser darkness,
the greater darkness even now – even now.
And when sleep warms you up, it resembles a mother's compassion,
  the sad lonely yoni of night the dark mother,
in the measured darkness, barricading, with compassion's soft warmth,
that horrendous cold, the darkness without conclusion –
for one more day – yes, for one more day.

  One more day! One more day!
Day comes to the sky once more, though it's dark.
The horizon's labour-pangs
are voiced by crow, sparrow, blackbird. Cries rise,
  keen, conch-shell calls in the dark – 'More day! One more day!'
In the face-smothering, breast-stifling darkness,
  in the quilt's cave, warm and secret,
night groans. And clinging to night, sleep gropes for the last dreams.
  But still they rise, more calls. Day breaks, yet another day!
Another day in that same room, in the darkness!
Day comes to the sky once more, though it's dark in the room.
And in that closed room, in darkness thick with sleep's breath,
immersed half in sleep, half in dreams,
I imagine
there's nothing,
neither sleep, nor dreams, nor day,
no, there's nothing – absolutely nothing –

except this love,
nothing except this love,
my fervent, frenzied, self-losing love!

        Therefore songs. Therefore even now — songs.

                                      December 1947

After Forty

Don't keep calling memory back,
it's much too heavy;
its larder's large enough,
but crueller still are its mice,
who pick and eat its shredded minutes.
And thus the heart dries.

From the original mouths of children learn
wisdom's initial glossary;
if what is not, and will never be,
becomes fierce thirst, then surely
what's been your lot in life's family
is absolutely all right.

If still you think there were errors,
vanish into the blue,
efface your usable name,
and as happy as the wind, flow
to the silvery dark of the stars.
Say to the wave, 'I am,'
and to the earth: 'I too was.'

                                      September 1950

Monsoon Day

The rain's theatrics right from the early morning:
the sky wiped out, the day veiled in dark.

From *Sheeter Prarthana: Basanter Uttar* (1955)

This very day, Srabon seems determined
to pay back all debts piled in dry Baishakh.
Pitter-patter the blind waters come down,
the earth's surrendered, rapturously drowned;
now it seems there's neither day nor night;
and time hides in cloud-land, stupefied.

The pavement slabs send off a watery spray,
the tall trees, heads bowed, are keeping quiet;
on a day when matter is melted, liquefied,
better if everything were washed away.
Yet the clock says nine, so I pick up my umbrella,
get on a tram to keep my tryst with the office;
the tram's a cage packed tight with clerical workers
and through its gaps come moist, soft caresses.

Even on a day so lost, private, eerie
the vast city vibrates with work's hubbub.
Men are mice, imprisoned in a trap
whose jaws are always ready to gobble us up.
The pull's decisive – we do as it decrees,
bobbing brollies quite blacken the streets;
nor are the affluent free to do as they please:
stern of mien, they proceed in motor cars.
I mingle with that crowd and walk, determined,
without a name, without an identity.

Someone has drained the marrow from my bones;
my shoes shame me at each step – they're so worn;
my crumpled clothes and the two-day stubble I've grown
body forth my life's futility.
When the rain descends like this, drowning life,
flushing out time, weaving dreams round the day,
and electric lights push Srabon out of the way
in a stuffy office where a hundred out-breaths flow –
then today simply takes a loan from tomorrow.

The day concludes; a drunken rain's-end haze
clings to the clouds, though the rain's been put on hold;
streaked with transient yellow, green, and gold,

the oneiric twilight craves the rain's next phase.
Ah, how beautiful is this earth, this life,
the most precious gift, for which I paid no price!
However the hellish lack of buying power
harasses the body, harries the bodied me,
in the unfathomable, the unreachable, my spirit's free.
No sooner had I been released from the machine
of earning a living, than Srabon placed on my breast
its dangling garland, strung with gold and green.
How lucky I am to be alive, to be living!

Bruised, weary, liberated, enthused,
to my little home's citadel I retrace my steps.
Still traced on the sky — the lingering memory-flecks
of a day that I will never again embrace.
The lane's hideous, slippery — twists and turns;
you have to be careful — pointed brick-chips poke;
curling like an argument ascends
the rain-bedraggled day's damp-coal smoke.
A sadness steals over me like a drug,
makes me numb, denudes me of my breath,
wipes the image of the universe from my mind.
— As I'm about to go in, my trance breaks.

Holding the door ajar with gentle grace,
there she stands, a colourful sari on —
its border drawn partly over her head
and partly so that it obscures her face.
The day's deceptions haven't robbed me of all —
there is still night, something is still left:
filling the drowsy cave of my emptied soul
with the plenitude of dream's draughtsman-sketches,
one thin wrist, bare, bereft of gold,
mimics an evening lamp's expectant glow.

I think I know her — but no, don't know her quite.
What can I say? And in what accent say it?
Through my poverty's sieve with its hundred thousand holes
gushes the monsoon's generous, unlocked flow —

in the blind alley blossoms a kadamba grove.
I have nothing to offer as my heart's metaphor –
no jasmine, no tuberose, no bel-flower.
I can only gaze at her face silently
and with my eyes touch her black eyeballs.
Unknown to me, the eternal she has travelled,
traversed the deceitful trickery of the trivial,
and softly whispers in my ears, 'My pledge
I won't forget, I will never forget.'

August 1944

30 January 1948

Impossible to grieve for ever. Stunned stone breaks
with the thirst for tears. In the stone's hidden, yet tense,
swollen, unbearable veins a torrent descends; to the heart's reddish lips
descends the pity of fatigue, the tears cease. ... After that?

Lakhs and lakhs of wordless grief trudge the streets.
On Ganga's bank the sunset's tenderness matches it gently, quietly.
Pained clamour in the press; voices choking on the radio –
all will cease, conclude, let's say – have come to an end. After that?

With lovely hands of compassion sorrow cups
this night's holy blood; the more it flows, the more the hands hold.
But the blood will drain away, and even after this weeping has ceased
dawn will, without fail, awaken home after home. – And then?

Will rekindle torment, the grim torment of living, the pressure of which
crumbles housekeeping, crushes kingdoms to dust, shakes ministers,
                              housewives, labourers.
This unforgiving business of living will send out questions again,
which must be answered. Then? ... What then?

1 February 1948 [Written after the
assassination of Mahatma Gandhi.]

Calcutta

Once upon a time Calcutta was matchless, marvellously beautiful in my
                                                                eyes,
like the beginning of a dream, a flower blossomed from imagination's
                                                                stem.
In its dust, in its wind, in its hot metallic breath
            my passions have screamed out loud.

Evening lights on the Chowringhee, midday's asphalt-scent,
massive, frothy, fast-flowing currents of motley crowds in the streets,
and the descent of blue clouds on a thousand white terraced roofs
            used to make me mad with delight.

When youth begins its years, the sails of its boat swell,
and far off, in the gaps of golden mists, a continent gleams —
that's what you were like to me: hazy, luminous, incredible,
            you, Calcutta.

I had come to you as a guest, with the shyness of virginity,
but you, heroine of a hundred thousand loves, broke the ice
and flung yourself on me — just as the boundless ocean opens itself
            suddenly before our eyes.

I remember those moments when the railway platform, solemn, sleep-
                                                                awakened,
would recede like a veil, and a bell would ring in my breast. —
You, you again! Your sharp, strong, hard-working dawn, freshly bathed
            in the water-jets of the municipal workers' hose-pipes.

I have drunk you with my in-breath, I have touched your pores,
spread myself all over you, as a mountain stream when it first falls on
                                                                the plain,
and with the taxi's pulsing speed have felt breezes of the future
            sweeping over my spirit.

No one can say to you — 'You are mine'. For you, enchantress,
are the daughter of commerce, to be shared by all the world.
But I found my liberation, did I not, when to the ears of your breezes
            I could say, 'I am yours!'

From *Sheeter Prarthana: Basanter Uttar* (1955)

Liberation! – Yes, that's just what I wanted of you, and obtained it too:
the dynamics of living, the freedom to be articulate. A river's liberation
when it hits its banks, a poet's when he finds his melody, and a short-
        lived insect's on a joyous day of spring.

You never promised me anything, only sent me a summons;
and I too had no special present for you, except my eager uncertainty.
Yet – or precisely that's why – at the turns of your roads the doors
        of my future swung open before my eyes.

What we call fate, the unseen, which we don't know, can't know –
it's we who create it ourselves, always – that's just what you taught me.
From your hand I grabbed my destiny, and grasped it in my fist,
        free from all doubts.

It wasn't easy, that winning. Many a time has that battle defeated me.
Despair has robbed my breast of speech, and dozing on a jolting bus,
I have said to myself, 'Let it not stop again, no need for me to get off
                                            anywhere' –
        that's to say, occasionally, on those odd middays of sorrow.

Sorrow! – No, no, what I had to give up for your sake was trivial,
of no value in the long term. And in return you endowed me
as grandly as a queen – in every layer of my being I have absorbed
        your munificence.

Whatever is deposited as memory's gold, whatever gives meaning to
                                            the past,
friendship, love, struggles, the joy of keen toil,
my work, my vocation, my life – all, all I have had
        because I had you, Calcutta.

Where desire is profound, where the blood is eloquent, where the spirit
                                            yearns,
that space within us which, if filled, cancels out the areas where we are
                                            cheated,
the source whence issues the awareness – 'I am alive' – precisely there
        you have fulfilled me, Calcutta.

That's why there was happiness in your sun's whip, wine in the skin's
                                            sweat,

and within your crowds the challenge to be uniquely myself.
All my bitterness has been wiped off when I have seen the light of
                                          civilization blaze
          in your evenings, Calcutta.

You gave me everything except peace, for peace would have
                            undermined the other gifts.
A few gifts you kept hidden, so that I would have to search for them
                                             again.
And thus have I had you again and again
                afresh, anew, Calcutta.

Because you don't soothe like a mother, but like a charmer, ask to be
                                                  won over,
because you invite magnanimously, reject cruelly, reciprocate lavishly,
therefore have I loved you – infinitely mysterious,
          sexy Calcutta.

I have found you repeatedly, found myself repeatedly too.
When I want to be myself, but can't, nor can ever be
anything else instead – that terrible thirst of mine you have not
                    allowed me to forget, Calcutta.

Through the churning of work, the tumult of conflicts, the intensity of
                                                           dreams,
keeping me awake with the rolling of your blood's ocean, setting me on
                                                                         fire,
you have given meaning to my existence – my Ujjayini, my America,
        – Calcutta!

Oh, it's been a long time. Like yellow leaves the years fell down.
In the stormy winds of the end of an era history shed its pages.
You decked yourself in a new dress – perhaps it was necessary
                    that we should get to know each other better.

Famine came flying. Sparks of a conflagration rushed forward.
Your nerves were taut, a tidal wave raced along your veins.
The last breaths of my years of youth mingled with panic, turmoil,
                zeal's overflow, and the weeping of skeletons.

From *Sheeter Prarthana: Basanter Uttar* (1955)

Your rain washed away the torn flesh of human beings;
the hum of your traffic drowned the feeble moans of the hungry;
in the blackouts, grass grown lush was uprooted,
        trampled underfoot by restless refugees.

The havoc of epidemics, the death of the heart, the darkness of anarchy,
divisions, separations, arguments like stone chips, ideologies gritting
                                                            their teeth. –
On Bengal's breast, split asunder, the poinciana regia of my last
                                                    summer
        blossomed, shed its petals.

Everything that we had cherished – the aura of intellectual aristocracy,
friendship, love, courtesy, the flowering of individual personality –
all broke up, one by one, and collapsed on the stones of your
                                                    pavements.
        The trees died. And there were no birds.

Where was the comfort? – In the moonlight shimmering like water on
                                            your tram-lines
when there was terror in your aircraft-filled skies?
Or in the ceaseless groan of lorries heard from a hospital on a sleepless
                                                    night –
        assuring us that you were alive?

Nowhere. – Perhaps I'll have to say good-bye to you one day.
No regrets either. Every possible happiness – who has ever found that?
But once upon a time I did find all my happiness within you –
        that's something I won't forget.

You don't remember anyone, you are just the shuffle of footsteps.
You don't pity the past, you are just velocity.
But those years of mine, maddened by the rhythm of that speed –
        how can I forget them?

Memory of me will gather in your dust. Your breezes will be keen
with the new breath of some other guest like myself.
But I, – under any other sky, my eyes on any far horizon, –
        will say – Come back.

Come back, Calcutta of my dreams — that's what I say even today. —
Shine bright, not just in my eyes, but in the eyes of the world.
Let commerce spread from the Ganga to the earth's shores
            in your treasures, in your thoughts.

May the fruits of human labour be gathered as food for humans.
May our thirst for deathlessness quench itself — may that pitcher pour
                              out joyfully.
May the laughter of beautiful women move restlessly,
            stirring ripples in your swaying evenings.

How much more must you be destroyed, to be born again?
How many more deaths will you summon? — Yet dreams do not die.
That civilization might be annihilated — I cannot accept at all.
            Hence the scream of this volition.

I have no other power, but will does have power.
The seeds of my wishes are dropping, scattering on your future.
Are you planning any posterity for them in some distant epoch —
            won't you even let me know that?

My sorrow in being away from you will be calmed, if someday
in a distant land, before my death I hear at least this much —
that you did not play deceptive tricks on the hungry, did not mock
                                            beauty,
        did not force your talented ones into exile.

                                                    April 1953
                                                       Mysore

Prayer of A Winter Night

Come, forget all your worries, your worries about money, about health,
            about what will happen after this, and after that;
throw away your fears about the future, and your regrets about the past.
Today the earth has been wiped off, all your habitual props
have crumbled one by one. There's only icy loneliness now, and the
                                      dark chilly night.
        Come, get ready.

From *Sheeter Prarthana: Basanter Uttar* (1955)

Night of snow outside. The wind is a witch whose pitiless whip
tears the flesh of your cheeks, rips the moon like a piece of paper
and scatters it in the mist, gouges out the sky, scatters the chill
with malevolent hands; with the choreography of a white, soft dance
        sketches death on the earth.

Your earth is sunk, your familiar landmarks are lost;
no flowers, no birdsong, no one calling your name in a mellow voice;
the land's unfamiliar, the habitation temporary, the spirit resourceless
                                  in an empty room,
and outside – it's dark, a northern winter, with wave upon wave of the
                                              polar wind.
        Now's the time. Pull yourself together.

Pull yourself together. Concentrate. Don't forget that the past isn't
                                              exhausted yet.
The past that is waiting for you – future is the name for that very thing.
You will go, it will happen, you will get it back. Moments of deception
are interested only in binding, in hiding. But your path
        has proceeded very far, up to the horizon.

Who put a hand on your hand that very first day – you still remember
                                              that, don't you?
In order that you may remember, and never forget, you must forget
                                              much else.
In order that you may travel without fear, you must divest yourself of
                                              rubbish, the burden of security.
You must become destitute, get rid of all that is familiar, so that at each
                                              turn of the road
        you can recognize the old again, know it afresh.

Come, tread softly, climb the stairs to your empty room.
It's empty, so that you can fill it. It's cold, so that you can make it
                                              warm.
Come, forget your one thousand worries, about money, about survival –
                                              and after that
your future will come forward towards you, and your past will grab you
                                              from the back.
        Come, be ready for death tonight.

That's what you really want, what you hunger for. It is in the hands of
                                                              this death
that all those moments of deception will be rent asunder.
Just as the earth died in front of you today — no flowers, all the green
extinguished, just hard white stillness visible all around you —
            even so you must sink, even you.

— Into death's darkness you must sink, or else how would you come
                                                              alive again?
Into the underworld you must vanish, or else how would you return to
                                                              the light?
Don't you know that man must die again and again, oh yes, again and
                                                              again,
that in the ceaseless swing of death and rebirth he must be swung
            if he must truly survive.

It is to darkness that we have given the name of death. Seeds die
when they disappear below ground, in some secret hidden hollow.
When winter comes the earth dies, leaves fall; grass, flowers, grass-
hoppers take their leave; wolves come out; in a black, black, cruel
                                                              burial
            life gets lost — under dazzling snow.

You are the same. For you too the sunshine died, fog hemmed you in;
leaving your world of light you came down to the underworld;
your colourful clothes became torn, your name was rubbed off; you
                                                              forgot your language;
all the eyes that used to know you once — eyes like a carnival — you
                                                              went beyond their ken,
            disappearing from darkness into darkness.

But piercing the soil's breast, the lost seeds return one day,
reappear in another name, in a new birth, with the riches of a heaped
                                                              harvest.
And as for this winter, you know that with each drop of snow it too is
                                                              piling its debt,
which must be repaid. Life, concealed, with unshakeable patience
            is staying awake the long, long night.

Not only staying awake, but secretly at work,
creating new birth in death's bosom, strange unreasoning shoots

that burst the grave, water that splits stone and flows, pulsations within
snow's still layer — when ripping that veil, the slender, hardy, bright,
                                        marvellous green
            will peep with spring's first kiss.

And so this death is your waiting — you must be worthy of it.
You must forget the penury of caution, the rubbish of a thousand
                                                    worries.
Don't doubt, don't protest. Stay put like a seed
within this hard, dazzling, icy stratum — where your eternity is waiting
                                                        for you.
            Offer, surrender yourself.

The night deepens. The thin moon is in tatters. The darkness is
                                            wolflike.
Gangs of witches ride the wind. The cold is as keen as an assassin's
                                            knife.
In the midst of this is your ritual sacrifice. To be offered: your life;
                        to be lit: your soul's fire.
To be burnt to ashes: what you thought was your future, and what you
                                        knew to be your past.
            Be cleansed. Wait.

Listen, the church bell. The hour draws near for the festival of this folk
in memory of God's unique, only son.
But you — your body is built of another clay, a different song
hums in your blood. Your history's firmament rings with the assertion
        of a different consolation.

You have known that every man is the son of the immortal — not just
                        one person, but everyone.
You have asked to be led from darkness to light, from death to
                                    deathlessness.
You have heard it said that birth after birth twists and turns like an
                                                            eddy,
leading towards immortality; and that this life — it too will not remain a
                                                    prisoner
        within the limits of its time, within the bounds of flesh.

That's what you know — that man must die again and again, in order to
                                        be born again.

Not just rebirths, but this death and resurrection happening within one
                              lifetime,
and not just for one, but for all men. The forest of the heart's longings
has always kept this hunger hidden – towards that are all our tears, all
                              songs filled with tears,
      lovers breast to breast, unsatisfied.

You are burning in separation, unsatisfied. Go on burning. Let
                  whatever's old in you burn out.
Let your world burst like an eggshell, and another world come out of it.
Climb down the steps of this underworld, into greater, and greater
                              darkness.
When you have lost everything, every familiar sign,
   only then will your past catch up with you,
      your future come forward towards you –
         all new, renewed.

It's time. Outside – formless darkness, the wind shrieking like a ghost.
The land's unfamiliar, the habitation temporary, the spirit resourceless
                              in an empty room.
Today you have nothing else – just a hazy road-gazing hidden in a drop
                              of your blood,
trembling, in this pervasive fog, like a faint, transient, concealed star.
      Get ready. Wait for your death.

That death, piercing which lost seeds return, unerring,
with the fervour of heaped harvests, the miraculous success of crops.
That death, shattering which flowers shoot, bursting the snowy burial,
glowing with the glee of green, spring's undying might. –
      Wait for that death – that new birth.

The name of death is darkness. But don't forget, the mother's womb is
                              dark too.
Hence time is veiled, what's coming into being is hidden from view.
Come, be tranquil. This icy night, when there's no light within or
                              without,
pray for a new birth from the unknown cavern of your emptiness.
      Wait for it. Be in readiness.

                              December 1953
                              Pittsburgh

From
Baromaser Chhora (1956)

Mimi, On Your Birthday

Mimi, on your birthday   tell me what I should buy.

'A red sari, a silken blouse,   a purple petticoat,
and a shiuli's shade, its flowers dropping,   when the night draws to a
                                                                                close.'

A red sari, a silken blouse   I can always buy from a shop.
Under-a-shiuli-tree in moonlight –   where can that be bought?

'Under-a-shiuli-tree with shiulis falling   if you can't find for me,
then off you go wherever you please   with your silken blouse, your
                                                                            red sari.'

O Mimi, I have this Dhaka sari,   this bright red petticoat –
'Dawn's bliss under a shiuli –   moonlit – where is that?'

Alright, you win. I promise you   I'll get you what you crave.
I'll bring you verses mixed with moonlight,   dipped in staying awake.

In these verses your red sari   and purple slip you'll find.
These verses be the dawn enchantment   of your shiuli-mind.

                                                            1 October 1946, night

From
Je-Andhar Alor Adhik (1958)

To Memory: 1

It's you I accept as Goddess. There's nothing that's not yours.
What I call the well-spring, the root cause, is really your sleep:
intact even on the horizon, stealthily it creeps,
but if, half glancing, you turn in bed, a lush wonder flowers,

and glossy grapes kiss the earth, turning it to wine.
So the canvas lies blank, stone's inert, the vina just a jarring whine
till you teach us how to cross the surf, navigate the main,
till you lead us beyond the track, the rugged terrain

of warring night and day, to eternity's peaceful plain,
from far to farther, to another birth, the prehistoric cerulean
where, in a matrix, like a cluster of stars, burn

man's destiny and your unending treasures.
Darkness is what you own, but greater than light is that dark,
and utterly valueless is what you idly discard.

6-7 May 1955

To Memory: 2

'Tree', 'flower', 'pond', 'cloudy day': are dry mathematical symbols,
merely abstract, till you raise the curtain and show that my eyes too are
yours.

The vine trails over my body, a field bursts into sudden yellow flowers,
dyeing the sky-line. And thus I come to claim the earth, stars, and all
                                                                                                           else.

War flares; the citizen runs abroad, roaming from shore to shore,
losing in an instant letters, pictures, manuscripts, all that cold store;
but still he won't lose you, for the pole star is your sign,
which never sets elsewhere and is of all hoards the inner gold mine.

On a straight road we walk. Ants in procession, along the diligent
                                                                                           miles,
carry the corpse of a huge insect through childhood, the youthful years,
even dragging from age to age documents, signatures, files, –

till gradually men's countless children grow old and disappear.
But through your heart must he walk – whoever wishes to go back,
for only you know that pathway – that fine, curved, effortless track.

                                                                           8 May 1955, afternoon

To the Sea: Spoken from a Ship

I too have become barren now – like you.
No shores, crops, villages, huts or gardens in view.
Just the restless waves, their sighs, the heaving whine,
and relentless hunger stretched to the vast sky-line.
As if in another life you'd had your heart's eternal darling
from God's own hand upon this understanding
that her whom you love you must leave and go away.
So no more peace. Just this held-down grief, this fray,
this brawl of a protest from wave to wave, these groans,
typhoons, hailstorms, drowned sailors' bones,
shark-torn agony's inarticulate moans –
and through it all – this blue blood's salt, this bitter brew.

I too have become a pauper now – like you.

                                                                                   10 July 1954
                       On board the ship *Queen Mary,* on the Atlantic Ocean

The Epiphany

Then came the angel. As I had imagined from books read, or stories
                                                                heard —
not a bit like that. Not etched on a red sword-blade.
Nor with wings of fire or any such supernal baggage.

More like a little bird — warm, brown, and soft —
that had crossed the hazy spume of the waves, the years.
Breast stained an autumnal yellow with boyish tears,
yet bearing between his beaks the nest's first grass, spring's luggage.

A bird like a small fist, full of infinite trust.

I was lying on the dry coast. In that desolate spot
where snails and lichen, pebbles, rubbish, dead fish
never respond to the distant smoke of ships,
right there his feather's touch resembled a kiss.
My painful death became his island of rest.

— But why? Because separation would cease?
Because exile would end, the home-coming breeze would purr?
Only they can think like that, who haven't yet loved.
His path is unending. He travels from one age to the next.
So he to whom he shows himself — nothing remains of him
save thirst's heat cracking the grave's earth.
                    And that's the salvation, the salvage.

                                        July 1954
                                        London

The Surrender

Rain falls on the river's breast,
                    here comes the tide;
like flickering hidden hopes
within the bamboo groves
now vanish, now glow
                    a few pale fireflies.
The sky's burden of clouds

From *Je-Andhar Alor Adhik* (1958)

                bears lightning's pain,
rumbles from time to time
                its foolish grouch in vain.
Formless, cruel, false,
the waters foam and slide
and recede at destiny's
                silent gestured calls; —
you I have left behind
                in God's own hands.

In a little room stares and burns
                an only lamp.
One hand gently rests
close to the trembling breast,
on a quilt, cold and damp,
                where memory's stitches are torn.
Remembering is magic
                that dims the door,
and into my hand then leaps
                the keenest sword.
The wind that was long lost
blows from another land;
in a dark night redolent
                with childhood's treasured scents
my love I have left behind
                in God's own hands.

The womb of the future swells
                in folds of billowing sails;
the pressure of what's to come
rattles the bones of the planks;
the prow sways from side to side
                like a fish that's terrified.
With grim hands the helmsman holds
                desire's rudder;
my corpse's sloughed off skin floats
                in the fickle water.
Within my heart with each tug of the oars
the deathless name brings a tempest's roar,

a drunken brawl between the waves
                        and the horizon's curve; –
my life I have left behind
                        in God's own hands.

My dark adoration flies
                        in a reverse direction;
on an endless blue somnolence
clings in pain to the stupid deception
of staying awake, which nevertheless
                        brings no liberation.
Yet there's a home where trellises hold
                        the climbing stalks,
and on a veranda sit and talk
                        our ancestors.
Let their gentle whispers fall
and guard you from all harm
in that blind unknown where a thousand fears
                        and doubts clash and clang; –
I have left you behind
                        in God's own hands.

6-9 September 1954
On board the ship Victoria

To Arjun: from a Nameless Woman

Others, since you were Partha the hero, reckoned they'd made it
when they were counted in your celebrity's pickings.
It was a child they craved, a mother's honour, a key to fame,
and when the child came, with a natural cheeriness,
without a worry they disappeared behind convention's frame.
In between your demotic affaires de coeur
you played the husband: a fifth of it, your legally apportioned role,
and were invincible as a protégé of that smart diplomat
who is sometimes referred to as Draupadi's friend.
In this story, – glamorous, to no purpose, – only one
burnt for thirst of you, with a smoulder in her blood,

From *Je-Andhar Alor Adhik* (1958)

knowing you to be Khandava enough for her fire —
not because of any other future gain, but because you were you.
Without a name, without a son, with no records or evidence,
she was negligently passed over by Vyasa the scribe,
yet I know, when faltering in the dark of your last exit,
you, world-conquering hero, had wanted one more time
a taste of that personal embrace, untainted, unfinished.

28-29 January 1955

To a Dog

Don't give me that look. I'm filled with separation-sorrow.
The more I thread this garland, the more they recede — the far and the
near.
The long-promised kiss to be shared by today and tomorrow
hits at last a glass pane — unrelenting, clear.

Rather, choose any one of those who've never been so daft
as to embark on a sea voyage, riding a paper raft.
You'll get a home, meat and rice. Cosy in a darkness of scents,
you can go to sleep in the afternoons, stroked by female friends.

You won't? So you suppose, stirred by sympathetic vibes,
I'll become a rare flute, burst into melodic cries,
paint scenes of memory on your antelope eyes?

... Only half of that's correct. That you are from paradise,
a fallen nymph, curse-trapped, — I know. But to pull you from that net
I haven't been called. I'm not poet enough yet.

13 April 1955

Sonnet of 3 a.m.: 1

Only what is personal is sacred. Such as light,
soft and shaded, in evening's depth; that darkness
which surrounds, like a sky, the hidden stars of yellowing pages;
or an unhurried letter, penned in the shy sleepiness of midnight,

aimed at a far friend. Do you suppose Jesus
was a benefactor of men, or Buddha the honourable, hard-working,
                                                    garrulous,
eighty-year-old dotard of a president of some association?
Those who think they hold the key to salvation

are busybodies, with sentries, swishing fans, drums,
but the great shun all that, are quiet, indifferent tramps.
So I say, let the world go. Wherever it wants to, there let it wander.

Be thin, invisible, inaccessible, and deaf with ecstasy.
All those bits of news which excite the do-gooders and drive them
                                                    crazy —
you'll gain much more than all that in half an hour of a woman's
                                                    languor.

18 April 1955

Sonnet of 3 a.m.: 2

This is not for you. Only your book still stays open.
Those who, with the clink of tea things, give us formulas and grins,
the same people, before bedtime, when the neighbours have turned off
                                                    their lights,
become the larder's cockroaches, or scurrying mice.

They fight for scraps, pick and eat them, thinking history's in the left-
                                                    overs,
not knowing the welcome with which a feast should be given.
Not for you. What flowers and fruit, the twelve months, the seasons
say as they turn — learn that. And don't leave anywhere

traces of your whereabouts. Rather, like spring, conspiring, lost,
                                                    forgotten
in vaporous, white, uncomplicated December,
go far, to another country, to the last remote island of the ocean:

nameless, careless, effortless, undeterred,
go hear, in a new language, in the stars' dazzling wine
the hum of all things and of all times in your veins.

22–24 April 1955

The Desert Journey

As long as there was a way to turn back, he didn't take anything in.
Then he gazed and saw the stark horizon: up to it only the sand,
with cacti, and spiders, and one or two camel-skeletons.
Circling the hamlet of language, the sky's gigantic band

by gradual rape reduced to ashes all thoughts
and then stood still. The heat cooked his flesh and fat
as if to reincarnate him in the underworld's vat;
while his thirst followed him, like a pack of dogs.

Finally, the veil of mirage torn, the first date-tree appeared,
and in black circles upon the sand the gentlest hints of birth:
he knelt, his fingers digging frantically for water –

only a little, not enough for his thirst. Yet that touch spread spores
of the new season. Hands were wet, fruit grew on his elbows' pores,
and pushing through his throat, calmed by that sight, burst the evening
                                                                prayer.

                                                        2-5 May 1955

Why?

Not involved with this, these: the great destiny of the masses,
their rise and fall, welfare, freedom, service.
No hand in history. Material and salvational progress
wasn't brought on by Valmiki, Sappho, Virgil. Why, why then?

To please frustrated lust and rage? To vent
veiled revenge? A disordered ego's cunning?
Or simply a ruse to be oblivious of time's drubbing
'cause there's naught else? Speak! I think this question's fundamental,
                                                        urgent.

No answer anywhere – least from the poet's own jaws,
his lazy accent, as if he'd never once bothered to frame
questions about his own motives, the chain of causes, his dedication's
                                                        inner laws.

Only – suffering from an oozing disease that was incurable,
while the earth was drunk on wandering, he burned himself like a
                                                                candle,
giving himself light – with an ancient nameless flame.

                                                        24-25 May 1955

'Two Birds'

When night descends – not your run-of-the-mill thing –
but the posh stuff: nakta, die Nacht, la noche, la nuit;
when shops' diurnal pitchers, and cars and songs all sink;
watched by red-eyed street lamps, the pavement acquires profundity,

lying as a calm tabula rasa; the rickshaw man, his conscience clean,
drifts to dreamless sleep, and burning to reach the same nirvanic
                                                                harbours,
writers, students, and couples cease their labours; –
then, like a poet, darkness's free offspring,

the cat comes out – soft, solemn, very remote, and fierce;
as if with hidden lusts forked on his brow's crooked trident,
off he wanders beyond this barely tolerable world of ours.

And then my dog, cosseted, safe, content,
stares at him, forepaws hitched on the balcony railing:
a householder looking at a sick artist with eyes of resentment.

                                                        2-3 June 1955

In Reply to the Seasons

Winter, summer, spring, rainy day: I have at last
conquered your grand caprices, and in my heart's gathering evening
come to know emptiness, who's rid of opportunities, whose fortune's
                                                                bust, –
I who am dead, sure of things, full of futurity, beyond all questioning.
That injustice strung with Poushes and Phalguns, swinging laughter and
                                                                tears,
pierces me no more. At the most I am merely aware

of bile, phlegm, rheum marking the almanac's acted scenes
with small numerals, as in an old palace sheer absence
points its finger at room after room, each with its rusty padlock.

In perennial autumn my heart today is lost;
mists, the moon's ghost, memories of lucent sunsets —
all merge and fill the shore of light with darkness.

Only, having dream-heard the sea's continuous voice,
    without seasons, always in the same cadence,
I know now: Winter, Summer, Spring, the Year — these are
    just *your* names, Loneliness!

9-12 July 1955

For My Forty-eighth Winter: 2

Draw the curtain in that window. In that field there's absolutely
nothing to see.
They only want to seduce you — grass, earth, pond, sky.
Throw away those dolls, flowers, pet birds, pots of precious cacti.
Sink into ennui that's without pique, ever in the same beat, and doesn't
cheat.

There's nothing in that yard. Become deaf if you can.
Who can teach you what's not yours already — what wise man?
Rather, take up on your shoulders Grandad Sinbad's pack,
go search all day for a rime or two, like an ass, like a hack.

Winter drops its anchor. Who needs anything else?
The blank wall wakes up, shows shores, islets, seas.
They all blend — hours, times of the day, change itself.

Casting into darkness its fancy particoloured shawl,
patched with sunlight and moonlight, the earth recedes,
knowing that on the shore of its motion you will re-create all.

3 November 1955, afternoon

Anuradha

In the afternoon I chanced upon
    the shore of a lake.
The ice had thawed. Diamond-glinting
    a few waves played.
Cold the day, pale the sky,
    gentle the wind:
like a veiled dancer
    the new season
was scattering the odd adornment,
    small, fluttering, gleaming –
green leaves uncurled,
    two red robins.
Everything was fine, but in the end
    for some reason
my eyes were fixed where the water
    met the horizon,
        and I thought, 'Ah, bother!
She hides on that other shore –
    my Anuradha.'

I am gliding now in the blue breeze
    on an aeroplane,
dragging with me the earth, its
    cities, woods, mountain-chains.
Clear the dawn, pink the sun,
    the ground a blur:
drifting over my open book the aroma
    of the coffee cup
crosses, as on a chess-board,
    churches, hotels, solitudes,
straggling snow-peaks – the gone year's
    focused moods.
I am looking at everything, true,
    but am wondering inside me
if this is a picture, then where
    might its original be.
        I keep saying, 'Ah, bother!

Perhaps she hides behind this —
    my Anuradha.'

I have stood on the shore of an ocean
    before the day is done,
where the menstruating world
    has its bathing fun.
Soft the day, vast the water,
    flecked with the sun:
and in a café's crowds I see,
    as on a canvas drawn,
golden hair, bluish eyes,
    perfect holiday, rest, contentment,
fatigue's tight fist gripping
    enjoyment's sari-end.
I am enchanted, yet suddenly
    my mind begins to think —
when will the curtain rise
    and reveal the stage's queen? —
        and it says, 'Ah, bother!
She hides in another guise —
    my Anuradha.'

An orange turns and turns
    and from its labours
a sweet-sour world of the senses
    everywhere condenses.
Short our lives, and ancient time
    is immeasurable,
yet the passionate motion
    of a single rushing vehicle
churns to froth seas, islands, cities,
    mountain-ranges, woodlands,
even the Milky Way's far atom-clusters
    in their braided brilliance.
I understand it all, yet again and again
    my mind just gropes
in this darkness that waves signals of a way out
    as it rolls;
        and I keep saying, 'Ah, bother!

She hides in her own shadow, does
   my Anuradha.'

June 1956

The Moment of Liberation

In a tight vest and a grey lungi, a fool's cap on his head,
in morning's Gol Park he begins his day's routine.
Eyes on the pavement, bending almost like a woman,
he walks the streets, raking the dustbins with thoughtful attention,

till in Kalighat the children return from school.
Garbage, bits of glass, rotting flowers, the delights of flies,
precious packets made of newspaper, more precious, the yellow news –
filtering his breath through such things, conquering cholera and
                                                       despair,

should he come, a bright half-rupee in his cloth's fold, to your slum,
mad with a gas-lit craving for its sunken cheeks and hanging flesh, –
sister, make sure you give him everything, all your essential truth,

your open, generous arms, the effortless spread of your thighs,
and a dark cavern, spacious, beyond disputes,
sinking wherein, he can learn from you

that there's more to this life than hunger and hard work:
there's death, the moment of liberation, and there's God.

20 February 1957

From
Morche-pora Pereker Gan (1966)

The Weeping Beauty

Who are you, belle, whose teardrops ceaselessly fall
and float away as lotuses in the river's rich streams?
What wet blue dyes you? What holy water mingles
the essence of your loveliness with its own waves?
Weeping Beauty, why do you cry? Why do your tears bloom as
                                                        lotuses?
Why does their golden journey not fade even on the horizon?
What magic makes this day endless? ... Answers the great poet left none,
but only stated that the gods were under your governance.

An audacity – but still let me say this. In some far former existence
you, it seems, were very familiar to me – intimate, unforgettable.
You wept my tears then! And I, too, my ears upon the water's murmur,
heard how the five elements ran, charmed by your commands:
they forgot to fight, took shape as rhythm's hand-cupped gifts – in the
                                                      sky, in the light.
Immense opulence was yours then – an unsullied, unfragmented
                                                      universe,
seasons, skies, sun – and yet you needed me.
As I recall, in that distant dream-world, in that hour of primal dawn
I gave you precisely what you still didn't know about,
what didn't exist in the flood of light, in the swirl of water:
a sense of absence, of hiatus, dreams, memories, heartbeats!
From then on you were the queen of the cosmos, and Indra became
                                                      suddenly helpless;

on the margin of heaven's deception that thrill of tears endlessly flows.
Only this: I sometimes forget it, and fall into pain's dark pit,
writhe like a speared pig in an ignorant striving for life.

March 1964
Brooklyn, New York

Life on the Margin

I give a sudden scream and cry,
but no one lets go of the tram's door-handle and stops boarding.
No one lifts the telephone or rushes to the address of an association –
welfare workers don't budge.

Fire Brigade! Ambulance! Caring police force!
Help! Help!
Take me to hospital, consign me to a loony-bin,
put me in prison – at least there are other people there, surely!

Minister for Rehabilitation! Sir! Won't you kindly check
if through a clerical error my petition isn't lying under a pile of papers?

Am I a refugee? Am I sick? Am I laid low by starvation?
– No, none of these!
There's just a hole in my heart under my rib-cage,
my back's wall has collapsed.

Yet why does this crying not trigger a response anywhere?
Does crying, then, have no sound?
Have I forgotten language, perhaps?
Or am I mute out of politeness?

A giant bank, it seems, has collapsed somewhere.
Now instead of hills there are only rows of holes.

'When the boat has left the canal and has entered the river,
and all familiar landmarks have one by one receded,
the boy keeps staring, but notices nothing –
remembers the smell of Mother's body,
the familiar musty smell of his quilt,

or doesn't even remember — it just merges with his pain,
which isn't pain either — just non-being.

It's as if I'd arrived at a railway junction, having travelled far,
after which one couldn't miss reaching one's final destination,
but you, holding someone else's hand, got on the wrong train and left —
my love, my all.

Or in an underground station
when one train has left and the next one hasn't arrived:
in such a vacant moment
in the spaces between the grey pillars, in the humid air
it seems there's no city above,
no earth anywhere,
there are no words, no movements, neither days nor nights:
or if anything exists,
then in a half-dark ghost-world
far removed from people's memories and eyes,
abandoned by the living, not known to the dead,
arrived at the margin of the underworld, hangs
just a gormless, creaturely,
dying, yet quivering
life.

6 March 1964
Brooklyn, New York

Other Germs

They say you don't exist. And neither do I.

For now thirty-three crores of companies cover the world,
all roads are straight, all engines are merciful.
There's no pain in toothache, none in the throes of death;
women giving birth don't gasp like koi fish any more.

Born under maternal hypnosis, drooping with tearless oxygen,
in the interim we are correctly cradled and rocked
by banking and insurance, while shrinks rid our hearts of cobwebs.
By murdering the past man survives in good cheer.

I look around me and see health, happiness, radiance;
my ears ring with Vishnu's heaven's slogan – 'Fear not!'
No one will extend an emaciated arm any more,
                     shadowy figures will not stand at crossroads,
won't become pale or desperate with exhausted panting.
Conflicts, hesitations – impurities of polluted minds –
                     will be eradicated with pills, two-anna anodynes.

In every direction stretch tracts, tidy and level;
the fierce beasts are tied up to long chains;
not a needle-point crack on any of the gleaming walls –
so in what hole would secret lizard-eyes hide now?

If only they could supply bliss in steady monthly instalments!
If one could really become immortal by giving up smoking!

If that terrible worm were not the air we breathe!

If cockroaches could be exterminated, it would be a great
common good. But they know – those who,
when water-sport is finished, when fireworks are over,
stare sleeplessly in the dark,
yes, stare sleeplessly in the dark,
lying alone in the dark,
lying beside their lovers, male and female,
listening to each other breathing,
limb joined to limb, yet devoid of warmth,
motionless, staring in the dark, alone,
motionless, staring, all alone –
those who, suddenly face to face with themselves, shiver
when such things as Rome, Burma, Parthenon, and belly-dancing
       in Cairo have come to an end –
they know that other germs remain, indestructible,
hidden in the blood, fast-rooted in the flesh,
that other pains remain, indestructible,
perhaps desire, too, remains.

Perhaps that very desire is
you.

April 1964
Brooklyn, New York

Icarus

A sparkling, immaculate day, the sea scarcely breathing,
the air ecstatic, drunk on sun-drenched blue:
so still, so calm – so comely –
   as if at the height of a summer filled to its brim
the world's effluence of pain had retrieved an effulgent identity.

The naked, round, infinite, lustrous sky
   melts in the infinite kiss of the naked, circular, unflickering horizon.

Brimful and mellow is the noontide, not a wrangle in the charmed sea,
as if this full-blown horizon was the luminous answer to all longings,
as if all success was a pledge of this translucent blue,
as if today, finally, on the darkness of men's thirsty eyes
the curtain would rise.

Far off floats
one grey dot: with its cargo of passengers, merchandise, and hope,
eager for the port.
Other than that, not a scar on the sea,
just the light's shimmer on the blue,
an unblemished Mediterranean day, a fountain of golden wine.

Suddenly a mad blow:
as though ripping the womb
of this too-ripe hour, a stream of secret seeds
was hurtling down along a fiery line.
This light – this brightness – the midsummer's furtive meaning
bursts the sky, drops with a meteor's velocity,
casting a whopping rebuke
on the very region where the sun and the sea are confluent.
Head down, feet up, weighed down with impotent wings,
accelerating without let, a whiplash swishing in the wind –
'Icarus, alas, Icarus!'
Only in his ears does this threnody ring, till his head
plunges into the water's deep abyss.
The feet still twitch for seconds longer, the memory of molten-wax
   teeth searing the pores –
no sound after that, and no more effort.

The momentary trespass forgotten, the sea is calm again;
solar exhilaration spreads once more in the air;
the sky is revised, resplendent.

On the ship a banquet is on; the port nears.
Feasting on ox-flesh, the passengers fill their wine-cups.
Some prick their prickly heat spots; others think:
'Tonight I'll sleep with my wife.'

In the city meanwhile
in a half-hour recess clerks in the secretariat
get into a lather over whatever's currently the main news:
which minister's been eclipsed, who with ten measures of gold
    has bought the post of the police boss,
which wrestler's going to get a prize in the upcoming festival.

And by then
gracefully waving their arms within cool interiors,
the ladies are throwing dice, or complaining
that the price of honey has gone up by twenty-five per cent,
or sinking into their naps.

But that very instant a decrepit, rheumaticky poet,
his efforts defeated, beyond the border of despair,
realizing that failure was the one thing that never deceived,
stifling his disgust, brushing off his useless rage,
was lying in bed, wrapped in the comfort he had earned,
between sheets of spotless white –
emaciated, desiccated, silently wise.

2 August 1964
Boulder, Colorado

Only by Holding on to You

Only by holding on to you do I survive, though I don't know
either your name or the lineaments of your face.
What are you – woman or man, sister or friend, revenge or hate?

Sateless lust? Or sadness – that swept by revulsion's tide,
now sinks, now bobs up, almost dead, yet deathless?

You take my heart and cook it in toxic salt,
my slumber's quilt you fill with the holes of remorse.
Like a loved woman someone signals in the dark –
is it you – or an old relentless ghost
who always says: 'There isn't' or 'It isn't time yet'?

(2)

Revulsion – for myself? Then why with contempt for all
am I lying on the bottom of a deep well, an assiduous mouse?
Pity – for myself? Kurukshetra rings with rebukes.
Alas, I've been through it all, and shall never be a Vidur.

Imprisoned in impotent screams, I always hear the sound of water;
I am my anguish, yet that fountain-head isn't far.

(3)

Sometimes I think you are that dead girl
    whom I've never forgotten –
like an unsullied union, dream-blossomed, in whose calyx
    moving time stands still
and in whose leaves road-weary wishes build a nest and go to sleep:
those naive, eager eyes seem to return,
    lotus buds, shy hand-offerings, drift away;
moist lips, cool arms, the world embrace-wrapped,
in blood's dialogue the synchronous pulsing of stars.

(4)

But my dream is shattered. I see a beast – unclean, grotesque,
pawing, playing with my days, seasons, years –
intimately, as if its dogged, immemorial smear
might ripen, in my food, drink, brain, a disease that's dire.
Even my tears turn into its saliva, are wasted, dripping down its chin.
It even winks at me – secretly, shrewdly, as if in dalliance –
so that I, swung between hope and terror, might forget my vain toil,
keep hanging in utter doubt, till in Act Five heaven and hell

broadcast a bloody dispute: 'Are you a cold, loathsome reptilian,
a she-vulture's patience, or hope's keen hunger, lolling out its tongue?
Or are you that blast of a thunderous flute, the Man-Lion,
whose lightning-claws pledge radiant redemption?'

27 October 1964
Bloomington, Illinois

From Another Land

Dead now – those lovers with water-lily breasts;
pond dense with cool grass, damp smell of snails –
small, but once beyond the knee-level, quite a storm.

Friends all dead. No generous evenings descend on balconies,
no light craft toss on conversation's waves,
beginning as sport, ending as sea-going ships.

Nature's dead too. Bribes are useless by the door of the beast's den.
The red tiger bows down to a moth;
no silly child wets you with its kidney-warmth.

Only – as long as witches shake their heads
in trees, and skewered pussy-cats scream, keeping the beat –
in a rain-obscured night on the pavement lies
a heart from another land,
sensing by touch, increasingly well-informed.

12-15 May 1962

Other Debts

Grant me leave, Lord. See how far westward the day leans.
My hair falls out, my teeth jiggle. And that unearthly bird –
dead, stuffed with straw, with no dearth of cosmetics –
is devoured by countless lice in a rich glass case.
Let me depart. I have other debts to face.

13 May 1962

You, Strangers, Who Write Me Letters

You, strangers, who write me letters –
young ladies and unhappy creatures,
young men fidgeting, bitten by the poetry bug:
you who, not getting a reply,
imagine the bloke's right arrogant, or that yourselves are at fault –

listen: it's neither what they call 'being busy'
nor any reluctance to write.
I read and re-read everything – what's explicit and what's left unsaid.
All the words in those letters,
                            sweetly jingling like silver rupee coins,
roll down gently, gather one by one in a dark safe.
I want to pay my debts.
From time to time I do remember I'm indebted to you all.
There are times when
the night in all its vastness descends
and far off in the darkness I see the lights in your windows
in Bankura, Gauhati, Barisal.
The sheer fact that you exist
                          and I too exist alongside of you
suddenly chirps like a cricket
and silences all sounds.

But – what's there to be said?
If that silver were to be melted, just what image might it shape?
I who fall down when I try to stand,
having fallen, climb high,
having run for miles with much effort,
right away chuck on the dust-heap whatever I've grabbed; –
I who, having probed the underworld once or twice,
have still failed to grasp which darkness begets light –
how can the hands of such a person make a neat puppet?
What scope is there for words
in his mind pressurized by 'or's and 'but's?

That's why – there's nothing at all to say.
A very hard task – this survival.

                                                1 December 1962

Hölderlin

[The German poet Friedrich Hölderlin (1770–1843) lost his sanity after writing some stunning poems in his youth; he survived in that condition for almost thirty-six years. I think of him as the perfect image of a deeply meditative poet.]

Completed as the moon, still,
yet someone whom the operation of celestial motion
slowly brings to our windows, tamarisk groves, park benches:
and also distant –
unmoved by the pity, contempt, blandishments
of those who wail, row, get knackered,
hunch their backs and hunt for bargains in flea markets,
or those who huddle to hatch plots
in the corridors of palaces, decorated with murals,
conspire with zeal in the spacious patios of temples –
farther off than all such, in a remoter expanse of blue –
as if history were no more than an obscene procession,
nothing but mummery, white and black masks, and buffoons –
with only this certitude
that in the effulgence
of a light that shines but causes no burns
the gods still linger,
indifferent, independent, non-effervescent.

Someone who, as if knowing that after this
the moon would wane, decay and darkness would be ineluctable,
composed himself in a copiously flowing, tormented
night of the full moon:
exhausted everything in one night, all his powers of immortality,
the tones of his vina, pierced by beauty's anguish;
all seasons of the year, swans of spring, all glowing apples,
the kisses of the clear waters in the icy lake.

24 May 1962

Song of a Man in Love

Now the entire world climbs right inside me:
people, tall buildings, clothes shops reeking of feminine odours,
drudgery, quarrels, streetwise youths spouting laddish obscenities,
and park benches, where old men sit together.

When it's past midnight
a sudden scream pierces me totally — soars up, then dies down.
Feet trample me, climbing up and down a thousand steps.

That beggar girl who limps
tears my nerves' ribbons and in naïve gladness ties her hair with them.
The husky voices of whores
raise the clamour of conch-shells to my infirm ears.

The beasts come too, crawling. They curl up, huddle together,
as if they'd chanced on the primal portico, just right for a squat,
unclaimed by others.
The huge buffalo that drags a cart
                    spreads his rug of fatigue and is well pleased;
the mongrel's graceful eyes are eloquent.

They come: far-off things, valleys, forests, fields,
roads, vehicles, bridges;
raising a rhythm from peak to peak along telegraph wires
                    the mountain wind sweeps over me in a great gust.

Everything is normal,
stable, certain, whole —
like events deliberately strung together in a play.
Only I have become
a current, a movement, an oozing:
a wound —
unending, gaping, red,
dripping non-stop from an infection past cure.

                                        17 May 1962

When the Burnt Day is Done

'When the burnt day's done, O gaunt coal, still smouldering,
what sacred water's the scene of your ritual bathing?'

'That lake's woman. There's rich comfort in store
in the body's abyss, moist with the heart's overflow.'

'But now your flag is down, your chariot's pulverized.
Sans vim, a stern, icy rebuff from Pushkar is your prize.'

'How shines the grape! Her bosom is benign.
What if she builds me a dream-dome, being so kind?'

'When vino's votary climbs salvation's steps,
sleep, just animal sleep's the last reward he gets.'

'Travel diverts us. Far scenes, winters of good omen,
or somewhere high summer ripening the red water-melon.'

'Misery's not longitude-bound. All countries are clones.
Wherever you go, it's yourself you'll drag to that zone.'

'I'll take on another name, another tongue. I'll have an alibi.
Disguised, I'll be suavely positive, with the seal of life.'

'The past will still weigh on your shoulders – you old Sindbad!
The earth's not so extensive that you'd escape from that.'

'Books by day, quiet reflection at nightfall.
Scholarship tires the body, but the mind's not palled.'

'Hypocrite! Isn't it a storm that you really pray for,
so your books and papers might be scattered, lost for ever?'

'In lieu of River Mayurakshi or Valmiki's hermitage
I'd settle for natural contentment in any Bengali village.'

'What you secretly look for is not in such childhood-dreamings.
Beasts don't talk, and trees are really dumb things.'

'All, all are alternatives! I always want something else!
Transient pleasure's all that hard work builds.'

'It's because there are alternatives that life continually flows.'

'I've known that oven's ardour, seen how that fire glows!'

'He who supplies the fuel is no longer an ally of yours.'

'Yet my conscience says I must transcend my limits.'
'Alas, vain commotion! That's also His cleverly imposed remit.'

'There's desire, the great truth. Is that also going to cheat?'

'Desire-tossed, you still don't accept the inevitable – that upstream
                    flow.
Count this as your blessing, post-tied beast, destined for the sacrificial
                        blow!'

5 July 1965
Honolulu, Hawaii

The Music of Mortality

(for Mrs Gauri Ayyub)

Nature, so dear to you, is really unconscious matter,
for ever bound in the iron laws of maths.
Water's not its own boss; what evaporates in Baishakh
returns as rain in Srabon; melted snow descends
with blind speed, hard-battered by mountainside;
rivers run unstoppably seaward, and the seven oceans
heave in their fullness, yet do not drown the earth,
just deck the beaches with waves. What magician pulls
strings to show the moon's play, breaks off to cast it beyond
the horizon's rim; dances the sequence of seasons
on a revolving stage – so rich in rhythmic threads,
so punctual, so unchanging, that it seems –
seems to man, uniquely born with the anguish of thinking power –
that there has to be an intelligence behind the show:
a goal, a purpose, a pursuit, the gradual expression
of an imagination – maybe even benevolence.

                          There's nothing.
Look, autumn is here. In the bluish sky
the sun dangles southward, rested and happy like a lover
whose lust is satisfied. The breeze blows gently, stirs
the urban coconut; flecks of sunshine glitter
in the upward-tilted leaves – like active hope, or the message-bearer
of the emperor beloved of the universe, who grants friendship, faith,
leisure free of conflicts, the pretence of success and well-being
of descending Agrahayan.

                         Meanwhile through nine doors
Saturn enters my house. Blood cells conspire
in an assassin's plot. In cobweb-smothered darkness
the heart pulses slowly, like an exhausted pendulum, lordless.
In the vast concourse of nerves the civil war
of the Jadav clan appears – they grit their teeth and tear
one another. The secretions of joints weaken; the failing liver
spreads foul odours; the bowel's stockpile of poisons
mingles with food, carries off the nutrition. The six deadly enemies –
lifelong friends – bring neither meanings nor agonies;
and in their ruined arsenal rats mate and shake the night with scandals.
A nameless terror descends; in the brain's royal treasury
descends inertia; the mine of thought lies empty. And, above all,
the heart, oblivious of its ancient pledges, sinks into ennui.
Like any other animal organ, like a diurnal kingshuk flower
the heart too is dying. Its once huge commerce
that conquered horizons, now – incredibly – bankrupt,
puts on the red light, broadcasts obscene stories.
Emotion's ur-Ganges, losing its leadership, its three-streamed flow,
is thinned, exhausted – gradually, mutely shrinking
into a muddy channel, where cold snakes swim,
the frolic of damp tadpoles raises bubbles
purveying evil smells, immobile garbage floats
in suffocating seclusion – pale, desperate, non-metropolitan.
Therefore in this autumnal hour, in this sunshine
a soundless scream rends the voice of that man
who is rooted in the earth, yet loves the cerulean:
'If old age is certain, then why was I born?
If I am for slaughter, why is the universe so beautiful?'

Good woman, wife and mother, if you think this is just the delirium
of a sick, demented man, know nevertheless this:
what you call beauty is not inherent in the multiform
five elements, picturesque plants, or sunset's colour-feast,
but exists only in my sense of the self. What are the facts? —
The union of man and woman, immemorial, repeated;
children, harvests, the cremation-ground. Locked in this cycle, life
is adequate and pleasant. Drunk on the pursuit of desires,
one may forget the deception of Nature, tongue-lolling, murderous,
the mindless Enchantress who inspires us primally, indomitably.
But I go even beyond Her and create
beauty and love, constructing with ethereal elements
a universe full of myself. Dreams, its by-products, scatter
seeds everywhere: above, below, in the sky, out of sight.
Fruits hang from a rootless, invisible tree, on whose branches swing
heaven, gods, the Supreme Self, reincarnation, and similar things,
illusory yet irresistible. So I, clutching to my breast
upcoming death, standing on ruin's edge, in stillness filled
with the absence of friends, in a voice raucous with protest,
still say: there's no universe without me, it's me who's mirrored
                                                                      everywhere.
Nature and Time are the cast, but I am the playwright
and also the audience — until with a final thunderbolt
they all perish — being, the cosmos, and God.

                        Begun 1954, completed August-September 1965

The Song of a Rusty Nail

[When the rains failed in the kingdom of Anga and famine stalked the land, wise men who could foresee the future advised the king that if the young ascetic Rishyasringa, who had been a forest-dweller ever since his birth, could be brought to the capital, the calamity would end. Rishyasringa, though young in years, was a front runner in ascetic power, and had never even seen a woman with his eyes; hence only he could accomplish that difficult task, but for that it would be necessary to rob him of his virginity. Commanded by the ministers, an old courtesan took charge of the project. Her own daughter, young and beautiful, cleverly caused the ascetic to stray from his celibate path, after which it was not difficult to bring him to the capital. As soon as he entered the city, it rained heavily. King Lomapada gave his daughter Shanta in marriage to Rishyasringa.

Many scholars think that the story of Rishyasringa is the original source of the older, non-Christian part of the European legend of the Holy Grail.]

There was this rusty nail lying, jutting out from a piece of rotten wood.
It was an Ashwin morning, with an old woman patting cow-dung cakes
                                              on a wall,
the bud of a red lotus stirring in the breeze, when it beckoned me —
that rusty nail jutting out from a piece of rotten wood.

I was on my way, but I stopped. Suddenly it seemed
before me was a prince in disguise, a fallen ascetic, stricken by a curse.
A curtain of amnesia was torn apart, and in the wind charged with the
fragrance of adolescence, a song rang out, piercing the sky's silence.

'Listen to me, I must speak. In my previous birth I was Rishyasringa,
but I didn't find happiness in Shanta's arms. It rained in the country,
                                    they brought in a huge harvest,
young women came with babies in their arms to pay me their respects.
I was a blessed hero, the saviour of creatures, the liberator of the rains.

'But to me the royal palace had no zest, nor did the princess, my
                                                                  wedded wife;
my days were colourless; my nights, made up of bitter lust, were
                                                                    loveless;
bitter was our sanctioned union, tormented the seminal flow
                                                    that had propelled the rain,
ripened the grain. In the very land where I had brought joyous showers
                                                                I alone was dry.

'I was a prisoner of their bullying, for they wanted to live. My
manhood was in bondage to them, for they were helpless. My penance-
power was their meagre subsidy, so that pumpkins might hang from
their trellises and their cows get pregnant. But I had another dream.

'I kept dreaming of that apparition, of that unsheathed dawn that broke
my sleep. I didn't know what woman was: she made me understand it.
I hadn't realized that I was male, until her touch ignited
a fire in my blood and sparks in my pores, and made a whole ocean
                                                                       roar in my ears.

"'Who are you, ascetic? A messenger of heaven, or a god in disguise?
What stringent discipline has given your limbs such a death-defying
glow? Why is your sight plunging me in a thrill of delight?"
– She laughed like a rill, like the gurgle of a sinking pitcher.

'Her voice tied me like a living rope, like notes from Narada's vina,
or chanting from the Sama Veda, to be drunk with the ears.
"I'm your friend, I'm a friend to all troubled mortals.
I've come from the nether regions to save the world."

' – With a sinuous gesture of her arms she came forward, quivering like
                              moonlight in a current of water.
Like particles of sunlight between leaves were the rays reflected from
                              her bangles.
Her neck was like a conch-shell, her ears were shaped like shining
                              water-cups,
the twin lumps of flesh on her breast were as smart and rounded as
                              ritual offerings.

'Like a shower of the post-monsoon season her gaze was limpid and
moist. Upon her face was the jubilation of a full-moon night of Chaitra.
The motion of her knees and legs had the rhythm of incantation –
thus did she come forward, until her breath touched me.

'It was more fragrant than flowers, joss-sticks, sandalwood, and ghee-
                              gobbling fire.
At her touch a meditative darkness descended on my eyes.
My heart stopped beating, all the senses shut their shutters.
My body and mind sank deep, deeper – from emptiness to a
                              profounder emptiness. –

'Where heaven, earth, and underworld are concentrated in one point –
                              still and indivisible –
where past, present, and future are one spotless level plain,
where all dualities dissolve, and there is none but you and me –
in her embrace in that Brahman-realm I found myself.

'And then they put me in a cage like an animal, in this cagelike
                              samsara,
so that they could bring forth children through sheer undented habit,

so that nothing would be unbearable any more, everything would
                                             become
pale and common through daily use. – But I had another dream.

'In my dream I still see that heaven, that unfolded moment when
eternity was bodied forth in the darkness pouring from the sun's heart,
and I was spread from star to star, from sea-wave to sea-wave –
I was grass, I was the banyan tree, both deer and tiger, the Himalayas
                              and the green cockatoo. –

'I was the gander, the flute's moan, wandering everywhere yet still,
both god-sage and primitive huntsman, five jewels and the Jatayu bird:
in that luminous flood of non-existence, screened by that splendour. –
– I don't even know her name. But I haven't forgotten her.

'I haven't forgotten her. I couldn't. That's why I am cursed.
From age to age heaven has been the goal of my desire.
So the gods punished me. I lie like a thing that's mute, inert.
You don't recognize me. But I remember.'

This is the song I heard one Ashwin morning,
and a centipede curled on the ground heard it too,
when on the earth covered with grass, dew, and adolescence
a rusty nail was lying – outside the seasons, beyond history.

18 August 1965

From
Ekdin: Chirodin o Anyanyo Kavita (April 1971)

Bloomington, Indiana

How quiet it is, this Sunday morning – not a soul in the street,
curtained sleep in house after house, rows of cars standing idle.
In this country no one wakes before ten on a Sunday morning;
the streets lie still like an artist's canvas, the silence of trees
on either side.

    But when I got out, I heard the sound of ringing behind me.
Cring cring cring. Rings spaced out with tiny moments of pause.
Again. And again. And again. The sound pierced the soft air
like a small pin – wafted to me, sharp, anxious, troubled; –
I walked on, and the sound followed me, as if without end.

    With what message does the telephone ring – in whose house,
for which hero, which friend, which lover? Is someone in torment
waiting on the other side? Has someone's loneliness become
unbearable? Has death crept in to stand by someone's bed-head?
Or is it some mute sorrow, some inarticulate grief
that at long last wants to resound like a conch-shell –
in this unstoppable bell of the telephone?

    But does no one hear it but me?
In this street am I the only one who wakes?
Awake, townspeople! Stretch your hand – hero, friend, beloved.
Awake, heart; awake, pain; awake, awareness.
Listen to that rising cry: 'Save me! Save me!'

For you, yes for you is that summons —
it's that same weeping that flows without cease through the world,
like a current with its secret crooning,
and has this day, this minute, revealed itself to you,
spreading itself in wave after wave.
Someone wants you, you are needed; — lucky you!

   I don't know when the sound ceased, nor if
anyone drowned in despair; all I know is this:
the person who calls is weak, the person who desires
is helpless. For every so often the telephone rings
in a room without response, some letters never arrive,
and the language of what I mean to say is hard to reach.

   Meanwhile in the sky the month of June is brilliant, the air
is once more whole and unpricked, the tree-leaves stir like breath,
and in house after house the slumber's still unbroken.

5 July 1965
Honolulu, Hawaii

The Dead

The living, I gather, weigh this earth down.
But the dead, I reckon, number many more.

   Which world is it, where they all fit in? Is it
an underworld, a firmament, or further still —
beyond our imagination?

   Do they float in some airless sky? Do they swim
in some abyss of water that's not wet and has no bottom?
Do they have lips? Voices? Do they know they are dead?

   A child, I think, finds his mother there again. Lovers walk
hand in hand — softly, softly — as if their feet
barely brush the ground, though it's really for them
that the ground is green.

Or maybe even touch is superfluous; they have become
twin electric sparks which flow like currents into each other.

Do they get hungry? Do they have clocks? Have they festivals,
public assemblies, centenaries? Do they come forward as a group
to greet a new arrival? Do they wave flags,
leaning against the railing of a bridge?

Or is each single one of them simply alone, infinitely
solitary? Or are the distances between them as interminable
as those between stars?

Once I saw a dying man – with huge toenails
and skin as rough as a frog's. He was a friend of mine
from hard times, but I didn't stand there too long.
Did he find solace in the land of the dead? Did anyone
clip his toenails?

Some dying people I didn't see at all. That unhappy fun-loving
lady weighing fifty-six kg, in whose sun
my sapling had grown tall. She was in a hospital
five minutes away, and I didn't go to see her.

Once upon a time in a village of Bengal there was a young woman:
the rapture in her eyes was quite normal, but her husband
was mad. She suffered many more afflictions because of me,
but I don't even know how she died.

Tell me, will we meet there? Will I be able to ask forgiveness?
Or even as the Queen of Carthage did, so will you too
avert your faces and move away, disappear behind the scene
like the lean moon? Just taking a look –
one little look, no more – can't I have even that?
Eyes, my twin trees of sight, can you not flower in another garden?

But no matter how hard I try, I cannot sort out
which is the land of the dead, nor imagine what they are like.
My senses, decaying as they are, hold me a prisoner.

So I open my drawers and secretly look at photographs,
pace in my room, light a cigarette;

recall a face that's blurred, a handwriting that's faded,
and the name by which I used to be called – the sound of it.
Can't believe there's nothing after this.

   Tell me, have you all kept me in your minds? Have you
memories? Do you know that I haven't forgotten yet?

   It rains outside in the evening. The earth darkens.
I stand by the window, all ears for an obscure answer –
but can hear nothing except the sound of the rain,
nothing except the sighing of the wind.

2 September 1965
Calcutta

Young Men and Young Women

All of a sudden the earth has filled with young people.
When I look at the streets I see only young men
and young women. I never thought they were so innumerable.

   Abundant as grass, winsome as moss, restless as ants.
They are always in the streets, and always busy. As if somewhere
an entirely untapped gold mine had been discovered,
or a ship's horn, muffled by fog, was calling:
'Come on over, come this minute!
Anybody for a passage to an enchanted island?'

   Or it's as if they'd all won millions at a lottery –
all because the sun gave warmth, and the wind scattered
the sound of their laughter.

   Winter now, and nearly every day I see
a funeral cortège. Waves foam on the pavements
on either side. A raft glides along the middle,
carrying a corpse that's tranquil, void of all desires.
But when I look at their faces, I am stunned,
for even death is powerless to rob them of their decrepitude.

From *Ekdin: Chirodin o Anyanyo Kavita* (April 1971)

Once in a while someone comes out with a walking-stick,
all wrapped up in a woollen scarf, without a face,
like an extra drop of shadow within the lamp-post's shadow.
I say to myself: I won't see him next winter.

Only young men, only young women.

But why don't I ever see any young man I know?
Those, whose lips were scornful, and hearts were Ashwin skies?
Their eyes, their laughter – nothing have I forgotten yet.
Where are they?

Could it even be that smouldering in jealousy's fire,
they are hanging as burning strings in betel shops
for any thick-lipped lecher to light his fag by?
Or is it they who have now become
sacks of fat and malice, each a great gang-leader in his block?

Maybe I'm on the wrong track. Maybe suddenly someday
someone will shed his mask – when on the train to Delhi
the rail-track curves, and evening descends, gigantic, on the plain.
Or when someone will be laid on a hospital operation-table.

Why don't I see those young women, who, with their college texts
open in front of them, in the verandas of the month of Chaitra,
would suddenly look up, as if letting fly a flock of birds?

I saw one once. I had gone out to post a letter.
She approached me and said, 'Perhaps you don't recognize me?
I am Kusum; my father's name is Suhrid Bhonjo.'
Instantly another face emerged from her face;
my eyes said: middle-aged; my mind saw a young woman;
a rainbow, arching between two edges, flashed
and immediately faded.

Yet within an instant I grasped that behind the scene
all was intact. Just the barrier of a thin curtain.
Thin, almost transparent. With sudden, fitful tremors.
But in no way can it be removed.

Alas, the famous gold mine, the enchanted island —
all, all are on the other side of that curtain.
It's with the intention of getting there
that the young men and young women have filled the streets.
My eyes tell me it's a young man; my mind sees an old man.
Nowhere is there a moment that stays put.
It's the same terror that makes them all run —
Fire, Wind, Ocean, Life, and the Fifth One.

1 January 1966
Calcutta

Shopkeepers

Sixteen years back, when I first came to this area,
its furnishings were of a different order. There was grass then.
Mop-heads of coconuts all over the place.
Everywhere gulmor pollen. And in the fields
puddles of rainwater, violet and green in the gas light,
pregnant with dreams and germs.

    And mosquitoes. Maybe fire-flies. And distances:
of shops and markets supplying our needs.

    All's changed now. Instead of fields, five-storeyed mansions.
Restaurants over buried pools. All day the dutiful traffic.
And when walking, instead of fallen leaves, mushrooms,
eerie twilights — now we find shops, many and varied,
growing right and left like public speeches. Brand-new
in shiny garish covers, or laid out on the pavement like
the volumes of a dated poet. Or sprung up like magic
on the narrow ledge of a veranda. In rows,
like the smiling teeth of development: shops.

    I love looking at these shops. Here undying avarice
and ancient arrogance play games; want and need
fight with each other; women, oblivious of modesty,
observe the shapes of their own breasts and arms;

so many desires beat against the glass windows and die
like flies.

    And the shopkeepers – I observe them too:
their flattering gestures, greedy and wary eyes,
and along with all that – the sheer patience of their waiting.
You think they only display and supply goods,
palm them off, keep accounts, count the money,
tot up the change? You've never guessed
the real thing? They wait, yes, they keep waiting:
that's their job, their true vocation.

    When one customer has left, and the next one hasn't
turned up yet – in such moments have I seen them:
elbows on counters, chins digging into hand-hollows,
staring at the street, gazing into the distance,
as if they were in the shadow of an obscure future.

    I think I then see sadness in their eyes, floating up
like fish in still waters. They have dumb eyes then – yes, just like fish.

    Gentle reader, can't you see any imagery at all
in those eyes? You and I – yes, all of us –
have set up shop, each in his own fashion, the oscillation
of waiting in our hearts. When winter comes, for summer;
when summer's here, for the monsoon; the dark waiting
for one's wife; waiting with curiosity, for the birth
of a child; for money, fame, a journey,
travelling, returning, perhaps for a hint
of fate to come – it's endless. Who will write us a letter?
In the evening, when the house is still unlit,
who will knock on the door? Boarding a tram
to Bowbazar in the middle of the day, which lost friend
might one meet with? Thus do our hearts swing
day after day, season after season, without cease.
And what's most terrible: sometimes there's indeed a knock,
we re-discover a childhood sweetheart in Florida.
But since we cannot stop, we stare again at the road,
gaze into the distance, at that hazy horizon where I, my

childhood sweetheart, the coast of Florida — all are vanishing
into a point.

    Man, man, afflicted man, do you know
who is the last object of your waiting? Do you know
it was for you that death was created?

Begun in 1953, completed on 4 September 1965
Calcutta

Day of Rain

Here comes the rain, the rain once more! Not the glamorous rain
of Baishakh, nor with the caressing touch of Srabon — but chilly rain,
black rain, autumn's rain that ushers in the cold.

    Ah, this is fine; this is just what I adore. Baring their
diamond teeth, Ashwin's glittering days left me this message:—
'Oi, you there! Interpolated pygmy! Perjury of the universe!
Just look at us — see how beautiful we are,
how mindless, ruthless, unconcerned!' — I was torn
by the cutting edge of their light, bent double
with the weight of their jibes.

    This day brings me comfort — this stooping, folding-upon-itself,
bodiless day. The hours have been wiped off; time's teeth
seem blunted — for a little while, at least for a little while
we shall have time off work, morning merging with midday,
midday folding into evening — without a trace, without emblazonry,
without arms — continuous, homogenized, grey.

    Today the clouds are spreading across the sky
like my own soul's blackness; and Calcutta lies
under this harsh rain like a submissive middle-aged
woman — dull, unresponsive, knackered,
crushed by the weight of her libidinous husband.

    I sit by the window. I stare at the dark day
and drown my dejection in eternity —

all those bitter memories, hyperactive regrets,
my lonely, soundless howl.

    Meanwhile in the human world the day advances. Some
open their shops. Some come home, their grocery shopping done.
And one by one people gather at the tram stop – with umbrellas,
with raincoats, with the solemn resolution to carry on living,
sinking in amnesia's generous consolation.

    What is it that they want to forget? The very fact
that they are alive. Can't you hear what the splatter
of the rain exhorts? – 'Escape! To the office,
to the factory, to markets where they speculate, or to any other
excitement – run off wherever you can! And in the evening,
when work stops, there's drinking, there's gambling,
maybe the illusion of conjugal bliss, or the refuge
of a misery that needs to be remedied. Wherever you can,
however you can – run, ill-fated creature, hide the curse
of your awareness, drown the rotation
of day following day – this killing wheel. For death
is not such a sad thing, the torment is
to know that you are dying.'

7 October 195

Night

Night, my love, grant me your favour, don't give me sleep!

    Do you remember, Night, the rituals of our union?
That pledge of nakedness, pledge of stillness, exchange of gifts?

    You gave me your moon, many moons, many more stars,
star-filled skies, burning fire-breathing darkness.
And a huge country, a continent, a crowded solitude,
and the sweet-and-sharp intoxication of insomnia.
And I gave you my love,
my spirit's essence, the perfume of my being.

Day, your sister, your rival, has with her fat bangled hands
pressed me to service, dragged me to her lanes and alleys,
ringing the bunched keys tied to her sari's end.
She is busy: hazy despite her abundant sun,
torn, dishevelled, formless. Her moments drop
leaden on the pavement, with inarticulate noise.
The fragments of her hours, pieced together, add up to nothing
but the humiliation of hunger, the misery of managing a meal,
inferior pleasures, dwarfish sufferings.

This Day I have accepted, I have endured,
followed her like a dog on a lead –
for you, for you alone, Night! Ah, that moment
when Day's grip slackens, the hydra-headed crowd withdraws,
and I, naked and pure, can discover you again,
bathe in your dark hair's unplumbed indigo waves
and say – 'I exist!'

You have given me your moon, many moons –
moons that have died and come back, darkness that breathes stars.
And I've given you my love, filled the cups of kissing
with the wrung-out extracts of my conscious being.

Do you remember?

I've played with your moons, as a lover lying in bed
counts the pearls on an earring: your curved moons;
thin, flat, dangling moons; white, green, yellow; shameless
as Urbashi's beauty; winter moons like teeth made of glass shards,
like God's forgiveness on the horizon. With two hands
I've churned your darkness, climbed its steps, rolled down
its joyous slopes, got tangled in its soft, hairy, never-ending
folds. Losing myself in your vast, liquid embrace, I've understood
that the stars are nothing but the manifested forms
of Negress-Night's consciousness – it's when you do your thinking
that the stars come out in the sky, O Wise Woman!

And I too have wished that my thoughts could spurt as light,
shine as stars – white, green, golden – sharp as eyes of ice,
streaming like a beauty's tears on the horizon. And in that hour
of your fullness, when none wake but poets, thieves, and sad men,

and the horse-speed of my own hopes has trampled me under its hooves
and sped off – then have I, within your heaving bosom,
trembled as if in a spasm, whispered in your ears
my mad desires, of desire's futility –
in your ears, Dearest!

You have not offered me consolation – mean consolation;
you've only said, in the mode of your humming stillness,
'Take this – this vast country, this vast solitude. People it
by scattering the seeds of your dreams upon it.'

This is what you've given me – in exchange for my desires,
my defeats – this seeded land, lonely land,
and the drunkenness of insomnia.

You've forgotten everything?

No, no, I know you too well, you Woman of Wiles!
You ditched me only to whet my manhood, jilted me
only to rekindle my thirst. Willingly you had once allowed
yourself to be caught, and today you challenge me
to conquer you, to kill Demoness-Death
and win you, Ageless Woman! And as I have
no other weapons but words, no other soldiers but songs, so
honing the steel of speech, I have shaped today
this song – Come back, Night, descend
on this death, bring me my agony in your bosom's cup –
give me dreams, nightmares, a poet's loneliness, like God's,
or joy like fever's delirium – give me any single token
of your eternal youth – only don't give me sleep,
no sleep please! Let me live within you,
disperse myself in your blue, crooked veins
and fill the whole sky, pulse with the breathing of stars,
ring with the rhythm of the breaking and building of your moons.
And then, at our love's intensest moment, when
jealous Day has burst the horizon like an egg,
may I discern, in the very last wink of your eyes
that are almost closing, how my lost time
is slowly becoming the future.

1952

Nostalgia

Which is that country, missing which I suffer so!
Was I ever there, or haven't I seen it yet,
or am I still there?

    Dangling from my eyes like fruit — are those memories?
Climbing up my body like a shrub — is that hope?
Once upon a time I had plucked out my heart and fed it
to birds. Off they flew in a flock towards that very country.

    Since that time I occasionally see their shadows:
when icy January descends, the sky fragments and
comes down in pieces, the snow falls silently; when,
having traversed a subway's darkness, suddenly I see —
like a sun-flooded portal — crossroads. Or in Calcutta's
midday rain, when the earth seems so small and intimate,
and I, at my desk in the corner, dim and fade away.

    I see the shadows of those birds — those who had flown off
with my heart. Experienced they are: they know all the seas,
have alighted on all the beaches, have friends in every city.
I have seen their shadows in Manhattan's East River,
flutter in Bavaria's lakes, and now I see them again
in Calcutta's overcast sky.

    Which is that country, where I want to go?
Would that be going away, or coming back?
Or just a search?

    The garment on my body is like the past, and the future
is the balcony where I pace. And the present
is an endless procession of ants who die under my feet.

    I remember the sound of snow melting in drips
and a thousand gloved hands on the window-pane.
I remember the smell of Jhamapukur Lane in Chaitra's sun.
One boy I remember — he was playing, then suddenly came
running, drank three sips of tea from his mother's cup
and ran off again. Why doesn't tea taste like that any more?

From *Ekdin: Chirodin o Anyanyo Kavita* (April 1971)

When it's time to go, I wish I could stay, and repeatedly postpone
my date of departure. It's as if I was in an airport hotel, between two
continents, where I arrived today and which I'll leave tomorrow,
and within this single torn fragment of time
I must taste all sorrows. All night through my half-sleep
I hear the expansive roar of an aeroplane –
neither here nor there, neither far nor near –
as if I was floating in cosmic space, journeying asleep,
and that journey too was motionless.

My birds, when will you come home?

8 September 1965
Calcutta

My Life

At times it seems that my life is a vast airport
where every minute a plane touches down,
a plane takes off.

Before me is the sea, behind me the city's roar.
In my breath hovers the smell of the sea, my cellar is stocked
with the quintessence of blue. None can overtake me
without partaking of that wine.

And as everyone wants to get drunk,
I am besieged by crowds day and night.

It's like the fairground of the chariot procession,
thirty-six ethnicities bubbling in one pot.
Blonde, brown, yellow, and black, they come;
merchants, warriors, and lovers come;
old women too, with curiosity in their weary eyes.
But they don't stop; they blow through me,
as unimpeded as air.

I have seen many moments of reunion
and scenes of farewell,

much weeping, many kisses,
many arms flailing like forest branches.

    What glittering festivals of light my nights are!
From star to star the signals are relayed.
How many luminaries are mine, how many crowns of distance,
how many meteoric tidings of triumph!
And how many orbitings, without pause! It's those who go off
who return.

    I am as extensive and simple as the dawn,
and an intricate fortress, a complicated palace;
in my inner rooms only the detectives are wise,
and those who deal in contraband.
I am as open as a public assembly,
and as secretive as a cave;
mysterious with stairs descending underground,
I am a hollow filled with the darkness of lengthy alleys.

    Don't I feel proud, when I hear thousands of feet
stomping on my heart? How gigantic is my hunger,
within which the whole world is gathered and turbulent!

    Then again I wonder: is this world me, or mine?
Or is it theirs – they who keep me sleepless with their footsteps,
are bubbles within my whirl?
Their dwellings are diminutive, their wines dilute,
but they have kinsmen and enemies, jealousies and attachments;
their hours are intimate with the impress of efforts and desires.
But I – I neither love nor hate, am beyond greetings or tears,
impartial, selfish. All that happens,
happens to others; all the drama belongs to others;
I am just a witness, an intermediary, an observer.

                                               10 September 1965
                                                         Calcutta

My Tower

Some say my tower is made of ivory. They are
wrong.

My tower is a shard-tiled shack in the slums of Behala,
a hotel of forty floors in San Francisco,
a majestic ship on the Atlantic,
or a soggy bathroom in Calcutta's rainy season,
where laundry scum floats on a tub of water,
and a spider wanders on the cracked wall.

In truth, my tower does not stand still in one spot;
it moves, it lives, it assumes many forms.

Some say I live alone in my tower. They are
wrong.

Here to keep me company I have many beautiful women,
many scholars, many gazelles, many rats from sewers,
beggars and whores from smelly alleys. Now and then
a magician's trick makes red and blue lotuses bloom
on the same branch. Once in a while
an aged vulture thrusts its neck through the window.

In truth, my tower has no bolts, no walls, no watchmen.
I don't even know the names of many of those
who crowd here. They chat amongst themselves
so that I can clearly hear what they are saying;
they eat up my food and go away.

Some say I am as secure in my tower
as a corpse in its coffin. They are wrong.

At times deadly germs fly over, epidemics
get going. Then my tower becomes a hospital,
and all night long I hear the patients groaning.
Sometimes bombs fall, soldiers with guns
take over my tower; I serve them like a servant.

In truth I can be very easily attacked,
very easily defeated. My tower is built
of an infinite vulnerability.

   But what is astonishing is that the tower is never destroyed –
neither by bombs, nor by germs, nor by earthquakes.
Sometimes it rises very high,
sometimes it is indistinguishable from the ground,
sometimes it dons camouflage and mingles with the enemy camp.
As sly and deceitful as a spy,
as invincible as a spider on a cracked wall,
as perennial as grass under snow
is this tower.

12 September 1965
Calcutta

The Constraint of Seasonality

If only there were no alternatives, how unburdened would
life be!

   Beyond my window a half-moon sea; carved in terraces
onto the hillside, a menstruating city; the sun-tinged rain
like pearl-drops; and after the rain, a world-dyeing rainbow.
And on the other side a sleepy garden, earth's bliss, ecstasy
of leaf, grass, flower: whose fragrance disturbs
my ascetic composure; where a young woman waters plants
hour after hour – bronzed by the sun's grace, covered
solely by her girdle and breast-cloth,
like the star Svati incarnate.

   My heart, wasn't this what you had desired
for a long time? This sea-distance, murmur of water
in a green and still afternoon, earth's perfume?
Then why must you still moan continuously: 'Honolulu,
why couldn't you be Napoli?'

From *Ekdin: Chirodin o Anyanyo Kavita* (April 1971)

Summer once more, now Colorado. In the bluest, clearest sky
an unflickering light, a transparency of immeasurable depth,
an unending day flooded in sharp sunlight, on far peaks the massed
radiance of snow. I go beyond the city by car, the loving dalliance
of cherries on my tongue, my eyes drunk on a thousand sights.
The road ascends in twists; below, the plain melts into the horizon;
and from an upper level the forest advances – dense, solemn,
enchanting. Sometimes a canyon approaches darkly, between
high rocks, rows of tall trees as guardsmen on either side –
no sky. And sometimes a bare, tawny mountain burns
in the fierce sun, like the statue of a nameless god
in primitive sculpting. In a secluded spot a stream descends and flows
through the green woodland's bosom, with as much spirit
as the fish that shelter in it. Suddenly from a peak leaps
a valley, as wide as imagination in evening's gold,
as hospitable as an affectionate hostess.

My heart, what more could you wish for?
This golden village, inn in an old stable –
cool wine, smell of fresh-baked bread, leisure suspended
from candles' chiaroscuro – isn't this the earth's limit?
If peace is to be had anywhere, is it not here?
Must you still be depressed – because you didn't have tea
in that 'Copper Kettle' place, with a veranda beside the spring?
Because you didn't go beyond the river's bend
and take another path? Are you forgetting
that you have just one body?

Five women I know – Chitra, Champa, Bishakha, Arundhati,
and Saraswati. One is dark, another fair-skinned; one has a face
with a quiet and wistful look; another is bubbly; yet another exudes
dreams, in some consciously concealed manner. When I look
them in the eye, desire's sure response I receive.
Any one of them I could have loved – but which one?
Whenever in my mind I welcome one, she merges
with the others. Can't there be a woman who is composed
of the elements of all five females – who is at once
dark and fair, merry and passionate, melancholy and with

a superb sense of humour? Someone who can be in turn
Bishakha and Champa, Chitra and Arundhati,
and Saraswati!

How happy life would be, if only there were no alternatives!

4-5 September 1965 [Revised: 11 April 1970]
Calcutta

The Expatriate

As she read the letter, tears streamed down her
cheeks. A strange noise pushed itself up her throat.
Moving to the window, she read every syllable again,
tossed and turned the paper like a hanky, as if it might
hide a different bit of news.

She felt she had to get out of the house.

The person she saw in the mirror was in slacks
and an orange shirt, hair cut like Mrs Kennedy's.
Was this the girl who, in Rajshahi, used to sit
on the pond's edge and call out 'Come, come' to the ducks?
Who used to be scared of her own shadow in lantern-light?

Coat and lipstick on, she came out. In the lift Barbara said,
'Hi.' Eileen Schnell made smiling eye-contact.
Dr David said, 'Good morning. How are you
this morning?' She replied, 'Fine.' Her lips smiled
a little. Many in this apartment building did indeed know her,
but none knew her Didi.

March outside. The wind sharp, the promenade by the river
deserted. No sun. Sky overcast with a cloud as fine as mist.
Lumps of ashen snow stuck to the ground and the benches.
The bay – with its pier, ships, huge bridge – was hazy; on the hazy
other shore were rows of skyscrapers. She stood, clutching the railing,
leaning over it, gazing through the mist into the distance,
where, on the Atlantic's horizon, another world beckoned.

From *Ekdin: Chirodin o Anyanyo Kavita* (April 1971)

Suddenly the words escaped her — 'Didi. My Didi.' A gust
of wind blew her voice away, as helpless and insignificant
as a piece of straw.

She had been saving up every month, for a trip back home.
How easily the years had flown by — these twenty-six years!
College, the great war, so many reversals in the world,
Rajshahi in another, incredible country. Two marriages
made and broken, a son in the navy, a daughter married
to a rich farmer in Arkansas. So much had happened —
yet how easy it all seemed now. Easy —
and somewhat hazy. Had she really been
Mrs Brown once, and another time,
Mrs Monticelli? Does she know those two ladies?
Her own name — wasn't it Annapurna, whom
everyone used to call Anni?

When she heard of her father's death, Annie Brown
didn't weep much. Anna Monticelli got over her mother's death
in a matter of days. But they had husbands, families,
youth. They didn't stow their hard-earned cash in the bank
every month, to make a return trip.

But now no reason for going back remained.
No one would know her.

Does that house still exist in Rajshahi? Does anyone know
that Anni lived there, that she and her Didi
slept in the same bed? The sound of rain, the scent of bokuls,
jamruls filled with a watery smell. But everything was wrapped
in her Didi — as if bokuls and jamruls were so good
only because of Didi — as if within that one
Bengali word was hidden all that today
was hard to believe. Hard to believe, yet had existed.
The face was now dim, but had existed: a concept,
a dream, the land of her birth.

It was as if there had been a shipwreck, with many jewels
sinking in the deep. But in this big city none else knew of it.
— Anni, you knew my Didi, didn't you?

Say something. Come home with me, stay with me
today. Speak to me. Anni, do you remember
those two girls, both young, but one even younger
than the other — as under their rinds
custard-apples fill with pulp, even so, concealed,
were they — as if under a cover, secret. And yet
in those days they wanted for nothing else.
Why did they have to become currents, flow over
all the world? Tell me truly, did they once exist? Did this 'I'
really spring thence?

 The wind pierced through her coat, needled her body.
She shivered and turned round. Started to walk, stopped abruptly,
and spoke out loud, 'I am in Brooklyn. This is nineteen-
sixty-three. It's freezing today.' She trudged over the slush
to the grocery store. Remembered that it was
Friday, the day for buying provisions.

8-9 September 1965
Calcutta

Ela-di

An old neighbourhood, far from the tram-track; beyond
hurry-scurry, crowds, and manual labour; solemn with the shade
of tall trees — there I go whenever I have time,
to see Ela-di.

 'To see' is quite the right phrase. For I am a kid, just turned
nineteen: what could I possibly say to Ela-di, that hasn't already been
murmured in her ears by all those lucky guys —
those who, having had the chance to have been born
a few years before me, have left nothing for me!

 A vast room. Beyond it, a veranda. Outside, a Chaitra afternoon:
where the sun's heat scorches, dust-eddies rustle as they circulate.
But here it's cool, pleasure for the eyes scattered in the dimmed light,
and there's no noise. Sheltered by green blinds is this veranda:
ribbons of sunlight tremble between the slats, into which bleed
the colours of the curtains and the walls; a picture, wall-hung,

From *Ekdin: Chirodin o Anyanyo Kavita* (April 1971)

casts a luminous glow; the light-green of a posh house-plant
is stood in a corner. It's a green radiance –
yellow, and green, and violet – an under-water glow
like clusters of grapes growing everywhere in the air, and as cool,
and as warm, and as suggestive of sensuality.

On a cushioned rattan armchair from Singapore reclines
Ela-di, her feet on a stool upholstered in Santiniketan leather.
Her feet are slender, paler even than her face;
the fine blue veins enhance their beauty: until I saw her
I never imagined even human feet could be so beautiful.
I stare at her feet, over which her sari-border trails
as blue as the breast of a peacock.
She leans forward a little and lights a cigarette.
When the smoke comes out of her mouth, I take a deep breath
and inhale the aroma of her foreign cigarette,
and at the same time the hypodermic syringe
of a perfume pricks me – who knows of what exotic name.
My head feels giddy – I feel so light that I fancy
I could fly off like a bird.

When a word or two fall from her lips, like dry leaves
from a tree, only then do I look at her face.
When our eyes meet, Ela-di smiles a little. The rows of her teeth
between her lipstick-dyed lips are so gleaming that I at once
lower my head – in case I transgress the limit of good manners.
Besides, other thoughts come into my head.

I remember my Kakima, who lives in ground-floor lodgings
in a narrow festering cul-de-sac, spending six hours a day in the
kitchen, her five children popping in and out in clothes which they have
outgrown. She is daily losing weight and looking paler and paler,
and yet the doctor is not being called, in case he detects
something seriously wrong with her. Yet even she once had
beauty – that gift of God which does not survive for long
without human care.

I remember our part-time maid, Horimoti, who washes dishes
from morning to evening, working her shifts in house after house,
who has only two teeth left – and those two

are huge, dangling, and dirty yellow. She no longer looks
like a woman; her body is like a plank of wood; and her face
is neither male nor female. She speaks very little,
just bends her back and gets on with her work.
Just working, just living, simply surviving somehow –
that's all she has time for. I'm embarrassed to look at her.

   And when Ela-di gets up in the morning, the car is already waiting
to take her husband to his office. She drinks her coffee; bath and
toilette take her to eleven a.m. After that she either goes shopping
in the car, or natters on the telephone, or else sits in this veranda
turning the pages of illustrated foreign magazines. Decorating her
house, her body; an hour or so of siesta in the afternoon; five or six
parties a week; rich and famous friends from many countries;
the occasional holiday in Gangtok, or Colombo, or Barcelona.
In response to all travail, all suffering, all stifling black holes,
Ela-di's indolence spreads itself like a beautiful tree,
green and abundant in foliage, where tinted flowers
blossom continuously, but never come to fruit.

   Still I say: Ela-di, stay as you are – always;
never ever do social work for any association;
don't give donations to those who save the world;
don't let a sudden pang of conscience make you rough.
Stay as you are now – happy and relaxed,
beautiful and scented, and yes, serving no purpose.

Begun in 1955, finished on 2-3 October 1965

A Farewell at Howrah Station

This life's a sea. How many jewels hide in it!

   By chance I picked one up once, having come
to see a couple off at Howrah Station.
It was half-past ten at night.

   Having married a little late, a friend of mine was going off
for his honeymoon. His bride Papiya was a favourite student of mine.

It was in my house that their courtship had flowered. So
shaking off my natural indolence, I too had to come
to bid them goodbye.

Facing their compartment was a group of relatives — grown-ups,
young married women, three budding adolescent girls —
movements, laughter, flashes of colour, repetitions
of gratuitous questions and answers
(Your money — tickets — luggage — water bottle —
is everything OK? Don't forget to write!),
and now and then a discreet joke, appropriate to the occasion.
Then a bell rang, and Papiya said, 'Five more minutes.'

She said it casually, almost wistfully, but I could hear
the lapping of her happiness. Five more minutes, and then
they would be alone in their compartment à deux,
with a delicious night in front of them, full of moving darkness,
and a new life too, full of grand possibilities. At least
that's what it seemed like to them at that point,
dandled, as they were, on nature's lap.

Showering my good wishes, I said goodbye —
taking with me a drop of the perfume of their bliss.
But perhaps it wasn't quite like that, perhaps the preface
of this short story is mostly my fabrication,
for within a few moments a different scene
gouged out from my mind both my friend and Papiya,
and the hopeful moment of their departure.

As I was walking out, I stopped abruptly.
In a square window of the train, framed like a picture,
was a woman's face. And on the platform stood
a middle-aged man. They were gazing
at each other — motionless, arrested, unflickering, mute.
Tears were streaming down their cheeks —
unimpeded, continuous, fluent, abundant — as if
this was as easy as breathing. They were neither making any attempt
to wipe their tears, nor moving their eyes away even for a moment,
but were simply looking — motionless, arrested, unflickering.
Their eyes were open, in spite of the deluge of tears.

Other people, hawkers, the miscellaneous noise of a railway station,
the sudden hoot of an engine – nothing interrupted
their attention. They didn't even see that I was looking at them.
Face to face, gazing steadily, weeping-wrapped: it was as if
each had now become the other's whole world,
and nothing else existed.

   I was surprised. Never before had I seen
a middle-aged man – tall, well-built, strong – cry
in that fashion. Nor had I ever seen a woman shed tears
so calmly, with such control, without breaking down.
I had no idea that one could weep such floods
so silently, nor that between two looking at each other there could
float up an unattainable heaven, to gaze at which
mind, heart, innermost soul would crowd into the eyes.
I didn't know that the tears of two could flow
in such unison, to the same rhythm, like twin
sad sisters gently consoling each other,
without saying a word, without the slightest touch. No –
they had no other gestures – not even the slightest,
faintest. Their hands, heads, necks were utterly motionless;
only the pressure of each other's eyes was crushing them,
they were melting into each other's tears. I was fascinated
by their patience, their almost inhuman control.

   To take in the scene, what it meant, it took me perhaps
a couple of minutes. And then, when amazement's first shock
had ebbed away, I felt a surge
of curiosity. I looked again, with a more discerning gaze,
at those two people, who were totally unknown to me,
but were nonetheless holding me riveted that instant:
I wondered what kind of daily lives they led, to which
social class they belonged.
From where I stood I could only see a half
of the man's face, but from his broad shoulders,
straight spine, and firm manner of standing
I guessed he was a hard-working man, one of those who could
make a place for themselves to stand upon
solely through their honesty and labours.

From *Ekdin: Chirodin o Anyanyo Kavita* (April 1971)

And the woman (I could see her fully) –
was no great beauty, whatever else she was,
nor was her toilette glamorous – just the conventional vermilion
on her hair-parting, the usual bangles on her
wrists, and upon her cheeks time had started its scratches.
Two girls sat on each side of her – one about six,
the other would be eleven or twelve. The young one
was trying to go to sleep, her head against her mother's shoulder;
her eyes were occasionally opening very roundly
and slowly shutting again; and the other girl,
leaning against the compartment wall, held
a film magazine open before her face. All this
I took in at a glance, and then another detail
caught my attention.

   On the seat on the other side I glimpsed another person,
another man, with his back turned to the platform, indistinct.
It was an 'inter class' compartment (so these people weren't well off),
with poor lighting: of this second man, beyond his back's curved line
and the slouching posture in which he sat, I could see nothing.
It seemed to me he was watching the goods train waiting
on the next line, and now and then puffing away
at his cigarette. But suddenly – even as I was looking –
that obscure figure moved, got up, advanced
towards the front door. A thin man I saw, his kaftan hanging
loosely on his body, his face suggesting he was unwell,
as if he'd wasted away from indigestion or insomnia.
He glanced once at the man standing on the platform
and once at the woman sitting inside the compartment:
those two, immersed in each other till the last moment,
didn't notice him. By then the little girl had fallen asleep
and the face of the older one was still behind
the film magazine.

   The guard blew his whistle. The long train, with all its
mysteries within it, disappeared into the night.

   Since then many days have gone by. So many friendships have
ceased to exist, so many delights have lost their zest, so many

memories have faded. But even now I sometimes remember
those three strangers: the extraordinary weeping of the two
and the glance cast by the other one – frightened as an injured animal's,
unsure, as if it hadn't found an answer – which had come from within
him and disappeared within him, and to witness which that instant
there was none there but me. No matter what any of you may say,
there's nothing as beautiful and holy and memorable
as sorrow, especially if it's another's. Or maybe our memory
is a discriminating sieve, in whose interstices
only sorrows stick – whether our own, or another's –
to be transmuted by some unknowable chemistry.

1969

One Day: For Ever

At times the afternoon feels like some other day.
As though it would open
at the slightest push. Just a little. A little more.

 Two p.m. Summer descends with ferocity. The heat
like an egg – as before; the stillness of brooding
all over the sky. This is the house: I recognize it
and get off the tram at Park Circus.

 Ground floor, wall-enclosed. Old moss on the steps.
Dry leaves fall on the yard. Softly: with the sound
of a torn-up letter.

 Or did someone breathe? Or whisper something?

 I have climbed up to the veranda – I am standing by the door.
There she is – she hasn't forgotten me –
she's lying down ready for me. Her body flows
like a golden current; her nipples quiver
like eyes.

 This moment trembles. This today, brimming-in-sky,
trembles. As if the curtain

would go up any minute. As if everything
was beginning all over again.

    Rain through dawn sleep, smell of frying cheera
in the rain. In a skycraft with a coloured cover
I travel to the lane of Potuatola
and alight. In the urinal
shadows tremble on the wall, booze smell
gives you gooseflesh. Kisses like pomegranate
granules, hidden in night's wrapping. My heart
like the pendulum of a giant clock
swinging from star to star.

    Her breasts, I sense, have lifted up,
are looking at me, with the innocence
of a young girl. Her body is a river, flows
with golden ripples in her pores.

    I bend down and begin to untie my shoe laces.

    But they get tangled – into knot
after knot. The more I pull,
the more firmly they grip me. My efforts grow
like a banyan tree; my patience is a stone
in my hand. I say to her: 'Hang on – just a minute –
from these dirty jeans a sword will
unsheathe itself. My fire will burn
in your flood-tide.' In response
she pushes off the pillow from under her head –
filled like a sail in a brisk breeze.

    Just a minute. Just another minute.

    But what sin, what curse entraps me? Why can't this plot
of shoelaces be unravelled? And why, lecher, do you still
lust?

    Sinking its teeth into my breast, the bell rings, the day
goes. Stubble grows on my cheeks; my trousers are in tatters;
grass shoots up from under my skin. Herds of goats
tear me up and devour me.

Even so, I return at times. That door, that waiting,
as though this moment were some other day. As if it was trembling.
A today, brimming-in-sky, is trembling. That's why,
lecherous, I still lust,
the disquiet of immortal eros in my bones.

March 1964
Brooklyn, New York

From
Swagatobiday o Anyanyo Kavita (June 1971)

Fishing

Farms fish, he does. Has a pond of his own.
That's his sport, his love, his living and daily yoke.
Rod cast, sits all day — not there, an absent bloke.
Thinks he sees great sholes tail-lash, giant bowals spawn.

A weird lot, his protégés. Smart guerrillas, they cheat him on a daily
basis.
Yet they will drunkenly swallow his bait, or else
send him signal after signal in bubbles, gestures, swells
from their hide-out in an unknown address in the lowest abyss.

Suddenly sometimes the sun ruptures the profound obscure
and the instant dissolves in a naiad's epiphanic gleams.
Or the instant hands out tidings of quivering limbs
when the wind blows, makes the water frisk in absurd furore.

– Fish? Or the fiery water's scam? Dream's conjuring trick?
But the water shivers again, becomes real, credible, incarnate:
there it is – the pulsing ray, compliant desire's true shape –
swims up, then sinks. He needs more finesse, more kick.

But it's hard work, is fishing. Demons and otters interfere.
Some years are barren. Or crippling rheumatism grips him.
No rest for him though. He needs patience, labour, and vim,
for honed by rivalry, the sly fish become even niftier.

Ergo, he turns selfish. Two tasks are very necessary:
sustaining, with daily subsistence, the general well-being,
and in this fickle world, with this tricky body, somehow surviving. –
For all would be lost, if death did the dirty on him – a sudden burglary.

14-15 January 1967

He and Others

A boy, he sees many dim figures in his dreams –
a group of grotesque magicians.
Long beards, some in loose tunics,
curly-maned, with sharp, pared faces,
sunken cheeks, bald pates, some with hand-drums, cymbals,
some dancing tumbling monkeys, or with grimacing pampered bears;
all of them carrying huge floppy shoulder-bags:
'This is the seed of datura that drives you crazy, and this
the lucky charm with seven metals, that wards off every sickness;
here's a tiger's claw, a musk deer's pouch, a beehive from Tibet,
and this is the snake-skin chemise of a sultan's daughter ...'
They show you things, coax you with winks, shout threats, open
mango buds with mumbo-jumbo, mix champak-scent with your breath,
sway to strange flutes and leave you with this message, 'Come,
come and join our gang,
this funfair, with songs, dances, games,
total freedom all day long,
an endless funfair, where all games are accommodated –
listen, kid, it's all for you, none but you, so come along!'
He's a little afraid – alone and small – lying in the dark;
stretches his hand and seeks his mother, clutches the sheet with his fist.
Wants to say, 'No, I won't go.' But his feeling of fascination's greater.
His ears alert, he sinks his eyes beneath his dreams,
while his future, the name of which he doesn't yet know,
twinkles in the dark like a little firefly.

Now he knows, therefore wholeheartedly
on the lineaments of those faces seen in childhood dreams
he draws divine characteristics –

to be obeyed compulsorily, and taken literally —
like rows of images in a living temple:
not mute, but articulate with gospels, full of mystery,
though indeed many haven't heard of them.
Off he goes to visit them, modesty flowering in both hands,
a ceaseless tremor beneath his breast — kneeling, yet fearless,
for to his heart newly opened with awakening chants
they bequeath lasting gifts:
smiles on the margins of their lips, gestures of fingers,
guardian angel gazes that enchant and do not blink,
and voices heard in the dark — sounds, reverberations.

But it's they who are his main enemies today — those merciful gods.
He engages in scintillating battles, rejections, diplomatic attacks.
Grandfather's shawl, embroidered all over, Father's hookah; deer with
eight-branched antlers, boar's head — souvenirs of some grey uncle —
a piece of Dhaka muslin touched by some distant great-grandmother —
all such items he discards, or hides in a warehouse; gets rid of
old furniture, ruthlessly shears the dense foliage of his garden;
gives leave to his servants, those who had known him as a boy.
By escaping from his extensive family estate
he thinks he will find his rich self.
He goes abroad, learns other languages, the customs of other countries,
learns with great care the names of foreign flowers,
sometimes with massive patience studies deep mathematics only,
sometimes crosses frontiers to spread
rebellions, secret addictions, banned music; —
seems gradually to attain security, his intolerably weighty past
shifting drop by drop — as dirty water drips away
through the hole of an unplugged water-tank.

'Say then, has this expedition been successful?
Have you performed patricide satisfactorily?
Killed yourself serially and been born in the wombs of new mothers?
Say, in which distant country did you find
two *kathas* of desired dry ground,
where, on a thin hostile tree,
despite drought, fatigue, lack of help,
you managed, with great difficulty, to grow
one or two original fruits, whose taste is now far-famed?'

He doesn't respond, doesn't hear so well these days.
Or is no longer interested in controversies,
as he's returned – exactly where the journey began.
Only for this, he muses, such a racket
so that he too in the end
can, in that deserted ancestral estate, find a place for himself –
in his own right – in a little room?
Light fades, evening descends. And in the dark they gather
round him – those others, who'd always been his companions
in speeches of exaggeration and protest, in travels and intellection,
though he'd not been aware of it, just as no one ever feels
the motion of blood in his veins,
or the work of the liver, that turns food to pure energy.
'Then are they themselves manure, seeds, and rain –
and myself just the thirsty soil? Within me, then, they too have toiled?
But if that is so, in which distant spark were they born?
Which promised friction-wood and shomi branch
rent darkness and lit the primeval fire, and when?'
– Such thoughts wear him out, and the night deepens;
he stares at them, sees how their countenances
change from time to time, as if merging into one another.
Sometimes he thinks he is really that other one,
or that other one is a previous draft of himself – almost.
And then an utterance, most ancient, springs to his lips:
'O Sun, I am but the flicker of a particle of your fire,
just a drop of your discharge, O source without beginning!
Take me back!'
            Thus it goes on from generation to generation.

1969

Lament

(for a young poet)

Are you too, then, a scion of that unlucky line,
naturally selected, in identity marginal and pale,
a thrilling example, just right to serve as a warning –
one of those who, after riding lightning miles

on famous horses, suddenly fall under their hooves:
might-have-been charioteers, all the more crushed themselves
under turning wheels, because they desired too much,
or who resemble meteors, whose velocity's luminous in fall?
Safe myself, entranced, I look at you
and think you've paid the price
for others to have thatch on their roofs, dal and rice on their plates,
or even on occasion to grow, in autumnal yards,
a few unabashed fruits on withered branches.
It seems because your opulence was innate
you, in the dusky glory of standing for others,
paid off all their debts and pauperized yourself.
But what we'd wanted in a deeper sense
was not your immolation of yourself,
not your altruism careless of consequences,
but your own harvest, well-ripened, more abundant.

Don't think I didn't get your heart's secret intention:
in response to the pain of separation,
anxious to do something in revenge straight away –
taking some sunset colours, some debates, some sorrows,
even more devious inventions as the occasion might borrow,
some realistic facts too, the tremor of nerves; –
chopping such ingredients, boiling them on fierce desire's fire,
in every bubble you saw an irresistible signal of coming together –
no, not just a signal, for your verve was sharper,
greater your daring: as if she whom you desired, who was not there,
was immanent in material goods that could be bound,
was eternally present in diverse mixtures and transmutations
(as salt in water, invisible, but present to the taste,
or salt in sea breeze, pervasive, but untasteable) –
so thinking, forgetting the difference between
art and artist, you wanted to enter and be conserved
in your beloved's most hidden inner chamber –
as a bird within an egg, or a foetus floating in womb-waters.
Or in some heated chemistry
burning and melting her down, you had her transferred
into your bloodstream, so she might never again
escape. But the pressure of that huge endeavour

fragmented and scattered your life so —
that you couldn't put it together again. Why could you not?

Yet you too know that our existence is not
simple like that of sardines packed in an airtight box.
Tearing open uteri, eggshells, the earth's interior,
we must be born, and so in our psyche, avid of rebirth,
that primal feeling of severance irresistibly recurs.
Love, song, beauty's intuition, urge to create —
there's nothing that's not rooted in separation, is not
a particle of radiance scattered between opposite pulls,
between the chisel and the stone.
And so
for ever we want to be
travellers in far, unspecified countries,
children in trouble, away from the shelter of mothers:
as if bruised by a nameless quest, we seek
that seductress, whose coruscating distance
provokes mad desire, but is never bridged.
This duality is our capital, the original law;
it is through conflict that life maintains its flow;
desire is all, not the acquisition. And you
had desire — fiery, ferocious.
Yet why, why could you not
be as free and lonely as a flying bird,
pulsing like an arrow released from a bow,
like a growing tree, capable of rising, though bound,
so that you could convert desire to power
and become richer, self-reliant, invulnerable?
The trap you laid for another — why did you let that trap you?

Listen, lad, I know how delicious darkness can be,
how apparently complete in itself, as if beyond contingencies.
But even the dark is not
still, stainless, uniform: it isn't fixed, but of variable register.
One can do some work with it, build with it:
that can be a lifelong labour, copious in responsibility and relevance,
can inform all future seasons, knowledge, experience.
There's memory, the kernel within, whence darkness is hope-charged.
Memory burns as a ray, blows as a mighty wind in every direction,

From *Swagatobiday o Anyanyo Kavita* (June 1971)

spreads in cavities, spectral colours dispersed on pitch-black;
scenes emerge, and language – cogitable, restless, dream-stirred –
tawny in the street lamp's gleam, or bluish white in rural fog,
or deeper blue, burning between clusters of stars –
all very disturbingly significant:
like a call, that wants to rouse you again,
demands from you an answer.
Once in a moving night train – do you recall? –
in hazy sleep, forgetting the location, the date,
you felt the immeasurable surprise of life and youth,
loaded, rich in possibilities,
as if all your travelling was towards that goal, and time
was beginning anew that minute. Likewise this.
The promise was you'd be both witness and scribe,
consumer and scientist at the same time;
engaged in embracing, yet measuring without error –
how blood pressure climbs during sexual intercourse,
how rapid the pulse becomes, how much the blood-vessels swell,
and how kisses forsake the proximity of lips,
riding the waves of who-knows-what insatiable lust,
and move far, farther – to beaches still beyond vision.
The promise was you'd find a flexible outer shell,
within which your fragile being would slowly gain
a fruit's density, whilst you in the street,
with as much self-assurance as anyone else,
your meat and paratha eaten, cardamom seeds tucked in your mouth,
would be pleased with the neighbourliness, were you to secure a place
to stand with a modicum of comfort in the bus's clayey crowds.
For there's the world: our rival, hard to conquer,
insuperable, unforgiving, who must somehow be hoodwinked.
You must put your feet on the ground – that's of prime importance –
hang interminably, without plummeting, without pique,
hang on, clutching any excuse – with your secret ruse.
– But you most horribly
when in the soft sun all petals of youth's blossom
hadn't even opened, like an incomplete flower
torn by a boy's hand, became exposed
in a single hurricane of the heart.
Like a trunk left behind in the wrong railway station

in a journey — you lost yourself, and closed all doors.
Hence my lament. On the other margin
winter comes down thick.

1969

The Aged Poet

His wife had called him an ugly slack-skinned lecher.
Even that was long ago. Now he's no longer on his own.
Has a constant companion — a strange and stupid newcomer,
ignorant of his language, an alien from another zone —
whom he'd first met after an operation, when in great pain,
and had thought: 'How odd! This is my body then!'

His books, meanwhile, have grown up and left home.
Wild, wicked, and shameless, in far-off parts they roam:
here — stirring up a riot, there — slapping a scholar's bald dome;
digging up shiny gewgaws in effortless sport,
stomping suddenly home with a 'Dad, see what I got!'
But he fails to understand why on earth they amass such trash,
doesn't understand this is fame, his long-sought stash;
puckers his eyebrows and moans, 'They shout so much!'

He's tired. He's cross. Of late, whatever he finds —
the morning's basket of letters, shoes kicked off by the door,
funeral crowds at birthdays, gatecrashing ahead of time —
everything hurts like a bad tooth, is a nuisance, a bore,
or a scrap of thread torn from his own past, moth-eaten.
Because today's world has fallen from its generative sign,
the womb of the golden One holds no conceivable Other —
both daughter and wife — so nothing happens any more:
neither amity nor anger, nor stepping into wonderment alone.
He spends the day in his armchair, curtains shutting out the light,
eyes closed, shaking his knees — inert, unassailable.

Nevertheless at times speech — a voice — erupts:
'Come, friend, let's reconsider:
is a point to be proved still left to any science?

From Swagatobiday o Anyanyo Kavita (June 1971)

Are there words worth speaking? Memories that remain memorable?
Thoughts, or feelings, that haven't been tasted, tried?
Or do all questions just grope a blind man's sky?'
Sometimes a scene opens, that he has himself contrived:
a food-glutted female, joy personified,
bares breasts, opens arms, laughs in filtered lust;
he makes her play, gives her another countenance,
scripts for her a different role of dalliance.
A lively breeze seems to return a living moment
till a deeper darkness swallows all sentience.

And sometimes a heart – smoky, immense,
rends sleep's veil, pierces the flesh, rattles the bones,
by the fiery force of ancient, inveterate habit
jerks into motion, emits sparks, then stops.

April 1967 [Rewritten 1 June 1967]

The Poet's Old Age

Far too long he'd been thrall to a strange disease;
life's rich gifts, that now come our way, now bid us goodbye,
all seemed to want to glow *through* him, piercing him,
with the radiance of a preternatural darkness.

Pleasures, dreams, languor, sensations, feelings of the heart –
it seemed they were not what they revealed that minute;
they sought to transform themselves in farther seclusion
and thereto claimed his help, his readiness.

But now he's recovered. Now he easily takes in
how cool palm kernel is, how lovely young women are,
for it's no longer necessary to translate every darned thing
dangerously into word-strings, goaded by bilious ire.

His constant companions – lust and rage, two handsome wolves,
whom he had danced in and out of the alphabet's hoops of fire –
are now mere worms. But no regrets. For in another sleek shelter
he is now positioned – as safe as a brahmin in his house.

Veins swollen with the pressure of hard effort he used to have,
back humped, nerves shattered, a quest that bashed its head on walls;
gradually new friends wiped off all that stress –
naps, games of ludo with granddaughters, detective novels.

Squeezing out the last drop who knows when it slid out,
the pearl that had clung to him so long – cruel, obdurate.
By now healthy, tranquil, immobile,

on the beach for ever resounding with the sea's waves,
in the path of any boy picnicking, curiosity-driven,
lies just a shell – the proverbial seven decades.

1969

The Death of a Prostitute

None but her sisters and co-workers bore her on their shoulders.
Heads lowered, beads of sweat on eyelids, fumbling in their footsteps,
like a group of girls turned serious, suddenly oblivious of play,
they were somewhat flustered to face the sky and others.

The day's expansive sunshine changed their looks.
All the faces looked alike. All the bodies were vexed by the breeze.
Covered by embarrassment – unfamiliar, uncomfortable, unexpected –
they cowered and shrank, leaning on each other for support.

In this different country they lost their identity. Their youth and
                                                    womanliness
became penniless, for it seemed nowhere were there any lustful men
                                                              left.
Just a dumb, still afternoon. And one person, seemingly in a drunken
stupor, drowned in unassailable sleep.

The smart-arse fire licks up all her wetness.
Spreads its gourmet tongue, swallows breasts, genitals, knees.
Invades even those secret cracks where no mad lover had descended
and greedily gobbles the remaining grains of salt.

Evening comes to the city. The rest of them trudge home.
The street lamps wink. The alley smells give encouragement.
Firm ground beneath their feet, the sisters stand upright once more
to be consumed in the fires of lesser hungers.

>   16 January 1967 [Rewritten 7-8 March 1967]

A Juncture of Time

My paternal great-grandfather's name I do not know.
My mother's name, never mentioned, I can just about recall.
She, a wife, a married woman, but really a girl,
struggling hard to bring me forth, succeeding, melting in the heat
of her recently activated youth, disappeared
and is totally forgotten today. Yet suddenly this midnight
she descends, spreads in my bloodstream. Mother, I salute you,
I kiss you, woman whom I never knew, never saw,
but who's still not peeved! I did see you once
in faded, obscure sepia — eyes closed, lip-lines asleep,
in the arms of a thin youth, as if you were still in this world,
and in the masses of your dishevelled hair, even beautiful — almost.
But tell me, were you already past then, rising on another horizon,
or floating like a dream in a consciousness both waking and sleeping,
suspended in the air like a dust-speck or a plant-fibre,
of this earth, yet homeless, unsure, without a sense of direction?
So then, was it at that time
that I, cleaving you, giving you pain, came down
that traditional path along which my father and ancient forefathers
had each blindly sowed his own death-seed —
came down from sheltered darkness to a splinter of light, to doubts,
from ignorant, immediate satisfaction to wild efforts full of struggles?
Forgive me, Mother. I pushed you aside — you whose breasts were of
no use. I sought, grabbed other nourishment, for life is irresistible,
whilst you, so controlled, so affectionate,
gently let me go, let me loose betwixt new moon and full moon:
fidgeting, whirling, dying, yet flushed with conquest-lust, enthused,
day and night in the arms of two lovers sporting eternal youth,

day and night automatically mobile through desire,
as though I was immortal, as though life was really great,
as though you never existed, or as though I wasn't
your very own unbearable labour!
Yet today, in the middle of the night, you seem to be
eager, restless, moving about.
As when at dawn the tramcar's noise tears dreams, the cave of dreams
is pierced by the street lamp's lingering light, and the fresh sun
rapes the curtain, trumpeting the new day's arrival
to the walls, to the table — even so, with the same ineluctability,
diurnal, repeated, like the next date on the calendar,
you too seem imminent, for ever begun
and for ever unfinished.

My paternal great-grandfather's name I do not know. But my paternal
grandfather, they say, was brainy, munificent, fond of his drink —
hence neither long-lived nor propertied. Did I inherit
his intellect or his penchant for reckless self-squandering?
I don't know. Don't know what's intellect or heritage.
Along what branching boughs, difficult to discern,
what pathway of water or seed, what alignment with distant fate,
or from what nameless, bottomless, inaccessible deep
spring intelligence, inclination, inspiration, one's own nature —
whence my sense of selfhood, my individual identity —
I have no idea at all.
Nevertheless, though I've walked many a long road
without directing towards you any dream, any thought,
yet in this still night, when I have neither company nor sleep,
it seems it's you who's the subtle drug in my blood, the strange
restlessness in my heart — you, Mother! Dead girl, self-giver —
in a literal sense, not in oblique signals like me,
for your sacrifice was no metaphor being constantly built,
constantly courted and rejected,
but performed beyond dispute in a unique toil.
Odd — how in sepia you are still just an adolescent, whilst I see
so many grey hairs on my head, teeth sadly missing in my mouth.
Yet odder still is how within myself
this and every minute
a child still wants to live, a youth still kindles the furnace of his heart,

an old man crawls on his knees towards his last bed.
As if every moment was a juncture of two moments, of birth and death,
the same moment being repeated for fifty-nine years –
a death, and at the same time, a new life.
Thus your death too is like an image, a hidden sign
whereby by losing you I've been empowered,
enriched, not impoverished;
I've filled the gap of that original, beneficent loss
by loving, all my life, poetry
and women.

Who are these two: slender young woman and ecstatic youth
who in the tender gap between touching each other
hold the whole world, or are perhaps the heralds
of the world still waiting to be born? The young man
is lovely of limb, but not athletic – half-born, being born,
knees fixed on stone, as if he's still half-imprisoned
in the bondage of primal matter, though his upper half
has already come to life and therefore can kiss.
But the girl is complete, radiant in her new-lit youth, very delicate:
in her very-soft finger and breast's touch
in her waist's extra-gentle bend
she bequeaths the necessary remaining vitality
to one who's fainted but is avid of life,
pours into his kissing lips
the essence of her own cool body,
milk, wine, honey –
so he, filling his breath with the fiery mercy of a first mother,
can become human, freed from the tyranny of matter,
can be revealed, ripened –
just as I too want to be revealed, as that still couple is revealed,
and in that couple is revealed an individual's genius.
In brief, I too want to be a creator.

Mother, don't laugh, don't think I'm full of myself.
I am just an ardent lover
of words, and of girls.
But love, on its own, is not enough. Knowledge and laborious research
are also needed,
though nowhere is there a final answer to our questions.

Sometimes I've thought that the artist is nature's rival,
making up for all its wants;
but if genius too is just a display of life, and life depends on the body,
then there's nothing, neither poetry nor art,
that's not under nature's rule.
Thus it seems that creatures can only give birth
and creation's shrouded in a mystery without beginning;
blessed, hence, are they who live just by pursuing their senses
and those who are in search of an ineffable light.
But those who are interpolated, like myself, in a half-way house,
residents of neither this nor that other shore,
but solely in quest of illicit chemistry
through travel and dialogue,
so thoughts can be apprehended by the senses,
and even what the senses bestow
can gain a thinkable dimension, become slowly understood:
what will you say about them? What's their goal, what do they
deserve, what's their destiny?
As for me,
when I was young I thought poetry itself was love,
or an overflow of desire,
a tastier butter produced by the churning of blood;
but nowadays other ideas
sometimes come to haunt me – especially
in a still night such as this, lacking company,
even poetry seems like deceit, a consolation, a mere alternative,
and the honey of a woman's body seems more desirable than poetry:
but I, an old man, have lost all.
But nothing's lost – everything abides, exists –
the event that's already happened keeps walking with us,
can even, perhaps, be retrieved.
Indeed our sole duty is just that – the retrieval.
If you say that's impossible, nevertheless the sheer attempt
at recovery is laudable, and he whose only resources are words
must perforce manage everything with words – however hard it seems.
And that's why I labour without cease.

Mother, please don't mind, this is my soliloquy.
I know you are inexperienced, a mere girl.
But you are dead, and the business of the dead

I understand so little that therein even imagination is pallid.
So I say, if at all possible,
please come once, let me see you;
with that youth of yours, just budded – so delicate –
give me your touch, the touch that is imperceptible.
And if in that other place by now you have learnt
something that is still beyond my ken,
that too, please
tell me before you leave.

23-24 November 1967

Welcome and Farewell

Along what distant evening's veranda does Aladdin light his lamp?
Brooklyn on this shore, on the other the skyline of Manhattan.
Between them a port, ships, a bridge's picturesque pose,
a helicopter flying hither and thither like fluttering hope.
I'm in a hotel room. Am used to it now. It's almost my own.
The season's summer, young and lovely June. At my window
the sea breeze. June it is, but Asharh is imminent.
Not evening, but a rain-resonant dawn, the sky blurred above the yard,
algae rejoicing on the pond, bamboo groves smoky in the rain.
'How delightful is this rain, so delightful to wake from sleep!' –
I hadn't learnt language yet, but the feelings were there –
sharp, freshly provoked, dispersed everywhere –
in the quilt's touch, in the wonder of seeing moss,
in the little but endless *Ramayan* wrapped in the caresses of words.
And this rain too was specially for me. My thrill was its goal.
Listening to its sound, I seem silently to cross
my self's demarcated boundary, and effortlessly recover
other such obsessed dawns – elsewhere – so many of them,
on Ramna's extensive grass, on tram tracks in Ballygunge.
Even on the pavement of Fifth Avenue
suddenly the other day
such a shower came down, with the deep clatter of thunder,
with the smell of dust and such cool damp gusts of wind
that I, stalled, immobile,

shaking for two or three prolonged minutes,
nearly retrieved certain things,
nearly went back to various familiar houses
which were really mine but were long lying empty,
were habitable, though no one lived there any more,
were perhaps ready, waiting even now for me,
though I would never get there.
And so
what was not so long ago a bright mass of ascending lights
gradually sinks in the sea mist,
the helicopter comes down like hope defeated,
an endless sadness comes down all over the evening's veranda
this June, in Brooklyn, in my mind.

But I don't go out, I stay put
(wherever I happen to be at any given time)
just in case any of you call – to spend Saturday afternoon with me,
or at ten in the morning, after dropping your daughter off at school,
hair down, relaxed, informal,
or late at night, spurred by some sudden emotion.
Come, each when it suits you,
come, whenever any of you wish to,
visit my dreams, my mind, whispering, or on the phone line.
Come back, let's return to your time and mine.
Know that every moment is a good time –
there's no such thing as an awkward time.
Know that whenever you come I shall make time,
know that I've no agenda but what's also yours.
There you are. Tea? I have Abed's biscuits for you.
(Do you remember setting feet in that shop and being immediately hit
by the bewitching smell of fresh bread –
subtle, beery, as if it wished to say something –
something else – beyond our comprehension?
And outside on the wall the ivy in heaps of green,
the path quiet and lonely, the Buriganga flowing gently,
its evening, soft and colourful, wishing to whisper something
in our ears – beyond our comprehension?)
Look, I've got everything ready;
day by day, by piecing bits together, working ever so hard,
I have constructed you – my friend – beautiful, golden boy,

and you, dearest, my beautiful, golden girl.
I have made time
by digging a secret tunnel into time,
as a puny creepy-crawly burrows a hole, turns it into his stronghold.
And where would you yourself find
lodgings after your own heart, if not here?
Come, let me take a look at you,
come, let me take a look at myself,
come, let me hear myself in your voice – say something, please.
Why are you silent? Don't you recognize me?
See, here's my hand outstretched, why are you far from my touch?
Why do you avert your face? Why do you fade away?
Then are you dead? Are you both dead?
Golden boy and girl, can't you stop for an hour or two – not even you?
Even the pair of you – are you no better than shiuli flowers
or lamp-lured moths?
You are nothing. There's nothing. The primeval sea-mist
rubs off Manhattan, Ballygunge, Noakhali, Purana Polton,
or tears that thread of consciousness whence they hang.
Which is why the letterbox is empty, the phone never rings, the lodger
never returns home, and from the balcony railing the yellow sari
hangs for ever, lacking a body to wrap itself around.
Survival – strenuous as it is – is only for
Elephanta, Parthenon, Altamira;
Ajanta's brighter in the dark, but the rest simply vamoose.

But nothing living craves
Ajanta's immortality, if you call it that.
Because they are rooted in death-awareness,
it's life the living are hungry for, instinctively –
thinking as long as there's heat in the body, there's no dying,
just as a foolish child, closing his own eyes,
fancies his enemy can't see him either.
Nor is death unique. He too plays in many guises, under many names.
It isn't just the body that's mortal,
the heart, the mind, love – all are transient, fragile.
Thus even those who are alive at the same time
do not breathe at the same pace;
sometimes they become dead to each other,

sometimes one is dead even to oneself
without knowing it, without mourning it, like a lantern at dawn,
or as steam from a boiling kettle
frees itself by losing its liquidity.
Take, for instance, that girl, with whom I once
shared a bunch of grapes – lip to lip, breast to breast,
yet didn't finish them off,
whom I've called Amita, Roma, Debjani, Kankabati,
whom I have decked with colours dark and pale,
with hair black and brown,
in whose eyes many a time I've seen
the enchantment of Bengal's rains,
flecks of ice-glinting northern sunshine,
in whose pursuit I've walked
who knows how many roads unawares, laid tortuous traps
with words upon words,
harried by how many nocturnal gales,
have swum across countless seas of loneliness –
who has nevertheless not yielded, hasn't grown with natural zest
like a tree in vigorous health,
but rather like camphor in a jar,
even under a sturdy, tight-fitting lid,
has, unknown to me, diminished in the darkness –
becoming less – and less:
until at last all that's left
is a sudden muted scent, or on the page of a notebook –
a faded address.
And what is almost incredible, that very sophisticated lover –
lord of colours, pleasures, divertissements, richer still in angst –
even he's left his kingdom of the heart now, and is on the run –
like an idiot. – Then was he really not me? Was he someone else?
The 'I' that I remember – does it not exist any more? Do I too die
every minute? And the line between 'am' and 'am not' isn't clear?
But look, I am not dead.
In that case,
this person whom I call 'myself' –
who is
he then?

He for ever bids you farewell, for ever welcomes you in.
Open your old scribblings –
maybe they're someone else's – but they're yours all the same.
You purse your lips a little now, but you were inside those words
and still are. Think, how often you have
re-written the old anew, woven into the same fabric
two layers of time, and still that cloth hasn't burst
under such pressure. Likewise
your being is inconstant, yet continuous,
present, absent, imminent, arrived.
Recall how many nights
were burnt on the desk of dreams, how many days
were pulverized by grinding metals,
still someone seemed to stand outside the door, gently knocking,
as if something new would begin.
Have you not grasped this yet –
that person wasn't a lover or a friend,
but just your next self?
It is for him that you have stretched your hand
this very minute, in this evening hour
charged with endless sadness, this June, here in Brooklyn,
or somewhere else, wherever it may be,
any minute, always.

Let go. Go forth. Get it back.

1967

A Poem for Savitri

Who is there, who has never, in an anguished moment,
or racked by the vibration between metal and hammer,
wished gently to lay his consciousness, debate-torn,
on the lap of simple death, with no pain?
              'With no pain!' The young, perfumed poet
hadn't forgotten to include this term. He'd wanted
a balmy night, a bed in a flowering garden:
to wrap himself in a quilt of sweet song that was creaturely

and sink into a pleasurable doze:
so his death might be a garland of springtime,
strung with the essence of flowers and the moon's rays,
with which the foreseeing Fates might wish to proffer him
advance honours.

But the end
came in traditional death-sweat, in blood-spewing.
He did not look out the window and behold
Hispanic steps bathed in the deep loveliness of blue,
didn't hear the dreamy murmur of fountains whispering of the past
or even the faintest approaching hum of his desired Fame.
He didn't grasp that this was Rome – proud city without a beginning,
where scattered aplenty here and there, brightly burned
images of that Beauty he had worshipped.
Didn't open Fanny's letter; in the end
didn't even remember that he hadn't opened it.
His unwritten, unfinished poems, disappointed protégés,
had long since left home. And around the last drops
of his awareness
the occasional firefly flickered like a needle piercing darkness –
sometimes his sheet burned him, sometimes he groaned in his cough.
At that moment he *became* his body,
just a body, a lump of agony, the breath of a stricken beast.
There was nothing else in the end.

Then is that the only barrier? Fear – that one might suffer?
Hesitation – in case there's horrible torment?
Only for that reason one endures
those two women, who with veiled faces thresh paddy continuously,
one with her foot on the pedal, very nimble,
the other briskly gathering with her hand,
rhythmically separating grain from husk,
following a rule that cannot be overturned,
garnering the grain, and discarding what had erstwhile been
the famous gold of fields across the earth?
Hence this secret unease, as if this little space
packed under the lid of day and night was too tight for us,
stifled us at times: or as someone revived

by complicated surgery might drag out
a few extra days with a dead stranger's heart inside his chest.
Or it's as though something which had been found
by digging in far Mohenjodaro and was on that account
most precious, dyed with history, mysterious,
all the more beautiful because of the loving gazes of many,
radiant under much research,
was suddenly, by indisputable proof,
shown to be a total forgery, and a trivial item at that,
a toy from the Chariot Festival fair, costing four annas.
                         But nevertheless a few spare friends
survive: as the first taste of sunshine in the sip
of morning's tea in bed, slowly floating up
from the darkness of non-being;
returning to the habits of a patient desk, books and papers.
Or that dead of night in Bhadra – returning home
to the moonlight sleeping on the veranda's concrete –
looking wet, almost transparent, so calm, extensive, and enchanting
that the solidity of surrounding objects melted
and weeds, gutters, slums – all became as ravishing
as a painted scene.
Or imagine suddenly hearing on the radio
a line of Tagore song
which was still stuck on the frontier of your youth.
These continue to be yours. And even perhaps
another kind of chastity isn't at least incredible.
Somewhere beyond the instability of circumstances
there does perhaps exist
personal love,
not given to self-advertising, yet felt
continuously, ineffably.

She had foreknowledge, being married to a man who would die.
Knew there was no difference between one year and fifty years.
So she told nobody, never wept even in secret.
Humbly, privately she just conserved herself
for three hundred and sixty-five days
in the oozing of desire, drop by drop – in hope, in faith:

as though her new-found love
was not accessible, not given, not a common wedding-gift,
but had to be earned like a poor man's plate of grub
day by day by the body's toil, with immense patience,
or was a studied pursuit
that draining her, would itself grow big and strong,
ready for the last challenging thrust.
And so in that juncture of time
it was not quite clear who shed lustre on whom:
was the girl lit up by the radiant person,
or the god by the girl's pure brilliance?

How much she had left behind – sunlight, the hillside in blossom,
the flourishing forest abounding in peacocks and streams!
The year's memories, grief shed by the year: forsaken;
the body of the man she had chosen to love: equally forsaken –
as though it was an eggshell, from which the bird had flown,
or the first draft of a poem, which the poet now ignored.
She never once looked back, did not lament,
nor trembled with terror at the epiphanic apparition,
but calm, free of doubt, welcomed that particular moment
as though it was another marriage hour – one she had waited for –
as though she'd once again become her father's maiden daughter
and had once more set forth on her journey,
her independent search for a lover.
Easily therefore
with no regret, no sighs,
counselled by her heart, in love's simple faith,
she laid down the dead man's head from her lap,
left what was mere inert matter,
and stood up, never thinking that what remained then to be done
was terrifying, strictly forbidden.

Night was then approaching. Grey and tawny in the twilight,
the forest landscape was delusory – motionless, as if it had no breath.
Not a leaf stirred. All trees looked unreal – like crafted stone.
No restless eyes, no moving animals – not even a trail.
Only that little spot where she might put her foot down
floated somehow to view and vanished with each step taken,
as the past moment fades into the next.

Thus they walked on, the pair of them:
a god incarnate, and a thwarted love.
                              God walked ahead
in slow steps awkward for him, casting the occasional
sidelong, backward glance,
trying to take in human language, to which his ears were unaccustomed,
answering prayers, not his usual practice –
since someone was following him, was at his heels,
almost brushing his wrap,
nearly causing flutters in his sovereignty
with the sweet smell of transience:
it was neither any Yudhishthir, heroic in truthfulness,
nor Nachiketa, rich in knowledge,
but a female in love – a mere girl.
                    She, however, didn't realize what a marvel this was:
this god, who had to be worshipped, was nevertheless
someone she could argue with too,
no longer unrivalled either, though for ever the supreme legislator,
and who, shrinking himself, making himself smaller,
was accepting parity with her. At least he pretended to,
pretended to listen when she became murmurous
like a sudden rush of wind sweeping through the still forest,
as if to meet her need an exception could be made
even in what was eternally ordained.
So she put her questions like a child, wanted an impossible gift,
forgot the unbridgeable gulf between herself and the god;
the farther he went, the farther she was eager to pursue him –
as though the love within her was so powerful in its upward surge
that the god of death himself, the all-destroyer,
must perforce honour her.

          How amazing though, that she didn't understand any of this!

But my mind, here's your chance to learn
the price of this thing we call mortality.
Because we lose all our loved ones, constantly piling the absences
within our inner vaults, the demand for compensation arises.
We feel we must fight, fight with the divine – at least have a dialogue.
I know you got love, without asking for it, without paying a duty on it,
and sometimes also got

a few lines of poetry, propelled by love's ecstasy.
But tell me, were they reliable?
Did they teach you how to survive from day to day?
There's still time, take this opportunity to learn:
what stays with you — such as the dead,
and the crowd of your own dead selves,
and that ready-made trap, a piece of white paper,
within which from time to time the dead are entrapped
and whence they fly away again,
whilst you, thorn-tormented, wait for their return —
by the use of such resources you too, at some moment,
may perhaps gain God's ears,
leap across that ever-widening hiatus.
It's that very hard striving that's called self-cession,
which begins with death and ends in resurrection.

1968

Notes to the Poems

It is necessary for readers of Bengali poetry to get used to the Bengali month-names and to the grid and associated images of the year's six seasons. The grip, on a poet's imagination, of the wild rainy season and the serene post-rains season needs to be understood. The months and seasons of the Bengali calendar are as follows:

1. Baishakh, summer (mid-April to mid-May).
2. Jyaishtha, summer (mid-May to mid-June).
3. Asharh, monsoon (mid-June to mid-July).
4. Srabon, monsoon (mid-July to mid-August).
5. Bhadra, post-rains (mid-August to mid-September).
6. Ashwin, post-rains (mid-September to mid-October).
7. Kartik, autumn (mid-October to mid-November).
8. Agrahayan, autumn (mid-November to mid-December).
9. Poush, winter (mid-December to mid-January).
10. Magh, winter (mid-January to mid-February).
11. Phalgun, spring (mid-February to mid-March).
12. Chaitra, spring (mid-March to mid-April).

In contrast to the Bengali names, which evoke the tropical seasons of his native land, Bose sometimes uses, very effectively, the month-names of the Christian calendar, such as December, January, or June, to convey the 'otherness' of the seasons experienced in other lattitudes.

BANDIR BANDANA (1930): The Bengali plural ending is not always physically present and sometimes has to be guessed from the context. In the title of this collection the word *bandana,* song or hymn of praise, is functioning as a collective singular, referring to all the poems, so the title could be translated with a plural as 'A Prisoner's Songs of Praise'.

'A Prisoner's Song of Praise': In the title of the name-poem the singular is obviously more appropriate. The word *bandi* can indeed also refer to a hired professional singer who chants a king's praise at a royal court, so there is an oblique suggestion to that effect in the title of the poem, but the poem itself makes it quite clear that within it *bandi* means primarily a prisoner. Let us say that there is a touch of word-play and paradox in the phrase *bandir bandana*.

'where the god of the fish-signed flag flies his pennant': The Hindu god of love, known by various names such as Kama, Madana, and Kandarpa, is supposed to fly a fish-marked flag that is his insignia.

'No Other Wishes': The twenty-first century girl reading (or rather, not reading) his poem makes an arch reference to Tagore's well-known poem 'Choddosho Sal' (The Year 1400, *Chitra,* 1896) invoking the Bengali year 1400: 'A hundred years from today / who are you, sitting, reading a poem of mine, / under curiosity's sway – / a hundred years from today?' (translation mine).

KANKABATI (1937): Kankabati is the name of a Bengali folk-tale maiden.

NATUN PATA (1940): The title, referring to the entire collection, should be understood as a plural: 'New Leaves'. I have translated the title of the name-poem too as 'New Leaves', as that poem talks about the publication of a new collection of poems, and a book will have many pages: *pata* in Bengali means both leaf and page.

'There Isn't Time': As a student of English literature, Bose would have been very familiar, of course, with Andrew Marvell's 'To his Coy Mistress'.

'Gods are Two: 1': Readers may wish to compare the statement of this poem with Tagore's critiquing, in some of his poems, of the same traditional Hindu notion of the sense-apprehended universe as a series of illusory phenomena; see, for instance, 'On the Doctrine of Maya', 'Play', and 'Renunciation' in *I Won't Let You Go: Selected Poems* of Rabindranath Tagore (translated by K. K. Dyson, Bloodaxe Books, Newcastle-upon-Tyne: 1991, UBSPD, New Delhi, 1992).

'Still the Koel Calls': The koel is the Indian cuckoo, one of the most indefatigable singers of the Indian spring, with a high-pitched, insistent, and intensely sweet song.

'Sea-bathing': This and the next two poems, 'Peace by the Lake' and 'Morning in Chilka', were written by Bose during a holiday in Orissa with his newly married wife (they had got married on 19 July 1934).

'Everest': Unsuccessful attempts on Everest in the thirties: Ruttledge (1933, 1936), Shipton (1935), Harold William Tilman (1938).

EK PAISAY EKTI (1942): The title of this collection could be translated as 'A Pice Apiece'.

'The Rains Come to Santiniketan': Santiniketan in Birbhum District houses, of course, the school and the university founded by Tagore, who was still alive when this poem was written; this would be his last rainy season. Bose visited Santiniketan with his wife and daughters in May 1941—the last time that he would meet Tagore.

'Farewell at Midday': For the background to this poem, and 'Padma' and 'Hilsa' from *Damayanti,* please see the comments in the Introduction. The place-names Narayanganj and Goalundo are also clarified there.

BAISHE SRABON (1942): The title of this collection means 'The Twenty-second of Srabon', commemorating the date of Tagore's death according to the Bengali calendar (22 Srabon 1348).

'For Rabindranath': Written on Tagore's birth anniversary (25 Baishakh) the year after his death. The image of the 'golden deer' is derived from the well-known episode in the Ramayana, in which Ravana kidnaps Sita after having lured Rama away from their hut with the assistance of Maricha. Maricha assumes the form of an exquisite spotted deer and wanders in front of the forest dwelling of Rama and Sita. Sita wishes her husband to capture the deer for her, alive or dead. Rama goes off, leaving Sita under the charge of his brother Lakshmana. The deer, when slain at a distance, assumes his real form, and imitating Rama's voice, utters a cry of distress. Hearing that cry, Sita insists that Lakshmana must go and see what has happened to Rama. Lakshmana goes reluctantly, and it is in that space of time that Sita is abducted. From a traditional point of view, the golden deer stands for life's illusory pleasures, chasing which we bring ruin upon ourselves. But by extension the image has also come to acquire a positive meaning, representing the yearnings and passions which make life worth living, whatever the cost. This meaning is enshrined in a popular song of Tagore's, which goes something like 'No matter what any of you may say, I want the golden deer ...' and which probably helped to consolidate the positive meaning. This is the sense in which the image is used here.

DAMAYANTI (1943): This volume is named after Damayanti, the wife of Nala, from one of the important stories narrated in the Mahabharata. Damayanti is an epitome of constancy, resourcefulness, and fortitude in adversity. Bose named his younger daughter after this character.

'O Africa, Covered in Shadows': This poem has an interesting genesis. Mussolini's aggression against Abyssinia in 1935–6 was the immediate trigger for the thoughts of many intellectuals turning towards Africa's plight. Amiya Chakravarty, who had met various thinkers in Britain who were deeply concerned about Africa, begged Tagore to write a poem about the continent of Africa, and Tagore obliged. At the request of Prince Nyabongo of Uganda, who was an Oxford friend of Chakravarty, Tagore later did an English version of the poem, which was re-translated into Swahili and disseminated in black Africa. For further details, see Naresh Guha (ed.), *Kabir Chithi Kabike*, Papyrus, 1995, p. 24 and p. 177 ff. Tagore's original poem exists in variant versions. The version in his collected works is from February 1937; another version was published later in the same year in the Ashwin 1344 issue (Sept-Oct 1937) of Bose's own magazine *Kavita*. This version must have inspired the present poem; the opening line of Bose's poem is a direct quotation from a line in that version of Tagore's poem. An English rendering of Tagore's February 1937 version of 'Africa' may be found in William Radice's *Selected Poems* of Tagore (Penguin Books, Harmondsworth, 1985, p. 102).

'Padma': 'with two arms she embraces Dhaka and Faridpur': I.e. the two districts of Dhaka and Faridpur on her two banks.

'fresh hilsa': The hilsa, a tasty sea-fish of the shad family that comes up the rivers to spawn, is a great Bengali favourite. See the poem 'Hilsa' in this volume.

abir and Holi: *Abir* is the red powder which merrymakers scatter on one another in the spring festival, Holi.

'Stars, scentless kunda flowers, open': The original adjective is *gondhohara*, suggesting that the flowers have 'lost' their scent. There seems to be some confusion about the kunda's status in this respect. Bengalis usually think of the kunda as a flower without scent, whereas botanists identify it with the *jasminum multiflorum* or *jasminum pubescens,* which is fragrant. I suspect there are two flowers, both white, with the same name, one with fragrance and the other without it.

'A Day of Asharh': Gaurisringa: Gauri's peak, the original name of Everest.

RUPANTAR (1943): The title of this collection means 'Transformation'. I have translated the very first poem of the collection, bearing the same name.

DRAUPADIR SARI (1948): The title of the collection means 'Draupadi's Sari'. The volume is named after the celebrated episode in the Mahabharata where Krishna's intervention saves Draupadi from the public humiliation of being stripped in court by Duhshasana: her sari is endlessly augmented, so that the more her tormentor pulls it, the more it unfolds. Draupadi's sari becomes a metaphor for the possibility of endless self-renewal.

'The Refugee': From the 1963 joint revised edition, *Damayanti: Draupadir Sari o Anyanyo Kavita* (Damayanti: Draupadi's Sari and Other Poems) to which some new poems were added while some of the older ones were left out.

'the Lake': An artificial lake, now officially known as Rabindra Sarobar, in Ballygunge, one of the southern districts of Calcutta.

Durga Puja: The annual festival of the goddess Durga in October, the most important religious festival of the Bengali Hindus.

Comilla District: Now in Bangladesh.

'Every day Satikanto sees all this': This may seem to contradict the previous assertion, in l.13, that Satikanto was walking by the Lake for the very first time. Actually, the poem proceeds in the manner of a short story. In the first stanza, Satikanto is walking by the Lake for the first time. By the third stanza, he is doing it on a daily basis. The fifth stanza asserts clearly that he is taking regular morning strolls by the Lake.

'Fog too could be handy at times ... on the boat, that very instant': The reference is to the story of Parashara and Satyavati in the Mahabharata. The sage Parashara created a veil of fog in order to make love to fisherman's daughter Satyavati on the boat on which she was the ferrywoman and he the passenger. The offspring of this union was Vyasa, to whom the authorship of the Mahabharata itself is ascribed.

Manoharpukur and Hindusthan Park are street-names.

'Come midday, I'm going to the Congress': To the headquarters of the Congress Party.

I am puzzled by the Dante reference: the only episode in the *Inferno* that Bose could be referring to is the story of Ugolino in Canto XXXIII, but the two stories do not match exactly. In Dante Ugolino has four sons, not two, and though they are all starving, there is no suggestion that the children are losing their sight, and no boy says 'Father, I can't see anything!' to Ugolino. There are three statements from the children, but none matches this one. Ugolino watches all the children drop dead; then it is he who goes blind and gropes over each child for two days, before dying himself. The mismatch could be attributed to the translation in which Bose knew the work, but if, as is likely, he knew it in the well circulated verse translation of Dorothy Sayers, available as a Penguin classic since 1949, we cannot blame it on Sayers' version, which is quite faithful to the original here. It is possible that he is conflating the story of Ugolino with another story altogether; in any case, it is Satikanto, the writer hero of the poem, who is making a slight error!

'Twenty-four Parganas': The name of a southern district of West Bengal.

SHEETER PRARTHANA: BASANTER UTTAR (1955): The title of the volume means 'Winter's Prayer: Spring's Answer'.

'After Death: Before Birth': John Donne's 'A Nocturnal upon St. Lucy's Day, Being the shortest day' might well have been the springboard for this poem.

The fair in Santiniketan refers to the Poush Mela, celebrated on the 7th of Poush, which tends to fall in the third week of December.

'this cold room, facing the north': The 202 Rashbehari Avenue apartment was indeed a north-facing one.

'After Forty': 'shredded minutes': The word 'minutes' for 'moments' introduces a marvellous double meaning in English which is so apt that I don't want to resist it!

'Monsoon Day': The kadamba tree flowers in the rainy season, bearing strongly scented yellow-orange ball-shaped flowers, which are really composed of numerous small florets. The bel is of the jasmine family and bears fragrant white flowers. All the flowers mentioned in the last stanza have strong romantic associations and occur frequently in the work of poets, including Tagore's.

'Calcutta': See the comments on this poem in the Introduction.

'Your ... dawn, freshly bathed / in the water-jets of the municipal workers' hose-pipes': During the British Raj it was customary for municipal workers to hose down the city streets with jets of water at dawn. The practice survived even after Independence; I have seen it myself in the late forties. The watering kept the dust under control and cooled the air too.

'my Ujjayini, my America': A fine example of East-West intertextuality, without a doubt inspired by John Donne's line, 'O my America! my new-found-land' (Elegy XIX, 'To his Mistress going to Bed'), and at the same time invoking Ujjayini (modern Ujjain) as a famous city of ancient India, especially as the seat of the Gupta emperors, and as associated with the name of the great Sanskrit poet and dramatist Kalidasa (circa the 5th century A.D.), who is supposed to have flourished at the court of Ujjayini as one of its 'nine jewels'. In Kalidasa's celebrated poem, the *Meghaduta,* where an exile in the highlands of central India sends a message to his wife in the far north by means of a wandering rain-cloud, the cloud is asked to make a slight detour so that it can pass over Ujjayini. Ujjayini as the city of Kalidasa, the home of sophisticated culture, has been much extolled in the poetry of Tagore. In one poem, Tagore speaks of having visited Ujjayini in a dream, to find his first love from a previous birth (see 'Dream', *I Won't Let You Go, Selected Poems* of Rabindranath Tagore, translated by Dyson, op. cit., pp. 119–22). In another poem ('Shekal', *Kshanika*) Tagore wishes he could have been born in the days of Kalidasa, when he might perchance have been the tenth jewel at the royal court, and as a favour from the king, might have asked for a house surrounded by a garden on the secluded edge of Ujjayini.

'the poinciana regia of my last summer': the Bengali name 'krishnachura' (Krishna's crest) can refer to two separate trees of the family Caesalpiniaceae: a) what botanists call the true krishnachura, the *caesalpinia pulcherrima,* a shortish tree (properly speaking, a large shrub) with flowers displaying shades of orange and red, and b) the *poinciana regia,* a taller tree (Hindi 'gulmor') which is a mass of dazzling red flowers in the early summer. The second is the more common meaning. Bose is undoubtedly referring to the second tree here. I have preferred to use the botanical name in the translation, leaving it, however, unitalicized, in consonance with the practice followed in this volume in respect of native flora. I must confess that I did agonize over this decision. The krishnachura is such a potent symbol in modern Bengali poetry that I am sure most Bengalis would opine that I should have written 'the krishnachura of my last summer'; however, translation is not really for the benefit of the native speakers of the source language. I felt the original Bengali name or the Hindi name would not convey to non-Indian readers who have not seen this tree in flower what a stunning spectacle it is—and the visual image is very important in this line—whereas there is an explicit acknowledgement of its grandeur in 'regia', and the Latin name also seals the identity of the tree in a transnational context. The Hindi name is sometimes written in English as 'gulmohar' or 'gulmohur', sometimes even as 'gold mohur', but these fanciful materialistic interpretations are likely to be corruptions from Anglo-Indian times; the *h* is most probably intrusive. The flowers do not really bear any resemblance to gold coins. Etymologically, 'gulmor' is most likely to mean 'peacock-flower': from *gul,* 'rose', 'flower', and *mor* (from *mayur*), 'peacock', and both the trees bear flowers which have a certain resemblance to a generic feather-shape. In poetry of the *bhakti* traditions Krishna is often imagined as wearing a crown of peacock-feathers; hence the name 'krishnachura' or Krishna's crest. It is not uncommon for Bengali writers to use the term 'gulmor'; Bose writes 'gulmor' in the poem 'Shopkeepers', also translated in this volume, and so does Tagore in a well-known poem in *Mahua*. 'Peacock-flower', by which name I believe the gulmor is sometimes known in Indian English, was an option for me, but I feared that the image might give rise to the false idea among non-Indian readers that the flowers were blue-green.

'Prayer of a Winter Night': Please see the comments on this poem in the Introduction, which will elucidate its background.

BAROMASER CHHORA (1956): The title means 'Nursery Rimes for the Twelve Months'.

'Mimi, On Your Birthday': Mimi is the pet name of the poet's elder daughter, Meenakshi. As Bose was a noted writer for children, I have included this poem as a sample of his writing for children. The shiuli, shephali, or shephalika is the *nyctanthes arbor-tristis,* with exquisitely scented star-shaped flowers which blossom at night and carpet the ground in the morning. The flowers are associated with the post-monsoon season and the Puja holidays, and epitomize the transience of beauty in Tagore's songs.

JE-ANDHAR ALOR ADHIK (1958): The title can be translated as 'The Darkness that is Greater than Light'.

'To Memory: 2': 'till gradually men's countless children grow old and disappear': Mutability and mortality are universal themes in poetry, but there is something in the phrasing that suggests that Bose's mind was echoing with the treatment of such themes in Anglo-Saxon poetry, e.g. in *The Seafarer* or *The Ruin*.

'The Surrender': Written when he was returning home after his first trip abroad, this poem begins with images of riverine East Bengal and of childhood which merge with those of the sea voyage being undertaken. In the second stanza, in the image of the sword leaping to the hand, there is a reference to a well-known Tagore poem about boyhood; an English translation of this Tagore poem, 'The Hero', can be found in William Radice's *Selected Poems* of Tagore (Penguin Books, Harmondsworth, 1985, pp. 68–9).

'To Arjun: from a Nameless Woman': Arjun, son of Kunti, is one of the five Pandava brothers in the epic Mahabharata, and a hero with many adventures to his credit. Kunti was also known as Pritha, hence Arjun's name Partha, meaning 'son of Pritha'. Draupadi is, of course, the wife of all the five Pandava brothers; 'that smart diplomat' is Krishna; Khandava is the name of a forest that burned down in the Mahabharata; and Vyasa is the sage to whom the authorship of the Mahabharata is ascribed.

'when faltering in the dark of your last exit': The 'Mahaprasthanika-parva' of the Mahabharata describes the last journey of the Pandavas, in course of which Draupadi and four of the Pandavas slip and die, one by one.

'Why?': Three poets from three lands, the Indian Valmiki, the supposed author of the Ramayana, Sappho, the ancient Greek poetess, and Virgil, the Latin poet, are cited in support of the thesis that poetry neither furthers man's material progress nor speeds up human salvation. Some may challenge this and maintain that listening to the tales of Rama's deeds does indeed further salvation!

" 'Two Birds' ": The title of this poem refers to a famous passage in the Upanishads (*Mundaka,* 3.1.1, also in *Svetasvatara,* 4.6) which speaks of two birds, for ever united, that live in the same tree, one eating the tasty fruit thereof, the other just watching: metaphors for the individual soul and the Universal Spirit.

Line 2: The word 'nakta' exists in the original line; it is the Sanskrit cognate word matching English 'night' and the other European words I have used in the translation, but these European words, from German, Spanish, and French, do not exist in the original poem: they replace some other poetic synonyms of 'night' which are impossible to parallel in English.

In the last line of the poem, 'householder' goes with the second stage of life in the Hindu scheme of 'the four stages of life'. But the idea of the sick artist is most certainly derived from European sources, especially writers like Charles Baudelaire or Thomas Mann. Bose effects a conflation between two dichotomies: the Indian one of the householder versus the wandering ascetic, and the European one of the bourgeois citizen versus the bohemian artist.

'In Reply to the Seasons': 'That injustice strung with Poushes and Phalguns, swinging laughter and tears': there is a reference in this line to a well-known Tagore song, echoed also in the phrase 'acted scenes' two lines below.

'Anuradha': There is a play of meanings in the name 'Anuradha', suggesting both a woman and a star-cluster. Anuradha is an asterism (the seventeenth of the twenty-seven Nakshatras) that is propitious to the traveller; a person travelling under the influence of this asterism is successful in his mission. The poem seems to remember some of the poet's travels in America in 1954.

'The Moment of Liberation': Gol Park and Kalighat: Calcutta localities.

In stanza 2, line 3, the original just refers to packets made of paper, but the next phrase makes it clear that packets made of newspaper are meant. Newspapers are routinely recycled into packets.

MORCHE-PORA PEREKER GAN (1966): I would translate the title of this volume as 'Songs of a Rusty Nail', referring to all the poems in the collection. The title of the name-poem, which lends its name to the whole collection, is translated as 'The Song of a Rusty Nail'.

'The Weeping Beauty': It was while teaching in the Comparative Literature Department of Indiana University in the fall semester of 1963 that Bose did a great deal of fresh thinking about epic poetry, comparing the Greek and Indian epics. His interest in the Mahabharata, always there, took a new turn. This poem, written while he was teaching in Brooklyn College the next semester (January-May 1964), takes off from a rather strange episode in the Mahabharata purporting to explain why it would be acceptable for Draupadi to have five husbands. The outline is somewhat like this. A group of gods going on an errand notice a golden lotus in the waters of the Ganges. As Indra tries to pick it up, he sees a woman of fiery glow standing in a deep part of the river, weeping. Her tears fall on the water as golden lotuses. Indra asks her why she is weeping. The woman leads him to a spot where a young man is playing a game of dice with a young woman. This young man takes no note of Indra, which enrages him. He blurts out that that the universe is governed by him, that he is its lord. The young man laughs and looks at Indra, whereupon Indra is immobilized. When the game of dice is over, the young man says to the woman who had brought Indra there, 'Bring him here, I shall crush his pride.' As soon as the woman touches Indra, he becomes numb and falls on the ground. The young man is none other than Shiva, who asks Indra not to be boastful ever again. Indra discovers four other Indras in captivity there, all punished because of their pride. These five Indras will be reincarnated as the five Pandavas. The woman who had been weeping golden lotuses is commanded by Shiva to become Draupadi, their joint wife.

Bose builds on the fact that though the woman seems to have a mysterious power, the story does not quite explain why she was weeping in the first place, or why her tears were falling as golden lotuses. He offers his own, modern interpretation, bringing himself into the story. Perhaps there is a link, in his mind, to the notion of *lachrymae rerum,* perhaps also to the Greek story of Niobe's tears.

'how the five elements ran': There is an Upanishadic reference here. See the note on 'Young Men and Young Women', *post.*

'Life on the Margin': It is interesting to note the mingling of geographical locations in the imagery of this poem. Passengers grabbing the tram's door-handle, who do not give up boarding just because they have heard a sudden scream, are most likely from Calcutta. The canal entering the river, with the boy staring as familiar landmarks recede, harks back to the poet's East Bengal childhood; the railway junction could be anywhere, but does have a whiff of the subcontinent about it; the underground station with grey pillars and humid air is taken directly from the urban American environment in which the poem was written.

'Other Germs': 'thirty-three crores of companies': Thirty-three crores represent the proverbial number of gods in Hindu lore, applied here ironically to the modern corporate world. The first half of the poem reflects the poet's amused observation of the phenomenon of American civilization trying to get rid of all suffering, physical and mental, from life.

'koi fish': This fish used to be—perhaps still is?—sold live in pots of water for freshness; hence its gasping has been a common sight to Bengalis and has contributed to certain idiomatic phrases.

'If one could really become immortal by giving up smoking!': The ironical comment of a smoker. Bose never did give up smoking.

'Icarus': See the comment on this poem in the Introduction for a very likely link between this poem and two items: a poem by Auden and a painting by Breughel. The story of Daedalus and his son Icarus is, of course, from Greek mythology. Daedalus was an ingenious craftsman to whom various inventions and constructions are ascribed, including the famous Labyrinth of Crete. Daedalus and his son Icarus were once imprisoned by King Minos of Crete in this very Labyrinth. Daedalus built wings with which to fly out. Icarus, however, flew too close to the sun, and the wax attaching his wings to his body melted. He fell to the sea and drowned, giving the name Icarian Sea to that stretch of the sea.

'Only by Holding on to You': Written while Bose was teaching for a year in the Wesleyan College of Bloomington, Illinois, this poem seems to have an underground spiritual connection with 'The Weeping Beauty' and 'Life on the Margin', *ante*. Kurukshetra is the battlefield where the great war of the Mahabharata is waged; Vidur is a wise man in the Mahabharata, son of Vyasa and a serving-maid. Intriguingly, Vidur is a linchpin in the story of the Mahabharata as interpreted by Protiva Bose in her heterodox deconstruction of the epic narrative (*Mahabharater Maharanye,* Vikalp, 1997). Following a suggestion made by Irawati Karve, Mrs Bose shows that Vidur could be the natural father of Yudhisthir, the eldest Pandava brother. Vidur is portrayed by Mrs Bose as a sly, ambitious man who ruthlessly plots to put his natural son on the throne. If, as I understand, Karve's book was published in 1969, the reference to Vidur in this poem could not have been influenced by it in any way. Later on Bose did become aware of Karve's work; in his *Mahabharater Katha* (posthumously published in 1974) he considers her hypothesis about Vidur being the real father of Yudhisthir. He finds the idea initially attractive, but does not accept it in the end. The Man-Lion, half-man, half-lion, is one of the ten incarnations of Vishnu.

'You, Strangers, Who Write Me Letters': The place-names suggest a span within which readership for a poet like himself might operate: Bankura is in West Bengal, Gauhati in Assam, and Barisal would have been then in East Pakistan and is now in Bangladesh.

'Hölderlin': The poet supplied a note at the end of the original poem, which I have translated and put at the head of the English poem. The last couple of lines of the poem strongly evoke the imagery of Hölderlin's poem 'Half of Life' ('Hälfte dess Lebens'), which Bose himself translated: the swans, the lake, the kisses are all there in the first stanza of Hölderlin's poem, and instead of Bose's glowing apples there are yellow pears. Indeed, it is a reference to that poem that really fully elucidates for us the last line of Bose's poem. There is a compound word in Bose's last line, *achchhodchumban,* which I had at first rendered as 'Achchhod-kisses', linking it to Lake Achchhod (Sanskrit *acchoda*), the famous meeting-place of Mahashweta and Pundarika in Banabhatta's *Kadambari*. Certainly a cross-reference to the seventh-century Sanskrit classic is willy-nilly there—the very word *achchhod* makes it mandatory for us to make the connection—and it is a cross-reference mediated by Tagore's famous poem 'Bijoyini', which opens with the compound word *achchhodsarasineere* ('in the waters of Lake Achchhod') and where, in the season of early spring, a woman sitting on a stone slab, breast-deep in the transparent water, caresses a she-swan, an image with which the 'swans of spring' in Bose easily link up. But after reading 'Half of Life', especially in Bose's own translation ('Madhyajiban', Vol. 5 of his *Kavitasangraha,* pp. 45–6), where swans, drunk with kissing, dip their heads in the pure and holy waters of a lake, I decided to render *achchhodchumban* as 'the kisses of the clear waters', invoking the etymological meaning of the lake's name: 'of clear, limpid, transparent waters'. The icy lake in the last line of this poem is both Hölderlin's lake, the waters of which are kissed by swans, *and* the Indian Achchhod of limpid waters, celebrated in *Kadambari* and remembered in Tagore's poem 'Bijoyini' (for a rendering of this poem see 'The Victorious Woman', *I Won't Let You Go: Selected Poems* of Tagore, translated by Dyson, op. cit., pp. 98–101).

Note that the name of a sacred lake can easily become symbolic in Indian poetry. See the note on the poem 'When the Burnt Day is Done', *post*. A variation of the image of 'glowing apples' occurs in a poem of *Je-Andhar Alor Adhik* not translated in this volume: entitled 'Still Life', it opens with the memorable question: 'Golden apple, why do you exist?'

'When the Burnt Day is Done': Pushkar: The sacred lake of Pushkar, about seven miles to the west of Ajmer in Rajasthan, one of the holiest of Hindu places of pilgrimage.

Mayurakshi: A river that flows through Bihar and West Bengal. The name means 'peacock-eyed', in the feminine gender, evoking magic and romance. Bose is undoubtedly remembering a poem of Tagore's, in which Tagore imagines his dream-dwelling by the River Mayurakshi: see the poem 'Dwelling', in *I Won't Let You Go, Selected Poems* of Tagore, translated by Dyson, op. cit., pp. 155–7.

Valmiki: The supposed author of the Ramayana; his hermitage by the River Tamasa near the Ganges, stands for peace and serenity. This is where the pregnant Sita is given shelter, when banished by Rama for fear of public calumny. There she gives birth to her twin sons, who learn the entire poem from Valmiki and eventually sing the verses in public in front of their father.

'The Music of Mortality': This poem is an interesting statement of belief, containing a passionate blast of ideas directed at the dedicatee, a woman noted for her understanding of philosophical issues, who at the same time had a strain of piousness which was not shared by Bose. Gauri Ayyub, née Datta (1931–98), a well-known educationist and activist, was the wife of Abu Sayeed Ayyub, a prominent Calcutta intellectual of the time (who is referred to in the Introduction of the present volume). When this poem was begun, she hadn't married Ayyub yet. She married him in 1956. It is possible that the poem originated in some real-life argument or exchange of ideas. Presumably it was then put to one side and fully developed many years later, by which time Bose's own convictions had thoroughly matured.

'Meanwhile through nine doors / Saturn enters my house': The influence of Saturn (usually regarded as an inauspicious planet) enters the body through nine entry-points. The nine orifices of the body through which malign influences can creep in are: the two eyes, the two ears, the two nostrils, the mouth, the penis, and the anus.

'the civil war of the Jadav clan': The destruction, through internecine conflict, of the Jadav (Yadava) clan, to which Krishna belonged, is described towards the end of the Mahabharata.

'The six deadly enemies': The proverbial 'six enemies' of the Hindu spiritual tradition, reminiscent of the Seven Deadly Sins of medieval Europe, are: lust, anger, greed, infatuation, pride, and envy.

'diurnal kingshuk flower': The kingshuk is the same as the polash tree, the *butea monosperma* (or *butea frondosa* of earlier classifications) which in spring makes a spectacular display of shapely flame-coloured or yellow flowers on its leafless branches.

'now—incredibly—bankrupt,/ puts on the red light ...': There is actually no one word corresponding to 'bankrupt' in the original, but I think it is implied in the image of putting on the red light, which seems to serve a double purpose, both hinting at the once mighty business being 'in the red' and linking its present enterprise with prostitution. Both nuances are ultimately derived from English and American usage, but they would be part of the furniture of a poet like Bose.

'three-streamed flow': The Ganges, in mythology, has three streams, one in heaven, one on the earth, and the third in the underworld.

'five elements': Earth, water, fire, air, and ether.

'Nature, tongue-lolling, murderous, / the mindless Enchantress ...': There is a conflation here of the philosophical concepts of Prakriti and Maya with the visual image of Kali.

'Supreme Self': *Paramatma* in the original, the ultimate reality, the Brahman of philosophy.

'The Song of a Rusty Nail': The note at the head of the poem is Bose's own.

Narada: A mythological god-sage.

Sama Veda: One of the four Vedas.

'five jewels': Sapphire, diamond, ruby, pearl, and coral.

'Jatayu bird': Jatayu, the king of vultures, who (in the Ramayana) tries to prevent Ravana from abducting Sita, and is mortally wounded in the struggle.

EKDIN: CHIRODIN O ANYANYO KAVITA (April 1971): The title can be translated as 'One Day: For Ever, and Other Poems'.

'The Dead': 'the Queen of Carthage': Dido. The reference is to the story of Aeneas and Dido, as narrated by Virgil in the *Aeneid*. Rome was supposed to have been founded by the descendants of the Trojan prince Aeneas and his followers, who escaped after the fall of Troy and eventually reached the west coast of Italy. In between, Aeneas had his love-adventure with the widow Dido, the Queen of Carthage in north Africa. Aeneas and his party, after a sea-storm, came to shore at Carthage. Aeneas and Dido fell in love and began to spend time together. Aeneas was then sternly reminded by a supernatural vision of his task to proceed to Italy. He and his followers sailed away from Carthage. Heartbroken at being abandoned, Dido cursed Aeneas and killed herself. Book Six of Virgil's epic describes Aeneas's visit to the underworld, in course of which Aeneas glimpses Dido through the shadows, recognizes her, and speaks to her tenderly and imploringly. But Dido is still angry and unforgiving: she keeps her furious gaze averted and fixed on the ground, and then flings herself back into the shadows, where she is comforted by her former husband.

'Young Men and Young Women': 'burning strings in betel shops': Shops selling betel and tobacco often hang a smouldering coir string so that customers can light their cigarettes from it.

In the original poem, there is a powerful explosion of meanings in the last line. There is a reference to a *sloka* of the *Katha* Upanishad (2.3.3), referred to, also, in 'The Weeping Beauty', *ante:* 'heard how the five elements ran, charmed by your commands'; but in both instances Bose is re-creating rather than simply quoting Upanishadic lines, and in this particular case doing it in such a way that the translator has to make some difficult decisions. In the Upanishadic source Yama tells Nachiketa that it is through fear of the Supreme Brahman that fire and the sun give their heat, and that through the same fear the following run: Indra, the wind, and death, the fifth one. The words for 'fire', 'sun', and 'wind'—*agni, surya, vayu*—double without any problem as the gods of the same elements. Bose omits the sun and Indra from the list, adds the name of the god of oceans, and personifies life.

On one level, his list works as a variation of the traditional Indian 'five elements', with 'life' instead of 'earth' and the nameless fifth one substituting for ether. The sun is presumably omitted to avoid duplication, since from the point of view of the 'five elements' classification, the sun and fire are the same. And the ocean-god is presumably preferred to Indra as a god easily identifiable with the watery element. Indra did have an ancient aspect as a rain-bearer, but most modern readers would simply see him as a vain and philandering 'king of gods' and no more. In these choices the poet is definitely leaning towards the concept of the five elements. At the same time, the first three words in the original poem, agni, vayu, and varun suggest the names of gods, which pulls *jiban* (life) into godhood too, and if life is the fourth god, who but death can be the fifth? But the poet does not name the fifth entity, leaves the naming to the reader's imagination. Even those who will not catch the Upanishadic reference may find a resonance with the idea of *panchatva-prapti* or 'reaching five-hood'—becoming the five elements, merging with them, i.e. death. Death, it must be noted, is also one of those running from fear. Death too is just one of the minor gods, like the others—powerful and powerless at the same time, with no ultimate power. Even death, the poet has already said, has not been able to rob the dead bodies of their decrepitude. Death has no power to ferry us to a new youth.

Bose's statement has an impact different from the Upanishad's. Yama wanted to teach Nachiketa that the Brahman was the ultimate truth. But Bose wants us to note that there is no still moment anywhere. For us that is the ultimate apprehensible truth, for we cannot reach the place where everything abides, is intact: we can never remove the thin, almost transparent veil between that locus and ourselves. Thus mutability is the real theme of this poem.

The line can be translated in several different ways. I could have written: 'fire, wind, water, life, and the fifth one', without initial capitalization, but if Bose had wanted to mean just the elements, he would have chosen plainer Bengali words signifying the first three, not agni, vayu, varun, which definitely suggest deities. Clearly, he wishes to personify the elements. I think that in a translation meant mainly for non-Bengali Indian readers, 'Agni, Vayu, Varuna, Life, and the Fifth One' would be fine, as they would recognize the godheads. But unless there is immediate recognition, such a version compromises the elemental strength of the line. Again, if Bose meant only certain mythological gods, it wouldn't have mattered that readers had to consult the notes before understanding his meaning, but it is the double meaning of elements and godheads that sparks the poetry. As a compromise I have decided that the three element-words are the best, with the initial letters of all five capitalized to indicate personification. 'Gods of ...' would have been intrusive and untidy.

The idea of the running *pancham* ('fifth') has other reverberations in the original poem. For instance, it suggests the fifth note of the octave, running towards the sixth. The song of the koel, the Indian cuckoo, is supposed to be on the fifth note, and it sounds as though it was always trying to climb to the next. 'Pancham' is also the name of an untouchable caste of southern India, a nuance which may not be altogether irrelevant.

In a poem entitled 'Open Letter to Kalidas', which I have not translated, written in October 1965, i.e. shortly before this one, Bose asks Kalidas (Kalidasa, the great Sanskrit poet and dramatist) whether any secret worm had not gnawn him, if pancham had not cast a shadow on the triumphal felicitations all around him. If pancham here is simply 'fifth' or 'death', then by making the two concepts completely equivalent Bose has gone beyond the Upanishadic line and endowed the word pancham with a new meaning not yet included in the dictionary, for here there is no list with four other items on it. Yet there remains the flicker of a suggestion that the shadow could have also been cast by an untouchable, which, in Kalidasa's time, would certainly have been regarded as inauspicious. The shadow of an untouchable fallen on a brahmin returning from his river bath or on a dairyman carrying yoghourt to market used to be regarded as a pollutant in the not too distant past, and untouchables used to run in order to avoid casting polluting shadows.

At least for a reader like myself, the diminutive shadow of such a meaning—'like an extra drop of shadow within the lamp-post's shadow', as Bose puts it—falls on this image. In the last line of 'Young Men and Young Women' there is a certain play on the notion of categories. Untouchables are outside the four castes, fifth in that sense. All those *within* named categories run; those *outside* the categories run too.

There is thus an explosion of suggestions that scatters us, makes us run metaphorically. In his mature years, Bose valued this kind of explosive power in imagery as a hallmark of modernism. In translation, the translator has to make his/her own choices; there is no mandatory path.

I also believe that there may be a distant echo in this poem of the Anglo-Saxon poem *The Seafarer,* the second half of which is dominated by the themes of old age, mutability, and death. Bose would have been familiar with the poem as a student of English literature and must have also known Ezra Pound's version of the poem. There is a certain resonance between the last line of 'Young Men and Young Women' and these lines of *The Seafarer*:

> Micel bith se Meotudes egsa,   for thon hi seo molde oncyrreth,
> se gestathelade   stithe grundas,
> eorthan sceatas   and uprodor.
>
> (Great is the terror of the Creator, whereby the earth turns. He established the mighty plains, the earth's surfaces, and the firmament.)

'Shopkeepers': 'gulmor pollen': See the note on 'Calcutta', *ante.* I have retained the flower-name used in the original, as it fits better than anything else in the sonic pattern of the English line.

Bowbazar: A locality of Calcutta.

'Night': Interested readers may compare the sentiments expressed in this poem with Rabindranath Tagore's lecture 'Din o Ratri' (Day and Night) in *Dharma* (*Rabindra-rachanabali,* the old Visvabharati edition, Vol. 13, printing of Bhadra 1393, pp. 341–8; and also the two lectures entitled 'Din' (Day) and 'Ratri' (Night) in *Santiniketan* (*Rabindra-rachanabali,* Vol. 13, as before, pp. 508–13). Tagore's emphasis is on the spiritual regeneration afforded by the interval of night between one day and the next; Bose's emphasis, expressed in a highly erotic language, is on the opportunity for creative work and artistic development that night affords a poet.

'the hydra-headed crowd': This phrase translates what in the original means 'the Ravan crowd', which is what I retained in many drafts. Ravana, the enemy of Rama in the Ramayana, had ten heads, and if a head was cut off, another sprouted in its place. Though as a rule I try to keep the original mythological references intact, in this case 'hydra-headed crowd' is such an accurate translation of the underlying meaning of the phrase that it perhaps serves poetry better.

Urbashi: A heavenly nymph.

'streaming like a beauty's tears on the horizon': Compare with the poem 'The Weeping Beauty', *ante*.

'Nostalgia': Jhamapukur Lane: in Calcutta.

'My Life': 'the chariot procession': The annual Rathjatra festival in the month of Asharh, when the image of Jagannath is taken out for a ride in a chariot pulled by devotees.

'My Tower': Behala: A locality of Calcutta.

'The Constraint of Seasonality': The title of this poem ('Tithidore') is also the name of a major novel by Bose (1949). It is most likely that the compound word *tithidore* was derived by Bose from a well-known song of Tagore's ('E pare mukhar holo keka oi', 'The peacock calls on this bank'), who probably coined it. It is this song which clinches the meaning of the word as the constraint imposed on us by seasonality.

Svati: The star Arcturus.

'The Expatriate': Didi: Elder sister.

Rajshahi: Now in Bangladesh, was in 1965, at the time of the writing of this poem, in East Pakistan. Does the poem hint that Anni's is a case of double expatriation? Her natal roots are in Rajshahi, East Pakistan, but has she migrated to America via India? She was clearly born before the partition of Bengal in 1947; hence to her Rajshahi is 'in another, incredible country'.

bokul: Star-shaped flowers with a pungent fragrance, the *mimusops elengi*.

jamrul: A small white fruit, crisp and watery, the *eugenia alba*.

'Ela-di': The suffix '-di' (short for Didi, elder sister) added to a woman's name, makes it honorific.

Kakima: Father's younger brother's wife. I retain this precise kinship term here because I feel 'Aunt' would be inadequate in the context. The different kinds of aunts and uncles and cousins have different social and emotional resonances in India. In the patrilineal extended family a Kakima would be an important member of one's immediate family, a daily available mother-substitute. The resonance continues even when large families have split up, as in this poem.

'A Farewell at Howrah Station': Howrah Station: the railway station at Howrah, a town facing Calcutta on the west bank of the Hooghly, used for westward journeys from Calcutta, including to Bombay, Delhi, and Madras.

'One Day: For Ever': Please see the discussion of this poem in the Introduction.
cheera: A rice cereal. 'Rain through dawn sleep, smell of frying cheera / in the rain': A memory of childhood. The detail is backed up by Bose's autobiographical novel *Anya Konkhane,* 1950, pp. 52–4.

SWAGATOBIDAY O ANYANYO KAVITA (June 1971): The title of this volume could be translated as 'Welcome and Farewell, and Other Poems'.

'Fishing': The shole and the bowal are two types of fish; the bowal is an especially big fish.

'He and Others': 'Two *kathas* of desired dry ground': The katha (pronounced with long vowels and a cerebral *th*) is a unit of land measurement.
'Which promised friction-wood and shomi branch ...': The wood of the shomi (Skr. *śamī*) tree was used to kindle sacrificial fires; indeed the tough wood of this tree was supposed to *contain* fire. Legend has it that Pururavas kindled primeval fire by rubbing together a branch of this tree and a branch of the peepul-tree.
'O Sun ...': These lines would seem to be suggested by the famous prayer to the sun in the *Isa* Upanishad (15–16), also in the *Brihadaranyaka* Upanishad (5.15.1).

'Lament': I wonder if this moving poem has some reference to a promising young poet of the *Kallol* era named Sukumar Sarkar, whose tragic story is recalled in Bose's *Amar Jauban,* reprint of 1989, pp. 41–3. This young poet, says Bose, fell in love with an actress much older than himself, printed her poems or her songs and sold them in the streets himself. He led a bohemian life, almost a tramp's life, and one summer fell victim to smallpox. Of course, despite the dedicatory phrase 'for a young poet', the poem could actually be a composite portrait, with elements drawn from more than one personality, not excluding the poet's own.

'A Juncture of Time': Please see the discussion of this poem in the Introduction, which will throw light on details that might seem opaque.

'Welcome and Farewell': 'June it is, but Asharh is imminent': an excellent example of the way Bose elicits meaning from the juxtaposition of the two month-names from the two calendars. Asharh begins half-way through June. It is important to remember that though he mentions Brooklyn and Manhattan, he is not in New York. He is not in America at all, but in India. This is a poem about memories.

'little but endless *Ramayan*': Some abridged Bengali version for youngsters.

Ramna: To the north and west of the old city of Dhaka. It is described thus in *A Handbook for Travellers in India, Burma and Ceylon* (John Murray, London, and Thacker, Spink, & Co., Calcutta, 1929, p. 494): 'a pleasant open place, with many trees, and a breeze which rarely fails to blow. There is a spacious Maidan, with a race-course, a golf-course and polo ground. The Club is to the N. of the Maidan; the Dacca University area lies mainly to the S. and W.' Many a time in my own childhood have I heard my father recall with nostalgia the delights of walking in the Ramna.

Ballygunge: The area of Calcutta where Bose lived for many years (where 202 Rashbehari Avenue is).

Fifth Avenue: In New York.

'I have Abed's biscuits for you': Biscuits made in a famous bakery of that name in Dhaka. Here and in the next few lines Bose is recalling a spot of Dhaka on the north bank of the Buriganga which he used to haunt in his student days. 'Sometimes,' he says in the second volume of his memoirs, 'we go beyond the Sadar Ghat and walk to the less crowded Wise Ghat at the time of sunset—past the smell of bread and biscuits from the famous bakery of Abed to that solitary border of the river where creeping ivy covers an old house, where an Englishman's name can be seen on the gate, but which appears to be uninhabited' (*Amar Jauban,* reprint of 1989, pp. 19–20). The old house was probably the Old Collector's House.

Buriganga: The city of Dhaka is on the north bank of the Buriganga.

'shiuli flowers': See the note on 'Mimi, On Your Birthday', *ante*.

Noakhali: Now in Bangladesh. Bose records that his very first memories were those of Noakhali.

Purana Polton: Bose spent part of his boyhood in this area of Dhaka.

Elephanta: The celebrated caves of the island of Elephanta, off Bombay.

Parthenon: The world-famous temple in Athens.

Altamira: The caves of Altamira in northern Spain, famous for their prehistoric murals of animals.

Ajanta: the Buddhist caves of Ajanta in western India, with their celebrated frescoes.

'A Poem for Savitri': See the Introduction for Savitri's story. In the Mahabharata Savitri is a woman who brings her husband back from death by holding a dialogue with Yama, the god of death.

'with no pain': A reference to Keats's 'Ode to a Nightingale': 'Now more than ever seems it rich to die, / To cease upon the midnight with no pain, / While thou art pouring forth thy soul abroad / In such an ecstasy!'

'The young, perfumed poet': Keats, of course. The adjective 'perfumed' refers to Keats listening to the nightingale in the dark, in 'embalmed darkness', smelling the 'soft incense' hanging upon the boughs, but unable to see the flowers.

'He'd wanted a balmy night, a bed in a flowering garden' etc: See especially the fifth stanza of Keats's 'Ode to a Nightingale', beginning: 'I cannot see what flowers are at my feet'.

'But the end / came in traditional death-sweat' etc: The whole of this stanza refers to Keats's death in Rome. Bose had just been to Rome and he certainly knew the famous Spanish Steps (see the discussion of this poem in the Introduction). The early deaths of Keats, Shelley, and Byron haunted him, and one of his poems, entitled 'Pratibimba' (Reflection, *Kavitasangraha*, Vol. 2, pp. 319–22), begins with a consideration of their deaths, opening: 'Keatser dak eshechhilo chhabbishe' ('Keats was called at the age of twenty-six'). Fanny is Fanny Brawne, the woman with whom Keats was ardently in love. Keats's tragic death from tuberculosis before he was fully twenty-six, the physical and mental agony of his last days, far from home, the intensity of his love for Fanny, his talent and the quality of his poetic achievement at such a young age: all these have had a great impact on the imagination of generations of Bengalis, ever since they were introduced to English literature and became familiar with the facts of his life.

Mohenjodaro: Now in Pakistan, the site, with Harappa, of the 'pre-historic' Indus Valley civilization of the subcontinent.

'Chariot Festival': See 'chariot procession' in the note on the poem 'My Life', *ante*.

'a god incarnate, and a thwarted love': 'A thwarted love' translates 'ek pratyadishta prem', a phrase which could have been interpreted in a number of ways. I have chosen an interpretation that matches the story best and also goes with Bose's preference for giving a modern tilt to the psychology of legendary characters. Other possibilities include 'a love that had received a divine message' and 'a countermanded love', but to me these do not seem as satisfactory as the other set of possible meanings: 'a love that had been thwarted, broken, undone, or rejected'. I think Bose wants to show that Savitri followed the god of death doggedly out of her personal love for her husband, because she was personally determined to bring him back, not because she had received any divine command or countermand about it. In the epic story Savitri had married Satyavan, knowing that he was supposed to die within a year, but what might happen after that death had not been predicted. The decision to follow the god of death when death did come to Satyavan was Savitri's own, and Bose highlights it. It was her gamble, and it paid off.

'as though she'd once again become her father's maiden daughter / and had once more set forth on her journey, her independent search for a lover': Savitri, a princess, had found her husband herself. Her father, the king, sent her on that very mission because no man had asked for her hand. Riding a chariot, accompanied by the king's old ministers, she set forth on her journey, visiting hermitages and places of pilgrimage. That is how she met Satyavan, who was living with his parents in exile, because his father, also a king, had been robbed of his kingdom. Savitri chose this young man and came home and told her father about her choice. (This seems like a variant form of *svayamvara* or 'choosing one's bridegroom oneself', available to kshatriya women in ancient India: more usually a princess chose from amongst princes and warriors gathered in a special assembly at her father's court.) Savitri was then warned by the heavenly sage Narada, who was at her father's court, that Satyavan, although an excellent choice in every other respect, was, however, destined to die within a year. Asked by her father to choose another bridegroom, Savitri persisted in her decision, but never told her husband or her in-laws what she had heard from Narada about what was written in Satyavan's stars. When the fatal day arrived, she dealt with it herself.

Yudhisthir: The eldest Pandava brother. In his last years Bose was particularly interested in this character. His unfinished book, *Mahabharater Katha,* posthumously published, sees Yudhisthir as the key character and the real hero of the Mahabharata. An English translation of this book was done by Sujit Mukherjee (*The Book of Yudhisthir,* Orient Longman, Calcutta, 1982).

Nachiketa: Nachiketas, who holds a long dialogue with Yama in the *Katha* Upanishad.

Appendix

Language, Poetry, and Being Human:
A Protest against the Report of the
Government's Language Commission

Only human beings have language, and all human beings have language. In the world of creatures no other species has language.

Nature requires of creatures that they continue their existence on earth generation after generation. To comply with this requirement, language is not necessary at all. Self-defence, reproduction, and child-rearing—all three functions can be managed without language, and managed quite well.

Indeed even humans can express hunger and thirst without the help of language, and for conveying or rousing sexual desire sidelong glances are more helpful than language. When men sustained themselves on hunting or warfare, war cries boosted their machismo, and our ancestors gave the name of love cries to the sounds that the throats of men and women still emit as a prologue to the procreative act. Neither war cries nor love cries can be called language.

Fulfilling the purposes of the deity presiding over procreation is not an issue that is dependent on language. Two partners can achieve parenthood without knowing each other's language. If nuclear weapons were to destroy the human race, leaving unscathed just a handful of black men and a handful of Eskimo women, then—should the two groups meet—they could arguably save the human race from imminent extinction. The fact that they could not communicate by means of speech would not present an obstacle to that noble task.

Other creatures too emit sounds from their throats. Hungry or hurt, swayed by the mating urge or by affection, most land animals use set collections of sounds, each species its own set. The male bird courts his mate with much coaxing and cajoling; all that sounds delightful to our ears, and we have bequeathed on it the name of 'song'. But human language rose on a different horizon, beyond the shores of those sounds.

Ants and bees lead social lives organized as groups; it has not been possible to deny their skills in building nests and hives. Scientists have discovered amazing facts about these creatures. They know how to form phalanxes, how to send news far and near, and how to forewarn members of their own species of approaching danger. That is to say, social life is quite possible without language.

2.

The Report of the Indian Language Commission which has recently been published has a Sanskrit statement in its preface which deserves to be quoted:

... yadvai vāṃ nābhavishyat na dharmo nādharmo vyajñāpayishyat na satyaṃ nānṛtaṃ na sādhu nāsādhu na hṛdayajño nāhṛdayajño vāgevaitat sarvaṃ vijñāpayati vācamupassveti. (*Chhandogya-Upanishad*, 7/2/1)

If speech [*vak*] did not exist, neither right nor wrong could be conveyed; truth or falsehood, good or evil, the pleasant or the unpleasant—nothing could be conveyed. Worship speech [*vak*].

If speech [*vak*] is worthy of worship, is it just because without it 'nothing could be conveyed'? Is it true to say that nothing can be known without language? If we receive an extract of neem in the mouth, we know at once that it is not pleasant, and the tongue gives us unerring proof of the pleasantness of honey. A gesture, a look of the eye can uncover a lie; that covering is good in the cold or that water is good in thirst is a reality that is conveyed spontaneously, immediately. The fellow who has just had his pocket picked does not need to have the scriptures read to him in order that he might understand the difference between right and wrong. Hence, though the statement is from one of the Upanishads, this definition of language is unacceptable.

But the fact that the Language Commission has chosen to ignore the many other pronouncements on language available in the Upanishads and has accepted this particular statement as its seminal mantra is not by chance, but is quite deliberate. This utterance comes closest to the attitude of most of the members towards language—what they mean by it—and embodies it in its most concentrated form. That attitude is implicitly operative throughout their lengthy discussion spread over 269 pages, and what they have kept implicit over 269 pages becomes boldly, unmistakably explicit in the last paragraph of the book:

Language is in a sense profoundly important and in another sense of little or no consequence! It is important at the level of instrumentality. It is a loom on which the life of a people is woven. It is, however, of no intrinsic consequence in itself because it is essentially an instrumentality: the loom, not the fabric; only a vehicle of thought and not thought itself; a receptacle for the traditions, usages and cultural memories of a people, but not their substance. It is not language but education that is aimed at in the schools; it is not language but good government that is aimed at in the field of public administration; it is not language but justice that is sought in the law courts. That which lends itself to the most convenience is the correct solution of the language problem in the various fields. Surely, there does not have to be heat and passion over the issue of Language, ever the instrumentality and not the substance! (The Report of the Language Commission: chapter 15, paragraph 18, p. 269)

In the first and last sentences of the paragraph it has been declared in the plainest fashion that the thing called language is not a thing at all, that it is of almost no consequence. To strengthen their message, its shapers have even pierced it with no less than two exclamation marks, as if to brush aside the whole business of language. My knowledge of English lacks that sophistication with which I might have appreciated the subtle difference that is being implied by their use of the word 'instrumentality' instead of 'instrument'; but it can be easily guessed that they are unwilling to confer on language even that modicum of status in its own right that would have been given to it, had they acknowledged it as an 'instrument'; they can just about accept it as an 'instrumentality'—which is completely abstract, not concrete at all, almost non-existent. But even if we were to desist from a fine analysis of their use of words, there can be no doubt that by language most members of the Language Commission understand an instrument or a vehicle, just a receptacle or an appliance, by means of which we perform various tasks! And I wish to state at once that this concept of language is essentially wrong, fundamentally false, a denial of man's humanity.

In so far as language is just a means, a 'means of communication', the other creatures have language too. Birds call, animals roar, ants and similar insects convey messages by means of touch. Humans too do not always need language just to convey messages. It is possible to communicate love, hate, pleading, prohibition, fear, disgust through the eyes; the touch of a hand can express service, desire, good wishes; and the same touch, its pressure augmented, manifests itself as violence. Human societies have a vast repertory of gestures that use the different limbs and their sections, and encode messages: pinching somebody is also a message, an act of 'communication', and the 'uh!' uttered by the person who is being pinched is also the same. If it is possible to communicate to this extent even without the mediation of language, enabling us to defend ourselves and to propagate, and even to have a social life, then why did human beings need language?

In reply it may be said that language is a communicator in a much wider sense than pinching, kissing or neighing; that only language—not touching, gesturing or roaring—contains enough signs to cover the adequate performance of the very diverse tasks that human societies must perform. Even though it may be possible to convey by gestures messages such as 'I feel hungry' or 'I desire (or loathe) you', without language it is not possible to say 'Vote for Congress', 'Ruin to imperialism', or 'We want the end of dictatorship'. 'The rains come after the summer', 'The present President of India is a propagandist for Hindi', 'Two sides of a triangle together will always be greater than the third side'—to make statements of this order we need language. And such statements can be made as effectively in Kannada, Marathi, Hindi, or Oriya as in Bengali: any differences can be no more than minimal. Something that is 'just a means, not the essential matter', has 'no value of its own'—what does it matter if it is Hindi or English or Russian? Therefore,— urge the majority of members of the Language Commission,—come let us accept Hindi all over India, by which means national unity will be strengthened and jobs of all kinds will be most conveniently managed throughout the country.

If the function of language was solely to convey messages, dish out facts, and to express crude emotions in the manner of slogans and advertisements, if its use was limited to the writing of government papers, reports, documents, newspaper articles, or speeches for addressing public meetings, then there might be no significant obstacles to the acceptance of this recommendation. If men used language to pursue nothing except history, theology, economics, law, science, and technology, even then it would not be altogether impossible to accept it. For history tells us that men have managed to do all these things in a foreign language. When in Mughal India Persian was the court language, ambitious individuals learnt it; in all the countries of medieval Europe, in Italy, Holland, England, France, and so on, scholars penned subtle, complicated discourses and substantial volumes in Latin; in nineteenth-century Russia French was not only the language of the court dignitaries, but also the social and familial language of the entire educated class, in which even a mother could utter endearments to her son or young couples carry on their love-dialogues. Within the past one hundred and fifty years in India many useful volumes full of valuable researches have been written, in many subject-areas ranging from history and archaeology to census reports, of which the language is English and the authors are Indian. Why should we not be able to do in Hindi what we have managed to do in English?

But a question remains. Why, in that very period when intellectuals throughout Europe thought in Latin and nothing else, Europe's poets composed, in their own mother tongues, innumerable romances relating to love and chivalry—of which the best examples are the circle of tales of King Arthur and his knights—and why indeed is the subsequent literature of the West suffused with the influence of that very vernacular literature? Why did Europe, flooded with Latin, discover its fundamental principle of modern lyricism in a language of the people like Provençal? Why was the language of the *Divine Comedy,* which is the greatest, most vital expression of the Catholic faith, not Latin, but the neglected Italian of those times? When Russian writers of the nineteenth century created imperishable literature, why was the language of that literature not French, but Russian, in which, if they could help it, they talked to nobody except to servants, peasants, and grannies? And why indeed, in the past one hundred and fifty years, in spite of having learnt English as best as any foreigner ever can, no Indian has authored an original literary volume which has been acknowledged as a treasure of literature?[1]

It takes no more than a moment to answer such questions. Human beings can manage to do almost everything in a foreign language, everything except the writing of poetry, drama, and fiction, the composition of creative literature. Why can't they? Because where literature is creative, the entire inner world of a human being becomes active—not only his intellect, his sensory perceptions, and his heart's impulses, but also his unconscious mind, the hell and heaven dwelling in his soul, the grey clusters of memory inherited from his forefathers. Whatever tasks we perform in the clear light of day as rational creatures and citizens—the rearing of children, the management of state affairs, the dispensing of education and justice—the sheaths of their conventions could accommodate almost any language, and if convenience so dictated, we could discard one and adopt another, without raising objections. If in mathematics and science signs are more convenient than human language, then surely those are what we must use. Where the goal is well fixed, where we want to distribute knowledge, to prove something, to defeat an opposing viewpoint, or to stir up a collective emotion such as patriotism, we may acknowledge the business of language as a mere means to an end. But besides these, man has another kind of life as well, without which he would not be fully human. That is a twilight life, a life of dreams that belong to the half dark. Even in this twentieth century sustained by science, in our dreams we become children or primitive men; there all our education received in daylight crumbles, our fears, hopes, efforts obey no dictates of reason: we have to move through a dimly lit tunnel, groping, crawling. If we can retrieve any mementoes of that unpremeditated journey, they can be embodied by means of one thing alone: the mother tongue. If we wish to strain and recover any translucent jewel from that primitive and murky darkness, if we wish to grasp and bring back to the surface any memories, discoveries, or souvenirs, that task can be performed only in that language which is an intimate of our unconscious mind, and in the folds of which the life-threads of all our ancestors, spread over many ages, are entangled. And this precisely is what the poet does: in the marriage of conscious life and the unconscious he acts as a go-between; he gives a conscious form to our wild, chaotic dream-self, endows our consciousness with fullness by bringing it into contact with the night of dreams. This is one human function that cannot be performed without language, and cannot be performed by a particular person except in a particular language. Therefore, until we have examined this function, we cannot grasp what language really means, how it relates to human life and being human. Language and literature are inextricably interrelated; it is not possible to discuss one without discussing the other. But the Report of the Language Commission, in spite of discussing many issues, has stopped just at the boundary of this particular subject. 'It is not language but education that is aimed at in the schools; it is not language but good government that is aimed at in the field of public administration; it is not language but justice that is sought in the law courts.' But if, after this, one had to mention poetry, one would have to say, 'It is not language but poetry that is the goal of poetry'—which would mean, 'In poetry our goal is language and nothing but language.' But the members of the Commission could not have said this, and have not been able to say it, because in that case all the reasoning of the gentlemen would have collapsed. Though the subject of their discourse is language, they have maintained a profound silence about creative literature from the beginning to the end. They have done well; they have thereby made it easier for us to realize that from the preliminary quotation to the very last paragraph their conscious aim, at every step, is the propagation of fallacies.

After we have paid our due respects to law, education, governance, and so on, and when we can hear the call of literature, our internal space begins to be lit up with another concept of language; this is one field where we realize, when we enter it, that language is not just some sort of means, but the very source; thought does not give rise to language, it is language that gives birth to thought. The pictures we see in our dreams may be called the imagery of a cosmic mythology, the original shapes of the human soul's clusters of emotions; when those transient, restless, and disorderly images cast aside their immediate emotive mobility and attained stillness, permanence, and transparence, only then was it possible for humans to do the job called thinking. Before that there was no thinking; there was just the thrust of emotions and sensations. Only when he is ravenously hungry does the tiger notice the deer; at other times the deer is non-existent to him. But even when a man is not interested in either devouring or caressing a deer, the being of the deer is absolutely clear to him, for he has acquired the word 'deer'. Precisely because that word exists, he can visualize that animal in his mind, that is to say, he can think about it, even when he is not driven by some personal emotion regarding the deer or is not directly experiencing the animal through his senses. If we had had nothing but the pictorial language of dreams, we might still have had mythology, but history would have been impossible. If man had remained bound by the immediate influence of his fleeting moments, even then the emergence of embryonic fairy tales would not have been impossible, but there would have been no science. That person may be called a poet, who, travelling from the physical impact of his emotions, liberates human beings from that impact, transforms sense-perceptions into that spiritual substance we call experience. This ur-poet of ours is at once the parent of poetry, history, and science: within his mind knowledge was first strained off from emotion and was then dipped again and revitalized in emotion; after human history was separated from cosmic mythology, history was once again given a stir in the flow of mythology and thus endowed with a new life. And he and language were born at the same hour; his being was dependent on language, very much so. That man has language is proof enough that his quintessence is that of a poet. If he had not been a poet, he would not have needed language.

For this reason the German philosopher Hamann had said: 'It is poetry that is the mother tongue of the human race.' Many of the world's mythological and religious texts would support this statement of Johann Georg Hamann,[2] under whose influence first Herder[3] and then Jacobi[4] laid the foundation of modern philology. In the simplistic Creation story of the Jews the portion that we need to think through begins at that point where God, after constructing the universe for six days and resting on the seventh, presents all living creatures in front of Adam for naming. Every creature needs a name, and it is Adam who must provide it. This very directive given by God makes us realize that Adam's fall is inevitable—a fall which God Himself has planned for him. For the human being who gives names has already gone beyond the condition of ignorance that goes with the Garden of Immortality; he has become a poet and a scientist at the same time. Desire for knowledge and desire for joy: these two human faculties are equally alert, and one is not complete without the other. 'O foreign flower, when I asked you—/ "What's your name?"/You smiled and shook your head, and I understood then—/Why did we need a name?/Who you are is in your smile/And in nothing else.'[5]—Though the author of these lines is Rabindranath, we cannot accept the sentiment as the utterance of a full human being; when we see an unknown flower, the first question we pose quite spontaneously is: 'What's its name?', and Rabindranath too had done the same. The connotation of that name is one thing for the botanist, another for the poet; but both of them need that thing called a name, and until a name is found for it that flower does not become a usable spiritual resource for human beings. At the end of the day human language may be called a collection of names; according to the Hindu scriptures this world is made up of names and forms. And different religious texts are also unanimous in their opinion that man may attain salvation simply by reciting the name of the Supreme God.

'In the beginning was the Word,' thus begins St John's account of the life of Jesus.[6] In the new translation of the Bible by Ronald Knox, the statement is made in a slightly different fashion—'At the beginning of time the Word already was; and God had the Word abiding with him, and the Word was God. He abode, at the beginning of time, with God. It was through him that all things came into being, and without him came nothing that has come to be. In him there was life, and that life was the light of men.'[7] And, according to St John, in Jesus 'the Word was made flesh,'[8] Jesus being the incarnation of this very Word [*vak*]. In the Upanishads the Brahman is called *akshara,* which in Sanskrit means both 'unchangeable' or 'imperishable' on the one hand and 'word' or 'letter of the alphabet' on the other. Here *vak* and Brahman have been thought of as one; they have been believed to be one. *Akshara* also denotes the *om-kara,* which is the very bow of the arrow that is the *jivatman* (*Mundaka-Upanishad*: 2.2.4); identical with the *atman* (*Mandukya-Upanishad*: 8); a prop for meditation (*Mundaka-Upanishad*: 2.2.6); the head of all the Vedas and the person of the Supreme God (*Taittiriya-Upanishad*: 1.4.1). Without a knowledge of *akshara* the knowledge of the Vedas is useless, for the *Rigveda* and all the other Vedas and all the gods reside in the *akshara* (Brahman) that is in the form of the Supreme Firmament (*Svetasvatara-Upanishad*: 4.8). In the *Taittiriya Brahmana* it has been said that the source of life for all creatures is indeed *vak*; beasts, men, and gods all depend on *vak*;

vak is without decay, the first offspring of the Eternal One, the Mother of the Vedas and other texts, and the navel of the cosmos. In the sacred book of the ancient Persians, where the conflict of good and evil has been imagined to be the fundamental principle of the Creation, the story of Creation has it that *vak* is God's highest power: *vak* pre-dates the Creation of the world and is an armour that protects against the power of Satan. In the myths of many primitive peoples too one encounters the faith that *vak* and the Creator are one, and that the Creation has emanated from *vak*.

The Creation has emanated from *vak*: in many areas of life we find no instances of this at all; rather, we can collect much evidence to the contrary. The proposition would have been hardly worth articulating today, had not the human race, giving the lie to Herbert Spencer's prediction,[9] let it be known unmistakably that it cannot do without poetry. The very fact that the being of poetry remains robust even in these times, when the machine and the doctrine of Utilitarianism have spread far and wide, indicates that man's ancient myths have not been wrong. The world has been created from *vak*: it is poetry which is the indisputable ground for this belief. When we read or remember poetry, we immediately realize that the value of language cannot be contained within its lexical meanings, that language is valuable for its own sake, that it is not just a vehicle but is itself a divinity. When a poet starts to write poetry, he immediately realizes that language is the very fountainhead of creation, that the poem he writes is created as much by his language as by himself; that far from language being an instrument in his hands, it is he who becomes, for the time being, an agent of language, and his success depends on how subservient, attentive, and focused he can be as an agent. And it is here also, in poetry or creative literature, that we witness the highest and true form of language.

3.

Let us now return to the Upanishadic sentence quoted by the Language Commission. 'If speech did not exist, neither right nor wrong could be conveyed; truth or falsehood, good or evil, the pleasant or the unpleasant— nothing could be conveyed.' The real meaning of this statement is not that language is just a means, for even a child knows that the difference between the pleasant and the unpleasant may be understood even without language; its real purpose is to alert us that the thing called language is double-faced. True and false, good and bad, right or wrong, what pleases and what distresses: language can simultaneously and indiscriminately convey all; it is a neutral publisher of all such opposites. A brother who has shot his brother dead is acquitted in court, thanks to his lawyer's language; during a war the propagandists of every country portray the enemy as demonic, which also is done by language. And a government commission can, through the sheer twisted use of language, declare as beneficial for the whole country a proposal which would aggrandize the few in number and thereby destroy the majority. The dishonesty of action is at once apparent; the dishonesty of language is more terrible precisely because it is subtle. This linguistic dishonesty is widely visible in commerce, worldly affairs, in the running of state machinery—not just now but in every age of history. Something that is so liable to distortion: how can we call it worthy of worship?

Perhaps this was what Hölderlin[10] meant when he said that language was 'man's most dangerous possession'. Language is easily distorted in the hands of a clever person; the cleverer a person is, the more he can distort language. The ideal creatures in the shape of horses that Swift imagined in the last part of *Gulliver's Travels* do not, in their limited language, have a synonym for 'opinions', for that extremely rationalist society of horses are very much the spokesmen of certainty and never have any differences of opinion among themselves.[11] We shall not express regret that man is not a rational machine as per the ideals of the eighteenth century, for we all know that just as man is under the power of enemies like lust, anger, and greed, so also he has within himself noble faculties such as the capacity for love, reverence, renunciation, and creativity, and that these two sets of instincts and faculties are mutually dependent. If he was not, at one end of the scale, lustful, envious, greedy, and so on, he could not, at the other end, be a saint, a hero, or a sage either; in Swift's society of Houyhnhnms everybody is morally good, in a dry sort of way, but none are marked by greatness. Where man is like an animal, he is irrational, and where he is godlike, he is too rational: his lowest and highest levels are equally beyond the bounds of reason. And because the existence of these two levels is usually simultaneous and continuous with each other, no such thing as pure reasoning is ever possible in human society; though it occurs as an idea in philosophical fantasy, in practice reasoning is always infiltrated by some instinct or affect, a selfish desire or a lofty idealistic emotion, and man's ambivalent nature is precisely the reason why it is not always easy to differentiate between those two things. No matter what the issue is, civilized men can muster almost equally powerful arguments on both sides; the college student gets applause in the debating club by arguing on behalf of a position he does not really believe in himself; whichever government wins power, civil servants do not lack arguments to propagate the views which are favoured by that government.

The devil can quote from the scriptures; the opinion of the populace on whether Julius Caesar was a hero or a tyrant can veer according to the speeches they are listening to, Brutus's or Mark Antony's.[12] More often than not what we call reason does not enable us to find the truth; that very language which is the vehicle of reason creates various delusions. Where language is a mere vehicle or means, its tendency towards corruption is beyond remedy.

But is there no area where language cannot be a liar, and if there isn't, where then does the specific value of language lie? In response to this question, I shall quote something else which Hölderlin said: 'Poetry is the least harmful activity of humans.' 'The least harmful'—he puts it mildly, minimally; to appreciate the real meaning of this phrase we have to ponder the relationship of language and poetry. Poetry is the least harmful activity in the sense that in poetry—in creative literature—and only there—does language become uncorrupted, beyond reproach, unerringly true. In the greatest moments of literature there is not a chance that the untrue will be expressed instead of the true, or what is morally wrong instead of what is morally right, or the unpleasant instead of the pleasant; yet even where law, or commerce, or the running of the state machinery is most highly developed, language can act falsely, and often does. For we understand by means of the intellect, and realize by means of intuition; if the intellect were totally reliable per se, there would be no such thing as misunderstanding in human society; to correct this falsifying tendency of the intellect, we have to connect it to intuition. What intuition realizes, it realizes without any error, but it lacks the power to express it; only when intuition accepts the intellect as its assistant does language become true, and poetry is just another name for that true language. This language, in which the whole inner self of a human being shines, can be nothing but that person's mother tongue. In other fields, we can change our language in accordance with the criterion of utility, as we can don different garbs according to convenience, but in the context of that literature where language is uncorrupted and true, by language we have to mean the mother tongue alone. The mother tongue is the mother of our thoughts, the directrice of our spiritual lives. And it is impossible to treat with respect any recommendations about language coming from those who maintain that *that* language is 'never an essential substance, just an instrument', and that there is no need to get 'het up or agitated' about it.

4.

But, some may object, if Hindi becomes the official language of India, why should that harm the other literatures? Just as in Europe, when it was flooded with Latin, poems were composed in the various mother tongues, just as the savants of nineteenth-century Russia were able to create authentic Russian literature in spite of the dominance of French, and just as in a part of British-ruled India there was a renaissance of the mother tongue and its literature, so also there need be no obstacles to the flowering of the different literatures of India even if Hindi is used for pan-Indian official business. If the mother tongue is indeed a spiritual affair, then surely its development is right in our own hands; what can the state do in that respect? Following a similar logic, in the days of British rule some used to maintain that the condition of political dependence was mere verbiage without substance, that even the effort to end it was quite superfluous, for even in a state of political dependence we might look at the sky's blue and be delighted, and there was nothing to stop us from sitting down in yogic meditation and attaining liberation thereby. And these days, following the very same logic, many are in the habit of saying that no one can snatch our inner freedom, hence there is nothing wrong with dictatorship. As regards language, the reality is that men cannot tolerate for long the dominance of a language which is not their own, even if that language is much more developed than their mother tongue: a language as powerful as Sanskrit had to admit defeat at the hands of various immature spoken dialects; the first radiant ascent of 'vernacular' literature in medieval Europe happened in Italy, the ancestral homeland of Latin; the glorious Elizabethan age of English literature and the rise of German literature in Goethe's time both share the backdrop of Biblical translation, the King James's Bible[13] and the Lutheran version,[14] that is to say, an emancipation from Latin in the field of religion; and one reason for the sudden and astonishing appearance of Russian literature in the nineteenth century was the fact that Russia, being under the Orthodox Church, had used the mother tongue for liturgical purposes from the beginning.[15] And in nineteenth-century Bengal, in spite of English education, or precisely because of it, an awakening in respect of the native language and culture took place, which ushered in a new era, and culminated in the *swadeshi* movement. It was at that moment of Bengal's re-birth that the foundation of modern India was laid: all Indians are aware of this, though nowadays many do not wish to admit it.[16]

It is necessary to say a bit more about the state of the English language in India. The very first thing we need to remember is that the British rulers did not impose their language on us by force; our own great men from Rammohan[17] to Vidyasagar[18] were interested in the introduction of English education in this country and laboured for that goal. Why did they? Because they grasped that India's white rulers represented the modern world and mentality, and that by adopting their language as a vehicle we might transport ourselves from the medieval to the modern age. The end of the Middle Ages took longer, or has not yet happened completely, in those areas of the country which at that juncture rejected the inspiration of Western thought—northern India redolent with memories of imperial Mughal rule. And for the same reason it is not proving easy to mirror modern life in an unconstrained manner in Hindi language and literature.[19] But even where doors opened fully towards the West, as in Bengal, the English language was adopted as a valuable tool, and no more; after Madhusudan's[20] futile efforts nearly everybody came to appreciate that we could not write poetry in English, that we could not express our soul in it, that to find our place in the minds of the rest of the world it was our mother tongue that we needed to cultivate.[21] And in that cultivation of the mother tongue English has never been a hindrance to us; on the contrary, it has given us inspiration, and is still doing so. At least as far as Bengal is concerned, the dissemination that English has achieved in the past one hundred and fifty years is far exceeded by the expansion of the mother tongue and the increase of prestige that has accrued to it. When Sir Ashutosh[22] introduced the M. A. degree in Bengali Literature at Calcutta University, the British Raj was still in the plenitude of its power; when Rabindranath composed his speech for the University's convocation in Bengali, the prospect of the British leaving India was merely imaginary; and when the mother tongue achieved recognition as a medium of instruction in schools in place of English, or when the first committee was set up to compile a glossary of Bengali technical terms suitable for official work, British rule had not yet come to an end. The English language ceded ground to the mother tongue in many areas, one by one, even when the British were still ruling.

But the manner in which Hindi has risen in the sky of contemporary, independent India's fortunes may with justification be called blustering and wanton. Its demands are huge, its ambition overbearing. Hindi has been recognized as India's official language in our Constitution; even the validity of that recognition may be questioned, inasmuch as the decision was taken not in the Lok Sabha, but in the Vidhan Sabha, with a very narrow majority.[23] Nevertheless, if the issue were merely one of Hindi being the official language, it might not have been altogether impossible for many to accept this recognition. But in the ten years since independence Hindi has been given pan-Indian publicity—not as the *sarkari bhasha* [official language], but as the *rashtra-bhasha* [state language], or as *jatiya bhasha*—the national language.[24] At the same time, a new adjective has been devised for the other major languages of India: 'regional', that is to say, *anchalik* or *daishik*. We totally reject both these terms [i.e. 'national language' and 'regional language']. A language may be called 'regional' when it is the mother tongue of a certain geographical region; and in that sense Hindi is just as 'regional' as Tamil, Bengali, Kannada, Malayalam; and Bengali, Telugu, Marathi, Gujarati etc are as regional as French, German, Japanese, Russian, and so on. So this adjective has no meaning at all; the motive behind its widespread use, which is visible in the Report of the Language Commission too, is simply to damage the prestige of the other languages of India besides Hindi. The phrase 'state language' [*rashtra-bhasha*] could be interpreted in two ways: the language used for state business, i.e. an official language [*sarkari bhasha*], and the 'national language' [*jatiya bhasha*], that is to say a language that is the mother tongue of all the citizens of the country. If we accept the first interpretation, the question arises: which government are we thinking about? West Bengal, or Madras, or New Delhi? That governments in Assam, Orissa, Andhra or West Bengal might conduct their business in Hindi—such a flight of fancy is possible only for someone whose mind-set is similar to Hitler's. Whether such a flight of fancy has appeared anywhere or not will be revealed in course of this discussion; at this point it is necessary to mention that the excessive zeal of the promoters of Hindi—which the President himself is continuously fuelling—is determined to push the second meaning of 'state language' [i.e. 'national language']; many of those whose interests are tied up with Hindi or who cannot think independently have assumed that the name of India's 'national'— i.e. sovereign—language is Hindi. This is not only wrong, but untrue; not only untrue, but false. India never had, and still does not have, one naturally sovereign language in the sense in which English is the 'national' language of the USA.[25] In no period of history has all of India spoken in the same tongue: this diversity is the hallmark of her history and the vital energy of her religion and culture; our current political leaders are pledged to safeguard this diversity. If we must use the epithet 'national', then we are bound to acknowledge that all fourteen languages recognized in our Constitution are our 'national languages'. The misguided manoeuvre to suddenly elevate one amongst these fourteen languages to a throne of sovereignty which has no foundation, and to conceal twelve other living, equal, and in some cases much more developed languages behind the unrealistic and humiliating adjective 'regional': this is only possible by applying the kind of logic which the British Government once used to intern many Indians indefinitely without trial. The British pleaded 'law and order'; the promoters of Hindi plead 'pan-Indian unity'. No doubt both goals are desirable and laudable in themselves; but just as the British then murdered justice in the name of law and order, so the promoters of Hindi now, in the very name of Indian unity, are about to wreck pan-Indian unity, the fundamental rights guaranteed in the Constitution, and the new-born democracy of India—all at one go.

5.

The Language Commission was set up with a very clear goal; its members would make recommendations to the Indian Government on what India's official language might be. But in practice the members of this Commission have exceeded their rights; they have not even held back from a generous discussion of a pan-Indian educational system. And as the readers and writers of literature are usually recruited from the ranks of the educated, this is the very section which we need to consider. On the basis of the principle that a foreign language should not be the medium of instruction, most members of the Commission have spent a lot of words against English; and we wholeheartedly agree with them about the removal of English from that role. The next question—'What should be the medium of instruction?'—has already been partially resolved; in most Indian schools today the medium of instruction is the mother tongue of that particular state;[26] English as a medium is still acknowledged in one sector only, in the system of higher education provided by the universities, but even then not everywhere or in every way. In the sphere of education the claims of the mother tongue are so irresistible that even the members of the Commission have not been able to push them aside; they have been forced to acknowledge them, at least on the face of it; and the friendly comments they have made, *en passant*, towards the Indian mother tongues ('regional' languages, according to their terminology) seem, in the light of their central tenet, about as merciful as a crocodile's tears. After admitting that the medium of education should preferably be the mother tongue, they are saying that all schoolchildren throughout India must be taught Hindi until the age of fourteen. They are not providing clear directives on what should be the medium of higher education; they are recommending that in some cases it could be the mother tongue, in some cases Hindi, and in some cases even English could be retained. Let different universities come to their own decisions as they see fit: this too they do not object to, on the face of it. It sounds so nice, but then, immediately afterwards, their real motives pierce us without fail, when they state: '... the principle of "autonomy of Universities" can, in the final analysis, have only a qualified bearing and the national language policy must ultimately prevail.' It does not take us long to understand what this means—no, not at all. If the recommendations of the Commission are taken as a foretaste of what is to come, if there are no fundamental changes in the language policies of the Indian Government, we can well imagine the kinds of recommendations and directives, carrots or sticks that will be reaching the universities from the official side: one does not have to be a soothsayer to imagine them. And the language that would become the sole medium in the Lok Sabha, in legislation, in the Supreme Court, and in pan-Indian governmental examinations, the language in which High Court judges would be compelled to give their verdicts, the language which would have the permission to be used in the examinations conducted by the state governments, and the language which would not be barred from use in the lower courts either—well, one can say without a doubt that it would not be too difficult to ram such a language down the throats of non-Hindi-speakers throughout India. Whether we liked it or not, we would have to lump it; we might die of it, but still we would have to swallow it. If as a result of this, in the course of time, education, freedom, and the quality of being human die an unnatural death in the major portion of India that does not speak Hindi, even then the 'rashtra-bhasha' must be given the highest place—'the national language policy must prevail'. What the special recommendations of the majority of members of the Language Commission boil down to—and the making of Hindi compulsory in schools is one of them—is a state of play in which a citizen of India who does not know Hindi will not be regarded as a citizen of India at all. Even after admitting the possibility that either the mother tongue or English might well be the medium of higher education, the members have tried to persuade us, with much demonstration of reasoning, that only if Hindi could become the sole medium of higher education throughout India, could we be sure of Indian unity; and that this path was therefore the most laudable. In this context they have said something else, reading which leaves us in no doubt whatsoever about their terrible intentions. Let Hindi be enriched, they say, by incorporating into it words from all the 'regional' languages of India, so that Hindi might become suitable for performing all kinds of functions, and so that, in the course of time, all the languages of India which belong to the same family might blend with one another and turn into one and only Hindi—a language that would be truly sovereign or national, and a lasting foundation for Indian unity. That is to say, most members wish that the other major languages of India become dialects used by the uneducated, that they slowly become obsolete, almost defunct, while Hindi alone flourishes with thirteen arms. And this is the motive working behind all their recommendations, explicitly or implicitly.

Needless to say, there can be no place for Sanskrit within this patriotic plan, for Sanskrit might become a major rival to Hindi in the field of education. There will be no Bengali, Assamese, Oriya, no Gujarati or Marathi; Punjabi and Urdu have already been subsumed under Hindi; Tamil, Telugu, Kannada, Malayalam will be restricted to the wise sayings of grannies; and even Sanskrit will find its resting-place in the cremation grounds of the museum. And the reason for one party stealing the property of others in this fashion? For sure, the preservation of Indian unity. I do not know if any other nation has heretofore chanced to experience a planned holocaust of languages on this scale.

I am not seeing a nightmare, simply translating the sweet dreams of the Commission members into the language of reality. If their recommendations on language are put into practice, and if, after that, the system initiated survives for a century or even half a century, the gradual decay of the other major languages and of the literatures and cultures dependent on those languages is inevitable. It is no longer true to say that a century or half a century is a very short time in the history of a nation; modern organization and technology have sharply increased the speed of so-called progress. Let us not forget the immeasurable might of the modern state; in no period of the past, not even in the days of the cruellest, most tyrannical emperors of history, was the state so powerful. The state was never so powerful, because no machinery or system had then been devised, by means of which the state could disseminate in the minds of its entire citizenry the influence it sought to spread—directly and indirectly, day in and day out, in every moment of work and of rest. Moreover, though the country is a democracy, the present state machinery of India has incorporated certain characteristics of dictatorship. In comparison with the Western democracies, here the scope of free enterprise is severely limited. Our commerce is not totally free, but follows the five-year-plan. Our system of education is not fully autonomous, because the universities cannot receive the support of wealthy patrons, but must depend wholly or mainly on the treasury for their funds. Our radio, being essentially monopolized by the state, is neither as self-reliant as in England, nor as free as in America. It is true that our newspapers have a freedom sanctioned by law that goes quite far, but we have received no proof yet that they always care to put that freedom to good use, or are allowed to do so; it is not that we have not seen them switch their fundamental principles or agendas overnight at some signal hidden from our view. And even in areas where authority cannot be exercised directly, our state is gradually putting in more efforts to spread its influence in an indirect manner. The institution of academies for literature, drama, and the fine arts is an example of this, as is the announcement of prizes for books and paintings, the organization of 'Sahitya-Samaroha' by the broadcasting authority,[27] and the inter-university youth festival. That our state has suddenly become very active in the patronage of literature and the arts, and has, to that end, established large offices out of tax-payers' money, is not a development that I, as a writer, can view as a good sign: in my opinion, the most generous treatment that a modern state can accord artists is indifference—a clean, unsentimental indifference. That good literature had been created in the past under the patronage of kings is totally irrelevant in this context; for the king of old was but one individual; his powers were, by modern standards, very limited; and occasionally he could be an honest fellow too. Furthermore, kings from Vikramaditya[28] to Frederick the Great[29] satisfied their personal sense of ego in patronizing poets, without harbouring any state purposes behind that façade. As a result, poets could, despite giving kings oral flattery— Voltaire denied Frederick even that[30]—maintain their independence in their work. But when today's state, impersonal, mechanical, gigantic, and invested with totalitarian powers, undertakes to patronize the arts, it soon comes to mean the narrowing and disappearance of that liberty which is the greatest treasure not only of the artist, but also of the country, the state, the society, and the civilization. The price that the state extracts from the artist in exchange of providing him with a pleasant means of livelihood is ultimate and unique; if that thing of value is destroyed, comfort, honour, and security cease to have any meaning for the artist: society becomes as well-regulated, rule-bound, and intolerable as a prison. It is freedom that is that thing of value: the freedom of thought, the freedom to say 'I don't accept this', the freedom to be alone, away from the pack. It is thanks to this freedom that the pulse of society responds to new rhythms from age to age, and the current of civilization can continue to flow. The present USSR has for long been placing in front of the world samples of that inert stuff, pleasing to the masters, that is produced in the name of art where this value is trampled, where the artist is fed and clothed and fattened but deprived of his liberty.

Seeing that the modern state possesses enough power to turn into its playthings even artists, who represent that sector of society which is normally alert and self-possessed, it is not at all beyond the realms of possibility that it might engineer the destruction of twelve or thirteen languages within a country, in order to aggrandize just one. This is a prospect that we must grasp as clearly as we can; the state really does have the power to convert to reality, within the next fifty or even twenty-five years, the happy dreams that the

Language Commission are currently visualizing on paper; the tremendous claims of the 'state language' can really and truly endanger the very existence of every other language—unless, that is, our positive intelligence, which is smothered in ashes, can light a spark now, this very minute, and put up a determined resistance. 'Let Hindi be the language of the Centre—no problem—we have the mother tongue within our state, haven't we?'; 'after all, how many people are going to join government service, and what would be the harm in letting those few learn Hindi?'; 'we Bengalis will forget to cultivate Bengali under the pressure of Hindi? you must be mad!': just a little bit of analysis would reveal the extent of self-deception which lurks behind such thinking, or rather, such lack of thinking. If—let us pick just two of the Commission's recommendations—if Hindi is installed without a rival on the official throne of India, and if every Indian citizen is forced to learn Hindi in childhood or from childhood onwards, what will happen is that the other languages, even though they might initially have the status of the king's fan-wavers or betel-box-bearers, will ultimately have to move off stage, away from the pan-Indian scenario to the greyness of anonymity. The inhabitants of India will identify Hindi as their language, and the whole world will think that Hindi is *the* Indian language. And it will not be long before this comes to pass, because already—by virtue of the publicity given to it in the ten years since independence—some countries outside India have accepted Hindi as another name for India's language, the study of Hindi is increasing in the West, and we ourselves—even Bengalis—have no problem in referring to the mother tongues as 'regional' languages and to Hindi as the 'national' language. Hindi is the only official language of India—if just this principle is accepted, and nothing else, then everything else will follow automatically; whether it is legally compulsory or not, students will learn Hindi off their own bat—not only those who have the ambition to become politicians or civil servants, to make a living from commerce or knowledge, but those also, who aim to live just that little bit above the painful thresholds of sheer survival, will find that they cannot advance themselves without Hindi. We must remember that the numbers of those who join government service directly or indirectly will before long cease to be a handful and become huge; thanks to the continuity of the Five-Year Plans, the subtle and twisted ramifications of the state will spread to layer after layer of civil life, and there will be few areas of livelihood left where the influence of the government will not have penetrated. Equally, it is impossible to forget—for already we are getting many indications of the phenomenon—that once ensconced as the 'state language' or the 'national language', Hindi will become the flagship of aristocracy, the refuge of fashion, a major article of snobbery, something one would need to have not only for getting on in one's job, but also to acquire caste, as it were; amongst any such lucky people who might remain, who are not compelled to learn it, many will opt to learn Hindi of their own accord. And in the minds of those too, the great masses of ordinary folk who will carry on with their humble occupations outside the fold of state-nurtured high caste, Hindi will come to occupy a special niche: like the national flag or the national anthem, the 'national language' too will become a symbol, an object of unthinking veneration and homage; peasants, housewives, small shopkeepers in the country towns—there will be nobody left who would not respect that language deeply, even without knowing a syllable of it or deriving any benefit through it. It is a good thing to respect all languages; but in this case the sentiment would be accompanied by a contempt for their own mother tongues, and that situation is dangerous. The power of such psychological influence cannot be measured and appreciated in a quantitative sense; no matter how Hindi's rights may be legally circumscribed, no matter how the other languages are given their status in the Constitution, the simple formula that 'Hindi is the national language or state language of India' will act like a spell in the minds of the masses. And we are getting a taste of this already; Hindi is already being taught as a compulsory subject in many non-government schools in West Bengal, though the government has not given any clear directives on this. The reasoning of the school authorities is presumably this: 'They'll have to learn it sooner or later anyway, so it's best to start right now.' Is it necessary to explain at length what a magnified form this reasoning will acquire as it spreads throughout the length and breadth of India—if what is a proposal today becomes a fact in a few more days? The masses never think through any issue thoroughly, plumbing its depths—and we cannot even expect them to do so—they will just surrender themselves to the 'national language' because of its symbolic value and nothing else. Besides, everybody wishes to get on in the world; people who do not wish to advance themselves and their families by climbing one more rung in the ladder are rare everywhere; and if advancement is impossible without a knowledge of Hindi, then no matter how mild the 'pressures' of such a situation are on paper, Indian citizens who do not speak Hindi will be willing or compelled to neglect their mother tongues.

Here let us consider the case of English once more: if in British times we have not neglected our mother tongues under the influence of English, why on earth would we forget our mother tongues because of Hindi? Many things could be said in reply to this; I shall mention just one circumstance. The way Hindi is wanting to take over the whole lives of the pan-Indian masses—the English language never had a claim on us as large as this, nor was it possible for English to press such a claim. British rule was foreign and imperialist; its connection with the masses of the country was slender; crores of rural people, completely unaware of events in Calcutta or Delhi, carried on their habitual lives generation after generation. But today the influence of the state is dispersed everywhere, and even the emotions of the masses are not free from that influence, because behind it is the glory of gaining independence, the pride of patriotism. Needless to say, the influence of the 'state language' will be as extensive as the influence of the state. Hindi has what English never had and still does not have: the stamp of being home-bred; that is its big advantage, and that is why it is so very dangerous. Most people will not be able to figure out that surrendering to Hindi will mean betraying the mother tongue, and it will be difficult to explain this to most. Urged by commendable patriotism, we shall accept Hindi, and without being aware of it, without formally understanding it, gradually begin to forget the mother tongue. We shall begin to forget it, because within a short time the view will solidify (it has already happened to some extent) that as Hindi is an Indian language, and we are all Indian, it is not wrong to think of Hindi as just our own language. From another point of view too the danger of the mother tongue's destruction is quite horribly palpable, especially for northern India. In one of his recent essays Sri Sunitikumar Chattopadhyay[31] has shown that precisely because Bengali and Hindi are very close to each other as languages, if the Bengali child is taught Hindi, the Bengali he will learn will not remain quite Bengali. The two languages have many words in common, but their spellings and pronunciations are different: being taught 'dash' and 'das', 'kahini' and 'kahani' at the same time, the child's sense of what is correct and what is not will be baffled. As a result he will probably learn neither Bengali nor Hindi well, but will mix the two and make up a Bengali tinged with Hindi or a Hindi tinged with Bengali. Every language of northern India will face this problem; nor will the southern languages be able to bypass this crisis altogether. And as according to the recommendations of the Commission, all Indian citizens will have to learn Hindi compulsorily, while speakers of Hindi will not need to learn any other language, the principal ingredient of this new dish with fourteen flavours mixed in it will be Hindi; the other languages will not be able to avoid the structures of Hindi, or maybe all the other languages will gradually waste away, feeding and enriching a unique Indian language, which perhaps will not be quite like the Hindi we know today, but which we shall nevertheless be able to recognize as

Hindi, without any doubt—we would never confuse it with Bengali or Marathi or Telugu. That is to say, the wild dreams of the Language Commission will then be fulfilled, and all the other Indian languages will simply dissolve and disappear in the body of Hindi.

A language that is the mother tongue of all or the vast majority of the citizens of a country can be called its natural 'national' language. Indians never had a common or 'national' language in this sense in any period of their history. And nobody had any regret about this either, because in no previous era were we a nation in the modern sense. We have no synonym for 'nation' in the Indian languages, and the word *jatiya* in the sense of 'national' still sounds unnatural and artificial.[32] Like many other things, the idea of nationhood was something that we acquired from the West, and now, after independence, in the evening of global nationalism, we are somewhat pathetically determined to become a fully-fledged nation, nothing short of a nation. As Indians are one *jati* or 'nation', therefore India needs a 'national' language as well: many are hypnotized by the mechanical usefulness of this reasoning. They may not support Hindi a hundred per cent, but will often say, 'Just because we didn't have a common language in the past, does it mean that we can't have one in the future? Isn't it a good idea to have one?' But if we admit that something is a good idea, it is surely our duty to work towards that end, and to say that a common or 'national' language is a good idea is quite simply to give our happy assent to the hegemony of Hindi. The real question is this: which is the better idea?—constructing a single 'national' language, or the gradual flowering of all our mother tongues, each at its own natural pace? Which alternative is more important for our sense of being human—the enrichment of all our mother tongues, or a language which will be usable by all in this continental land of India? Another related question has to be posed too. Which alternative is likely to be more favourable to the nourishment and expression of the Indian mind: diversity or uniformity, harmony or chorus? And whichever of the two is the more desirable, if the other one is diametrically opposed to it, what should we do?

If we give our assent to the main proposals of the Language Commission, we may be able to possess a 'national' language very likely within the next twenty-five or fifty years. If we accept those proposals—and not just accept—if we all work together to apply them, only then can it come to pass, not otherwise. If indeed a 'national' language seems the more desirable option, then we should give up paying lip service to the mother tongue and accept Hindi whole-heartedly. Let no one make the mistake of entertaining the illusion that both the development of the mother tongues and the rise of a 'national' language are possible in the land of India at one and the same time. In India a 'national' or common language can be built only on one condition, namely, that the path of every other language will be blocked, and it is precisely those who may be called the offspring of the various languages who will help in that blockade. If that dire day ever arrives, if the inhabitants of India are ready to sacrifice even their vital juices in the boiling cauldron of nationalism, then one out of two possibilities may be regarded as a certain outcome. One possibility is that we might forget identities such as Bengali, Marathi, Tamil, and so on, and all enter a half-imaginary category named 'Indian'; denying the great truth of our fundamental humanity, we might become mere citizens, useful creatures, or not even creatures, just microscopic fragments of a vast state machine. Or, since identities such as Tamil, Marathi, or Bengali are vital substances, behind which are particular streams of concentrated becoming, spread over many ages, there is also a strong likelihood that after some time, witnessing the humiliation and decay of their languages and cultures, the whole of non-Hindi-speaking India will rise in separatist revolt. Of the two possibilities the first one is antagonistic to our humanity, and the second one will be a blow to our integrity as a state. The first means a rejection of India's history as it has unfolded through the ages; the second means endangering India's future. The first will uproot that very pattern of diversity which is the salient characteristic of India's genius, and if the second happens, it is doubtful if our independence will survive intact. Neither of the two can be called desirable. Therefore in resolving this problem neither a compromise nor a delaying manoeuvre will yield any profit; the best would be to make some suitable arrangement right now, whereby we may feel ourselves to be Bengalis, know ourselves to be Indians, and above all, not forget that we are human beings and individuals, not puppets made in a state factory.

1957

This essay was originally published both as an independent pamphlet and in *Kavita* (Ashwin-Poush 1364). In 1960 it was incorporated into the second edition of Bose's volume of essays entitled *Swadesh o Sanskriti*. The present translation follows the definitive version published in Bose's collection of essays *Prabandha-sankalan*, 3rd printing of Dey's edition (Dey's Publishing, Calcutta, 1995). The selection of essays had been made by Bose himself and the volume had been first published in 1966.

End Notes

1. Readers who may feel inclined to raise their eyebrows at this comment must take into account the date of this essay.
2. Johann Georg Hamann (1730–88), a contemporary of the philosopher Immanuel Kant, was a very eminent thinker of the German Counter-Enlightenment. The nature and origin of language was one of his major preoccupations. Most Enlightenment thinkers viewed language as a useful tool devised by human beings out of their rationality and thinking powers. In Hamann's view it was the other way round: language was embedded in the Creation and preceded, or was at least simultaneous with, the emergence of man's reasoning and thinking faculties, neither of which would have been possible without language.
3. Johann Gottfried von Herder (1744–1803), German philosopher and literary critic, whose essay on the origin of language ('Abhandlung über den Ursprung der Sprache', 1772) helped to lay the foundations for the comparative study of philology, religion, and mythology.
4. Friedrich Heinrich Jacobi (1743–1819), German philosopher, was a critic of the system of Spinoza and emphasized the importance of faith as a unifying force in philosophy.
5. The opening lines of the well-known poem 'Bideshi Phul', from Rabindranath Tagore's collection *Purabi* (1925). The poem was written in Buenos Aires on 12 November 1924. The fragment is presented in my translation.
6. *The Gospel According to St John,* 1.1, quoted from the Authorized Version of the Bible (1611). Bose quotes this in his own Bengali re-translation, and translates 'the Word' as *vak*. From this point onwards the word vak occurs several times in Bose's text, in a diversity of contexts, Christian, Hindu, and Zoroastrian. He uses it to stand for 'speech' or 'language'. For convenience and clarity, I have often retained this word in my translation.
7. Bose quotes in his own Bengali re-translation. I have quoted directly from Ronald Knox's version of *John,* 1. 1–5, from the one-volume edition of Knox's Bible published by Burns & Oates, London, in 1955. Ronald Knox (1888–1957) was a distinguished Catholic intellectual of his time who was first ordained as an Anglican priest and then converted to Catholicism, subsequently becoming a Catholic priest. He translated the Bible from the Latin Vulgate, 'in the light of the Hebrew and Greek originals', and his version was approved of by the Catholic hierarchies of Great Britain. His translation of the New Testament first appeared in 1945 and of the Old Testament in 1949. Knox was interested in offering clarity and intelligibility to a contemporary audience, but as readers of the scriptures often prefer familiarity of diction, even if meanings are obscure, his translation raised controversies and was sometimes unjustly criticized. However, the Knox lines quoted here are actually quite close to

the version given in the authoritative *New English Bible* of 1961, which was prepared by a panel of translators and was approved of by the major Christian bodies of the British Isles excluding the Roman Catholic Church. This version was an attempt to present the meaning of the original, as understood by the best available Biblical scholarship of the time, in as clear and natural a language as the subject-matter would permit. For readers who are interested in the issue of translation, I quote the relevant lines from this sixties version (*The New English Bible, New Testament,* Oxford University Press and Cambridge University Press, 1961): 'When all things began, the Word already was. The Word dwelt with God, and what God was, the Word was. The Word, then, was with God at the beginning, and through him all things came to be; no single thing was created without him. All that came to be was alive with his life, and that life was the light of men.'

8. *John,* 1.14, Authorized Version. This phrase is quoted in English.
9. Herbert Spencer (1820–1903), a major British intellectual of Victorian times, one of the proponents of the theory of evolution and well-known for applying evolutionary theory to philosophy, psychology, and sociology. It was he who coined the phrase 'survival of the fittest', which was subsequently adopted by Darwin.
10. Friedrich Hölderlin (1770–1843), the great German poet whom Bose helped to bring to a Bengali readership through his translations.
11. 'I remember it was with extreme difficulty that I could bring my master to understand the meaning of the word *opinion,* or how a point could be disputable; because reason taught us to affirm or deny only where we are certain; and beyond our knowledge we cannot do either. So that controversies, wranglings, disputes, and positiveness in false or dubious propositions, are evils unknown among the *Houyhnhnms.*' Quoted from *The Portable Swift,* ed. by Carl Van Doren, The Viking Press, New York, printing of 1961, p. 495.
12. The reference is, of course, to Shakespeare's *Julius Caesar.*
13. The Authorized Version or King James's Bible was, of course, not published till 1611, but the main point that Bose is making here is correct: the Reformation generated a substantial movement to free religion from the domination of Latin, and English translations of the Bible kept appearing throughout the sixteenth century, including the versions of William Tyndale and Miles Coverdale, a version commissioned by Henry VIII, the Geneva Bible produced by Calvinist exiles in Geneva, and one issued in the reign of Elizabeth I, known as the Bishops' Bible. Shakespeare's Biblical quotations are drawn from the last two as well as from a third source. The Authorized Version was really the culmination of a long process.
14. Martin Luther (1483–1546), the leader of the Reformation in Germany, translated the Bible from the Latin into German, and his complete Bible was first printed in 1534. The Lutheran Bible had thus been around for two centuries prior to the birth of Johann Wolfgang Goethe (1749–1832).

15. This does raise the interesting question of why, in that case, the flowering of Russian literature had to wait till the nineteenth century. Conducting the business of religion in the mother tongue must be only one factor amongst many that lead to a flowering of literature in the mother tongue.
16. Making a connection with the previous point, we can see the complexity of these cultural processes. In India too, the emergence of the various *bhakti* movements in religion went hand in hand with a flowering of the mother tongues and their literatures. The great explosion of modernity in the nineteenth century was, however, set off by the contact with another civilization and a re-discovery of India's own classical past.
17. Rammohan Roy (1772–1833), the great religious and social reformer, the founder of the Brahmo movement of Bengal and a close friend of Dwarakanath Tagore, the grandfather of Rabindranath Tagore. He brought a petition to England in support of the abolition of suttee.
18. Ishwarchandra Vidyasagar (1820–91), the eminent Bengali scholar and activist, who dedicated himself to the cause of the legalization of the re-marriage of Hindu widows.
19. This comment, made in 1957, opens up interesting questions about the present time. The situation has surely changed now—at least to some extent?
20. Michael Madhusudan Datta (1824–73), who began with the ambition to be an English-language poet, then gave up that ambition to devote himself to the mother tongue, becoming a pioneer of modernization in Bengali verse and drama. His most famous work is the epic *Meghnad-badh Kavya* (1861), in which he introduced blank verse into Bengali.
21. Interestingly, to find their 'place in the minds of the rest of the world', Indians are now writing in English.
22. Sir Ashutosh Mookerjee (1864–1924), distinguished educationist, Vice-Chancellor of Calcutta University from 1906 to 1914.
23. This reference to the Vidhan Sabha is perplexing. Could a decision about the official language of the Centre have been taken in the Vidhan Sabhas or legislative assemblies of the states? Could this be a slip for Rajya Sabha? Does Bose mean that the decision was taken in the Upper House and not in the Lower House of the Indian Parliament?
24. Here and immediately afterwards I have retained some of the original terms for the sake of extra clarity.
25. Right now, of course, native speakers of Spanish in the USA want greater recognition for their language.
26. He must be talking about state schools; private schools, including those run by missionary foundations, were more autonomous. Thus in the Calcutta school run by a missionary foundation which I attended myself, between 1948 and 1953, we were taught in the medium of Bengali up to Class VI, switching to English for the last four years of schooling, Classes VII to X.

27. A big all-India literary gathering in Delhi organized by All India Radio.
28. In this context no doubt to be identified with Chandragupta II, whose rule over most of northern India stretched from c. 376 to 415. He is traditionally regarded as having been the patron of the poet and dramatist Kalidasa.
29. Frederick II, who ruled the eastern German state of Prussia from 1740 to 1786.
30. Voltaire (1694–1778), the celebrated French writer and philosopher, a rationalist and an outspoken critic of religious obscurantism, spent some years (1749–53) in Potsdam, near Berlin, at the invitation of Frederick the Great.
31. Sunitikumar Chatterjee (1890–1977), one of the most eminent linguists and philologists of the twentieth century.
32. In the beginning of the twentieth century Rabindranath Tagore began to discuss these issues in 'Nation Ki' and other essays, which were subsequently included in his collection of essays, *Atmashakti* (1905).

Bibliography

Below is a list of those works of Buddhadeva Bose which I have read or re-read or consulted in some way in the immediate past, in connection with the present project. It excludes the material I have absorbed in the past, including novels, stories, scattered articles, and all those issues of *Kavita* I read in my formative years.

(Ed.), *Adhunik Bangla Kavita* (anthology of modern Bengali poetry), M. C. Sarkar & Sons, Calcutta, 1963.

Amader Kavitabhavan (the third part of his memoirs, unfinished at his death), Vikalp, Calcutta, 2001.

Amar Chhelebela (memoirs of his boyhood), M. C. Sarkar & Sons, Calcutta, 1973, reprint of 1989.

Amar Jauban (memoirs of his early youth), M. C. Sarkar & Sons, Calcutta, 1977, reprint of 1989.

An Acre of Green Grass: A Review of Modern Bengali Literature, first published in 1948. Reprinted by Papyrus, Calcutta, 1997.

Anamni Angana o Pratham Partha (two verse plays), first published in November 1970. Dey's Publishing, Calcutta, 1996.

Anya Konkhane (autobiographical novel), New Age Publishers Ltd, Calcutta, 1950.

Desh-deshantarer Kavita (poetry from different countries translated by him), Vikalp, Calcutta, 1999.

Kabi Rabindranath (essays on Tagore as a poet), Bharabi, Calcutta, 1966.

Kalsandhya (verse drama), first published in 1969. Dey's Publishing, Calcutta, 1991.

(Ed.), *Kavita, Jibanananda Smriti Sankhya* (the Poush 1361 issue of *Kavita* dedicated to the memory of Jibanananda Das), facsimile edition, Vikalp, Calcutta, 1998.

Kavitar Shatru o Mitra (mainly essays on poetry), M. C. Sarkar & Sons, Calcutta, first published in 1974. Third printing, 1997.

Kavitasangraha (collected poems), in 5 volumes, edited by Naresh Guha, Dey's Publishing, Calcutta, 1980–94. The first three volumes house his own poetry and the last two poetry translated by him.

Kolkatar Elektra o Satyasandha (two plays), first published in 1968. Dey's Publishing, Calcutta, 1991.

Mahabharater Katha (essays in interpretation of the *Mahabharata*), M. C. Sarkar & Sons, Calcutta, 1974.

Maya-malancha (play), first published by Kavitabhavan in 1944, reissued by Vikalp, 2000.

Nepathya Natak / Kaththokra (two plays), Vikalp, Calcutta, 2000.

Pata Jhore Jay o Anyanyo Natak (plays), Vikalp, Calcutta, 1999.

Punarmilan (play), first published in May 1970. Dey's Publishing, Calcutta, 1991.

Raat Bhorey Brishti (novel), M. C. Sarkar & Sons, Calcutta, first published in 1967, seventh printing, 1990.

Sab-peyechhir Deshe (memoirs of his visits to Santiniketan in 1938 and 1941, and remembering Rabindranath Tagore), first published by Kavitabhavan in 1941, reissued by Vikalp, Calcutta, 1998.

Sankranti, Prayashchitta, Ikkaku Sennin (three verse plays, the second after a play of Yeats and the third after a Japanese No play), first published in 1973. Dey's Publishing, Calcutta, 1991.

Tagore: Portrait of a Poet, first published in 1962. Enlarged edition, Papyrus, Calcutta, 1994.

Tapasvi o Tarangini (play), Ananda Publishers Private Ltd, Calcutta, first published in 1966, seventh printing, 1994.

Tithidore (novel), New Age Publishers Private Ltd, Calcutta, first published in 1949, sixth edition, 2000.

To this list should be added the essay 'Bhasha, Kavita o Manushyatva' from *Kavita* (Ashwin-Poush 1364), translated in the Appendix of this volume, and 'Ingreji o Matribhasha', *Kavita,* Year 22, No. 2, Poush 1364.

Below is a very selective list of other volumes similarly consulted, i.e. specifically for this project. Again, it excludes numerous relevant books—individual collections of poetry as well as critical works—which I have otherwise read over the years or have in my personal collection, and which must have shaped my ideas and opinions.

Ayyub, Abu Sayeed, *Pather Shesh Kothay* (essays), fourth edition, Dey's Publishing, Calcutta, 1992.

Basu Singh, Damayanti (guest editor), *Boidagdhya,* special issue on Buddhadeva Bose, May, 1999, incorporating the contributions of many critics and scholars.

Bose, Protiva, *Jibaner Jalchhabi* (Mrs Bose's memoirs), Ananda Publishers Private Ltd, Calcutta, first published in 1993, third printing, 1996.

Bose, Protiva, *Mahabharater Maharanye* (essays in interpretation of the *Mahabharata*), Vikalp, Calcutta, 1997.

Chakravarty, Amiya, *Kavitasangraha* (collected poems), Dey's Publishing, Calcutta. Vol. 1, third edition, 1995. Vol. 2, 1979.

Chattopadhyay, Shakti, *Gadyasangraha* (collected prose), Vol. 1, Dey's Publishing, Calcutta, 1996.

Chattopadhyay, Shakti, *Padyasamagra* (collected verses), Ananda Publishers Private Ltd, Calcutta. Vol. 1, second edition, 1996. Vol. 5, 1997.

Chattopadhyay, Shakti, *Sreshtha Kavita* (selected poems), seventh edition of Dey's Publishing, Calcutta, 1996.

Das, Jibanananda, *A Certain Sense,* his poems translated by Various Hands; Translation Editor: Sukanta Chaudhuri; Introduction: Sisir Kumar Das; Notes: Sumita Chakrabarti. Sahitya Akademi, New Delhi etc, 1998.

Das, Jibanananda, *Sreshtha Kavita* (selected poems), Navana, Calcutta, second edition, 1956. Enlarged edition issued by Bharabi, Calcutta: second printing of 1968.

Datta, Sudhindranath, *Kavyasangraha* (collected poems, including his translations of foreign poems), Navana, Calcutta, 1962.

Datta, Sudhindranath, *The World of Twilight,* Oxford University Press, Calcutta, 1970.

Dey, Bishnu, *Sreshtha Kavita* (selected poems), Navana, Calcutta, fifth edition, 1985.

Dey, Bishnu, *Tumi Rabey ki Bideshini* (translations of foreign poems), Navana, Calcutta, 1986.

Gangopadhyay, Sunil, *Kavyasangraha* (collected poems), Visvavani Prakashani, Calcutta, 1974.

Gangopadhyay, Sunil, and Chacraverti, Sounak (editors), *Prasanga: Shakti Chattopadhyay* (essays remembering Shakti Chattopadhyay), Vikalp, Calcutta, 2000.

Ghosh, Sudakshina, *Buddhadeb Basu* (biographical monograph on Bose), Pashchimbanga Bangla Akademi, Calcutta, 1997.

Guha, Naresh (ed.), *Kavir Chithi Kavike: Rabindranathke Amiya Chakravarty, 1916–41* (Amiya Chakravarty's letters to Rabindranath Tagore, 1916–1941), Papyrus, Calcutta, 1995.

Gun, Suman, *Buddhadeb Basu o Samar Sen: Sakhye Samipye* (on the friendship between Bose and Samar Sen, with Sen's letters to Bose), Vikalp, Calcutta, 2000.

Ray, Sibnarayan, and Maddern, Marian (editors), *I have seen Bengal's face: A selection of modern Bengali poetry in English translation,* Editions Indian, Calcutta, 1974.

Sen, Arun, *Bishnu Dey, E Brotojatray* (critical study of the poetry of Bishnu Dey), Aruna Prakashani, Calcutta, 1983.

Sen, Arun (ed.), *Ei Moitree! Ei Monantor!* (Sudhindranath Datta's letters to Bishnu Dey and a study of their friendship based on these letters), Asha Prakashani, Calcutta, 1977.

Sengupta, Samir, *Buddhadeb Basur Jiban* (biographical monograph on Bose), Vikalp, Calcutta, 1998.

Seely, Clinton B., *A Poet Apart: A Literary Biography of the Bengali Poet Jibanananda Das (1899–1954),* University of Delaware Press, Newark; Associated University Presses, London and Toronto; 1990.

Tagore, Rabindranath, *Chithipatra,* Vol. 11 (Tagore's letters to Amiya Chakravarty and to Chakravarty's mother Anindita Devi), Visvabharati, Calcutta, 1974.